THEMES AND CONVENTIONS
OF
ELIZABETHAN TRAGEDY

BY

M. C. BRADBROOK

*Fellow of Girton College and Reader in English
in the University of Cambridge
and Mistress of Girton College*

CAMBRIDGE
AT THE UNIVERSITY PRESS
1969

PUBLISHED BY
THE SYNDICS OF THE CAMBRIDGE UNIVERSITY PRESS

Bentley House, 200 Euston Road, London, N.W.1
American Branch, 32 East 57th Street, New York, N.Y. 10022

Standard Book Numbers:
521 04302 6 clothbound
521 09108 X paperback

First edition	1935
Reprinted	1952
	1957
First paperback edition	1960
Reprinted	1964
	1966
	1969

First printed in Great Britain at the University Press, Cambridge
Reprinted by offset-litho by Unwin Brothers Limited, Woking & London

CONTENTS

NOTE ON THE 1969 REPRINT

In the thirty-five years since this book was written, many of the plays have been re-edited, discussed and performed, In the modern theatre not only Shakespeare's greater and lesser works, but those of his contemporaries can be presented. At Chichester or the Mermaid Theatre an open stage is provided; the Royal Shakespeare Theatre and the National Theatre have staged brilliant versions of Marlowe, Tourneur and Webster; the tragedies of Middleston and Ford have also been seen in London.

University departments of drama have arisen where the plays are studied in workshop conditions, but also in relation to their European background. Much that had once to be laboured can now be taken for granted. My plea for re-interpretation has received such reinforcement from the live theatre as could not have been anticipated thirty-five years ago.

This book may be looked on as the first part of a general history of Elizabethan drama which has been expanded in subsequent books on comedy, and on Shakespeare as poet and craftsman. As the most social of the arts, drama demands for its interpretation a wide range of skills; criticism must therefore of necessity draw on the resources of many studies.

At Cambridge, at Stratford, and in many other parts of the world, I have learnt both from my masters and my pupils. The boundaries of knowledge are being pushed forward now by such writers as George Hunter, Glynne Wickham, Clifford Leech, Anne Barton, V. A. Kolve. No perfromance that I have seen, however inadequate, has failed to give me an insight into the play that imagination could not supply. To Cambridge, and to Girton College, my debts have grown with the years; not only this book, which I wrote as a research fellow, but anything achieved since, is the fruit of that seed plot.

M. C. BRADBROOK

Cambridge, 1969

PREFACE

In the following pages I have tried to present an apparatus of approach to the Elizabethan drama, and in particular to tragedy. The first part deals with general informing conditions, the second with the uses to which they were put by the great dramatists. Thus the full significance of the first part can only be seen through the light which it throws on the second part; and this is the explanation of an arrangement which may seem to some readers rather severely insistent upon work first and playing afterwards. The reader who is not particularly devoted to the Elizabethan period may find the first part duller than the second, while the scholar with an appetite for work may object that the first part is neither detailed nor extensive enough for him. My defence would be that I have not attempted to placate either at the expense of the other, hoping each would concede a little to the other's frailty.

It seems at the moment as if criticism of the Elizabethan drama were entering a new and brilliant phase. The body of distinguished work represented by the names of Professors Caroline Spurgeon and Wilson Knight, Mr T. S. Eliot, Mrs Woolf, Miss Elizabeth Holmes and Mr G. W. H. Rylands reveals a tendency towards a unification of the scholarly and the critical forces. I am especially indebted to the first three of these writers. Also I am under no small methodological obligation to Mr W. Empson's *Seven Types of Ambiguity*, and more particularly to a lecture on *Plot and Subplot in the Elizabethan Drama* which he gave to the Heretics at Cambridge in the Lent Term of 1931.

My thanks are due to Miss Enid Welsford, of Newnham College, for invigorating discussion of my work. Miss H. M. R. Murray, my former Director of Studies, has encouraged me throughout by her interest and advice and by many personal kindnesses.

It is difficult, though it might be salutary, for those who read in the English School at Cambridge to try to estimate how much of what they produce might fairly be labelled "All my own work". It is no less difficult for me to count up my many debts to Girton College, from the award of the Research Fellowship, which made my work possible, to those gifts whose description would only be practicable where it would also be redundant, that is, among Girtonians.

M. C. BRADBROOK

1934

PART ONE

THE THEATRE

CHAPTER I

Introduction

THIS work was written as an attempt to discover how an Elizabethan would approach a tragedy by Chapman, Tourneur or Middleton. It has long been felt that Elizabethan drama was a very specialised form of art; but there has been no systematic attempt to discover what its peculiarities really were, or how far they helped or hindered the great dramatists in their work. It is hardly sufficient to make vague references to the influence of the *Commedia dell' Arte* or to compile a list of the number of times a Revenger says "Curae leves loquuntur, ingentes stupent". Something more comprehensive is needed, which would be at once an explanation and a justification. This book is meant to show that, beneath what may seem very arbitrary and trivial conventions, there was an underlying unity which makes into parts of a coherent whole, much that has seemed difficult to explain. It fixes the plot and subplot of *The Changeling* in a definite relation to each other, and reveals the structural methods of Tourneur. An attempt to understand the conventions as a whole has revolutionised my personal outlook on the Elizabethan drama.

The case is very complex and yet a single case. If any parts of the argument appear rather novel, they should be judged in relation to the rest. It is true that the development of the conventions has been only slightly indicated, but that would have required a much longer time than I could afford to give.

It is very necessary to approach the Elizabethan drama without any of the preconceptions about the nature of drama which are drawn from reading Ibsen, Shaw, Racine, Dryden's *Essay of Dramatic Poesy* or Aristotle's *Poetics*. It is necessary to regain the particular angle (even the particular limitations) of the Elizabethan point of view. The unity of their conventions was not at all like the unity of the Rules or of a strictly formulated code. (It is impossible to say how far they were conscious of the unity themselves: it seems obvious that Chapman and Jonson were particularly conscious, whereas Marston, for instance, swam with the stream.) The reader must not approach the drama with the *a priori* conviction that Jonson's plays are shapely and Chapman's shapeless, because the shape of Jonson's plays is immediately perceptible to him. Perhaps his consciousness of the shape of Jonson's might be modified by a realisation of the shape of Chapman's.

If this seems to imply a kind of critical anarchy, it can at least be urged that it finally produces order. The present system, which begins with orderly judgments, too often ends in critical anarchy.

The crucial question is the nature of Elizabethan dramatic speech, and the chapter on it forms the keystone of my argument. It was because he misunderstood the technique of the Elizabethans' dialogue that William Archer could misunderstand their whole dramatic structure. *The Old Drama and the New* has been more often attacked than refuted. Archer's attitude may seem absurd, but it is the logical outcome of the normal attitude towards Elizabethan drama, which implies that the technique, even when successful, is "primitive".

Expository speech is still stigmatised as undramatic.

Writing in 1890 Alfred Hennequin criticized many of the best plays for containing passages of this sort. In 1909 Archibald Henderson claimed it as the greatest innovation of the leading modern dramatists that they had succeeded in identifying action and exposition. The discredit into which the soliloquy and aside had fallen—until reclaimed to new uses by Eugene O'Neill—was largely due to the fact that they were generally employed to convey information, a method which critics, from the first century B.C. on, have objected to. The German scholar Kilian called it "a lame makeshift", and Brander Matthews denounced it as "false in psychology" and "primitive in dramaturgy". "Inartistic" is the mildest adjective applied to it.[1]

Brander Matthews can write in the following strain:

Iago and Richard III when they are alone on the stage talk straight to the spectators, to the gallants on their threepenny stools and to the groundlings standing in the yard. Both of these bold, bad characters unbosom themselves in soliloquy, revealing their dark designs and letting us see into their black hearts.[2]

This facetious rallying of Shakespeare seems unwise. *Othello* wants not Eugene O'Neill to support it: if the Elizabethans wrote great drama, it is only by taking nineteenth-century standards of dramaturgy as absolute, that it can be called primitive in any sense.

It may be added that "marvels of construction" can be produced by anyone who will take a little pains. William Archer noted this, but it did not lead him to suspect his own standards. He admits that "any good competent writer" can produce plays which are "better" than those of the greater Elizabethans.

It may seem unnecessary to defend the seventeenth century against this kind of attack; but there is too often a tendency to think that the Elizabethans were less dramatic than modern playwrights, but made up for it by being more poetic. It must be insisted upon that poetic drama may have a construction as efficient as, and far more complex than, prose drama and that to condemn it (or to acquiesce in condemnation by excusing it) is to betray the duty of a critic. The only way to gain recognition for Elizabethan methods of construction

[1] Doris Fenton, *The Extra Dramatic Moment in Elizabethan Plays before 1616*, p. 87. Pennsylvania, 1930. [2] *Ibid.* p. 92.

is to analyse and formulate them, and give them an independent status.

A great deal of preliminary work has already been done. There are innumerable monographs on different and isolated conventions: these give a body of support to any attempt at generalisation. It remains to see these little idiosyncracies in relation to each other, for whilst each of them, considered separately, may be only arbitrary and curious, in conjunction they form a body of conventions which constitutes the Elizabethan stage tradition.

A convention may be defined as an agreement between writers and readers, whereby the artist is allowed to limit and simplify his material in order to secure greater concentration through a control of the distribution of emphasis. Conventions which are acknowledged have usually been erected into a system of Rules. The neo-classic conventions, which were largely the creation of Renaissance critics, were considered to have the authority of the Ancients and to constitute the only right method of making plays: they were prescribed not as a convenience but as a duty. The value of such a system of Rules is that it imposes consistency, and only allows one set of conventions at a time.

The Elizabethan conventions have never been acknowledged because they were not formulated (except in so far as a parody implied a convention to be parodied). The neo-classic creed was the orthodox one: though the dramatists did not adhere to it, they could not construct an alternative one. It might have been possible to distort the Rules until they fitted contemporary practice, but Elizabethan criticism was not sufficiently advanced for so large an undertaking.

It was nevertheless impossible that writers who worked at the speed of these dramatists should not evolve a convention. They relied partly on the Senecal tradition (which derived from the Italians) and on the practice of greater dramatists like Kyd and Marlowe. In this way a body of incidents, types, tags grew up upon which anyone could draw. Such a body of common material is of little value in itself. It saves the writer's time but also tends to make his work lifeless and mechanical. Those dramatists who used it in an unenlightened way produced shapeless and incoherent plays.

But in the hands of the greater writers the stock material formed a true convention. The Revenge plays have in common a certain "criticism of life", and the common form is only a convenience for expressing it. The imagery and idiom of these plays is the means by which the convention is unified and made poetic. The essential structure of Elizabethan drama lies not in the narrative or the characters but in the words. The greatest poets are also the greatest dramatists. Through their unique interest in word play and word patterns of all kinds the Elizabethans were especially fitted to build their drama on words.

The lesser writers, who could not unify their plays through speech, relied upon spectacle and the coarsest stimulants of melodrama and farce. Since the observance of their conventions was purely pragmatical, there was nothing to prevent the combination of several conventions in one play (as in Dekker's *The Honest Whore*). A structure which was purely poetic offered nothing to the lesser dramatists, whereas our contemporary dramaturgy is equally useful to the mediocre writer and the good one.

The raw material for studying the conventions can be found only in the plays themselves. Since the greater dramatists often borrowed from lesser ones to build up their personal conventions, the whole of the drama must be considered.

Finally, the way in which the dramatists built up their plays may be most easily elucidated by a comparison with contemporary non-dramatic literature. Some consideration of the influence of other arts is helpful also. The mental habits of the age were very different from ours and, in some respects, much closer to those of the Middle Ages; particularly in the taste for allegory and the attitude towards rhetoric. The less important the dramatist, the more essential it is to see his play primarily as Elizabethan literature, and only secondly as a play. The Elizabethan drama has been so often compared with the drama of the Restoration or the nineteenth century that to approach it in its relation to *Euphues*, the *Arcadia* and *The Faery Queene* might at least have the justification of novelty. There is the further inducement that, without forgetting the distinctive qualities of the dramatic *genre*, it is easier to judge writers who worked in an age when the *Arcadia* and *The Faery Queene* were not regarded as stilted or complex or unusual, but as normal literary productions, by reference to such works, and not by reference to the works of writers for whom Browning and Meredith were normal and typical.

An equally necessary proviso is that the plays of Shakespeare should be, as far as possible, excluded from the mind when the lesser Elizabethans are being considered. Shakespeare can be judged by nineteenth-century standards (or any other dramatic standards, for that matter) without suffering an eclipse. He is so different from his contemporaries, particularly in the matter of characterisation, that it is unfair to judge them by him. Spenser and not Shakespeare was the typical Elizabethan poet, and the Spenserian standards are much safer to apply to the dramatists. To approach Shakespeare through his contemporaries is enlightening, but to approach his contemporaries through him is to set up false preconceptions. The difficulty is that everyone knows Shakespeare's plays the best of all, and a conscious effort to set them aside is not often made. It is very salutary to take three or four mediocre plays (say Day's *Humour out of Breath*, one of Heywood's plays of adventure, Yarrington's *Two Lamentable Tragedies* and a chronicle history), and to realise that the Elizabethan public would regard such plays as the norm and judge other writers accordingly.

CHAPTER II

Conventions of Presentation and Acting

I. LOCALITY

THE form of the Elizabethan theatre is so well known that it is not necessary to describe it in detail. The projecting main stage was backed by an inner stage, the "study" (in private theatres the "canopy" or "trophey") closed with a curtain (the "arras" or "traverse"). Above was a balcony, also curtained. There were three or more doors to the main stage, with windows over the side doors; and in the public theatres a third storey, the "top" or "turret". In the private theatres the upper stage was smaller; it was known as "the music room". The stage was provided with several kinds of traps, and with machines for descent from above, called "thrones".

The chief characteristic of the Elizabethan stage was its neutrality and its corresponding virtue, flexibility. There was no inevitable scenic background, or any other localising factor, such as a Chorus provides.

It followed that far more weight attached itself to the persons and movements of the actors. In short or unimportant scenes no indication of place is given, either by properties or by the speech of the actors, and no place need be assumed. It is the result of oversight rather than a deliberate device: the author was not compelled to locate his characters and, for a short scene between first and second gentlemen, there was no need to do so.

The scenes of a comedy were often located vaguely within a given town; and the short scenes of battle plays could all be covered by a general label.[1] It is uncertain whether the

[1] *Alphonsus of Aragon*, 2. 1, 2: the last three acts of *Edward III*.

entrance of a fresh set of combatants meant a change of place or not.

Vestiges of the older method of continuous staging (*décor simultané*) remain in a few plays of Lyly and Peele, such as *The Arraignment of Paris* and *The Old Wives' Tale*.[1] Marston apologises for the "entrances" in *Sophonisba* because "it was given after the fashion of the private stages". This might explain how in the fourth act the characters go from a bedroom to a wood and back again without in each case leaving the stage.

The private and the common stages could not have been very different, from the ease with which they pirated one another's plays. But Marston's plays, in particular, seem to indicate that two places could be shown at once: there are further instances in *Antonio's Revenge* and *The Fawne*.

In the "split" scene properties were set on the inner stage to indicate a fixed locality, and when the curtains were drawn the characters remaining on the main stage from the last scene were attracted into the new setting. Conversely, if the curtains were closed the characters left on the forestage were delocalised. The first kind of split scene occurs in *Bussy D'Ambois*, 4. 2, and *The White Devil*, 4. 3; the second in *The Massacre at Paris*, Scene 5, and *Othello*, 1. 3.

It is clear that the actors were the really important means of locating the scene. They were not set against a background real or imaginary; the audience did not visualise a setting for them. Shakespeare is misleading in this respect because he nearly always suggests a background for his characters, but no other writer did it with such consistency.

It was quite permissible for a character to bring his locality with him. In *The Devil's Charter* Lucrezia Borgia brings in her chair and sets it down like any humbler character: there are the notorious directions about thrusting out beds,[2]

[1] *Vide* Chambers, *The Elizabethan Stage*, III, pp. 48, 135–42.
[2] *Ibid.* pp. 66, 113.

though the idea that the royal chair of state was lowered by a pulley on to the stage has been dispelled.

There is one definite method of showing that the place is changed by the movement of the actors. When a character announces his intention of going somewhere, and then goes out at one side of the stage and comes in at the other, it is assumed that he has finished his journey. The two doors often indicated two localities.[1]

Besides the split scene, there are reminiscences of continuous setting in processional scenes and extended scenes. In processional scenes the characters walk about the stage, and are imagined to be travelling for quite a distance. Instances are *The Play of Stukeley*, Scene 1; *Romeo and Juliet*, 1. 4; *Merchant of Venice*, 5. 1; *Arden of Feversham*, 3. 5; *A Warning for Fair Women*, Act 2, ll. 476–96; *The Witch of Edmonton*, 3. 2. The march of the army round the stage is one of the commonest spectacles.

Processional scenes merge into extended scenes. In Roman plays the senate often sit above while the lower stage represents the street. In *Titus Andronicus*, 1. 1, the tomb of the Andronici is shown below and the senate sit on the upper stage.[2] Places further apart may be shown, such as a street with several houses or two opposing camps.[3] In *Eastward Hoe*, 4. 1, the butcher climbs a post and describes a distant scene of shipwreck offstage, and there is a similar scene in *The Captives*. The most notorious case occurs in a dumb show at the end of *The Three English Brothers*.

The sense of exact place is blurred in early plays by the figures of the induction. The presenters were in one definite locality, in *The Taming of the Shrew* (the Lord's house); the play was in another (Padua and the country round), but also

---

[1] *The Gull's Horn Book*, ed. McKerrow, p. 41.

[2] Chambers, *op. cit.* p. 58.

[3] *Soliman and Perseda*, 2. 1; *Arden of Feversham*, 1. 1; *The Fawne*, 4. 1; *Catiline*, 5. 6. *Vide* Chambers, *op. cit.* pp. 54, 99, 117.

in the Lord's house where it was being witnessed as a play. Conjuring produced something of the same effect, when Friar Bacon showed the Oxford scholars their fathers in Fressingfield or the Conjuror revealed the death of his wife to Brachiano.

The presence of allegorical figures, for whom time and place are irrelevant, and the confusion between induction and play in *The Old Wives' Tale*, *James IV* and other early dramas, even though they were not consciously felt by authors or audience, would help to establish a vague and unlocated scene. Of course these devices were rejected later, but not for their effects upon localisation.

It is also doubtful how far each scene was a unit. If there were no scenic pauses, the transference from one scene to another would be very much slurred over. In the second act of *Charlemagne*, the place shifts from Paris to Ganelon's country house during a series of short unlocated scenes, so that it is impossible to say exactly at what point the change is effected.

It was not the habit of the audience to visualise precisely (as the choruses to *Henry V* rather suggest), or unlocated and split scenes would have puzzled them. The author was not always conscious of implications of locality. In *King Leir*, Scene 24, and *The Blind Beggar of Alexandria*, Scene 3, banquets are brought on in the middle of an open desert. This could hardly have happened if the audience filled in the background for themselves.

On the early stage title boards were used with the name of the place painted on them. This custom may have survived in the private theatres for a short time.[1] A scene will often begin with some flat declaration of place, such as "Well, this is the forest of Arden".

There were certain properties which localised both generally and particularly. Tables, stools and a "state" indicated

[1] Chambers, *op. cit.* pp. 126, 154.

a hall; a bed, a chamber; a tomb, or altar (which may have amounted to the same thing), a church. For country scenes there were a bank of flowers and a river bank. As characters sometimes leap into the river, a painted board before an open trap seems the likeliest method of representation. There was an arbour which could rise through a trap, though the inner stage also served as a bower or cave.

In the histories, particularly for the fulfilment of omens, a very definite locality was often needed. The scene is frequently a familiar one as when Cade strikes his staff on London stone, or Queen Eleanor sinks into the earth at Charing Cross and rises at Potter's Hithe.

The two most popular scenes were the orchard or woodland scene and the city gates. The orchard scene must have been more realistic than most, though the exact nature of the trees is uncertain, and the method by which they were disposed on the stage has been much disputed. But they were solid and practicable trees on which verse, or more tragically, corpses, could be suspended (*The Massacre at Paris*, Scene 8; *Hoffman*, 1. 1, 5. 1). The woodland set was sometimes used for battle scenes, and as late as Shirley it was used to locate a scene out of doors when trees were not really needed.

The city gates were represented by the central door of the stage, the upper stage being the ramparts, and the main stage the surrounding fields. Sieges were the most popular episodes in chronicles: *Henry VI, Part II*, contains thirteen. The two levels of the stage were the most effective means of securing theatrical grouping, and were an equivalent, if not a substitute, for more realistic settings. Shakespeare's use of the monument in *Antony and Cleopatra* may be cited. It is clear that the stage was not the "bare board" that Coleridge thought, and certainly not a bare board from choice. Both writers and audience enjoyed spectacle, but there was no consistence in the degree of realism, and therefore there could have been no complete and permanent illusion. The introduction of elaborate spectacle did not prevent unlocated scenes, and the lack of a background did not prevent realism of detail.

II. TIME

The sense of time is partly dependent on the sense of place, and so it is not remarkable that in Elizabethan drama it is frequently disordered, and more frequently omitted. In split scenes, where characters are instantaneously transported from one locality to another, time is telescoped; while unlocated scenes are divorced from the clock.

Some shortening of time, or rather, acceleration of the pace of action, is necessary even in the most realistic plays; the degree of obtrusiveness determines whether the reader passes it over unconsciously or accepts it as an overt dramatic convention.

A simple departure from the actual time sequence is shown in the final scene of *Faustus* which is supposed to take exactly an hour, but requires about seven minutes. There is a similar scene at the opening of the fifth act of *The Changeling*. *Cymbeline*, 2. 2, opens at "near midnight" and ends at 3 a.m. Orders and journeys are executed with the speed of Puck. In *Appius and Virginia*, a late play, Icilius goes several miles to fetch the body of Virginia while a few lines are spoken: the trick is much commoner in the earlier drama.

In these cases, the telescoping is inevitable on any stage, and could be paralleled from any period. The instantaneous conception of very elaborate schemes of action is less natural. Barabas plans his revenge in a moment or so: the Duchess of Malfi evolves the plan to accuse Antonio of theft on the spur of the moment. Such a situation, however, is dependent on conventions of character rather than of staging, and is related to instantaneous conversions and love at first sight.

In the early plays there are very few references to the

passage of time. There is not one in *Alphonsus of Aragon*, *The Battle of Alcazar* or *Locrine*, so that no time scheme is possible. It was only with the introduction of a close-knit story, where events are causally and consecutively related, that the definite time scheme was necessary, and so it did not appear in the chronicle plays as a rule.

Marlowe was acutely aware of its possibilities. In *Faustus* he used a simple one, but in *The Jew of Malta* his intrigue is more complicated and less satisfactory. The manner in which characters come on to inform the audience that something has just happened when in fact it was the last thing enacted is awkward and calls attention to the lack of the time gap (*The Jew of Malta*, 1. 2, 3. 4; *Edward II*, 1. 2, 1. 3).

The phenomenon of double time can be found in many plays of the period if they are examined sufficiently closely. Sometimes it is only a matter of a scene or two (*Richard II*, 1. 3, 2. 1) but many plays have two time sequences throughout. There is a striking case in *The Atheist's Tragedy*, when Borachio orders his disguise at the end of the scene in which Charlemont departs for the war, and appears wearing it the same evening to report Charlemont's death at the siege of Ostend.

The combination of plot and subplot often leads to double time sequences, for the subplot may be only an anecdote, and yet it is interwoven with a long story; but as the passage of time is not important, these discrepancies are not noticed. The writer often slips through a desire to link up his scenes neatly. He might connect up the actions by a reference backwards or forwards to "last Tuesday" or "next Wednesday" while in the interval some action of a greater length has occurred, or the total action may require more or less time than the sum of the intervening acts. Thus in *Charlemagne*, between the dispatch of Didier to poison Orlando and his decision not to do it, so much has happened that he must have lingered for about a year on the journey.

The use of dumb shows and inductions also helped to confuse the time sequence. Lengthy acts were presented in dumb show symbolically (*Antonio's Revenge*, 3. 1, 2; *A Warning for Fair Women*, Act 2 (Prologue); *The Changeling*, 4. 1). The figures of the inductions, when they were allegorical, were outside time or space: moreover, they can predict the action which is to follow.

The Elizabethan audiences were not trained to put two and two together in the matter of temporal sequence, and so these difficulties did not exist for them. The rapidity of decision and quick movement from plan to action so characteristic of this drama was not a matter of hurried time, but only of increasing the speed of the narrative and of heightening suspense and attention. The excitement justifies the logical contradictions, and the well-knit appearance of a play like *Othello* is its own explanation.

In some tragedies flexibility of time and space provides the very structure of the play. This is so in *King Lear*, where things stop during the storm, *Antony and Cleopatra* with its forty-two scenes, and *The Duchess of Malfi* where, in the fourth act, things also stop.

In the late Jacobean and Caroline drama time references again become scarce. There are few in Fletcher or Massinger. In *Valentinian*, for instance, the general impression is that everything happens in a short time, but there are no indications in the text.

III. COSTUME AND STAGE EFFECTS

The costume and make-up of the actors is what might be expected from the method of setting. Clothes were as gorgeous as possible: a cloak might cost £19, and a gown to be worn in *A Woman Killed with Kindness* £7. 13s., which was not an unheard-of price for the text of a play.[1] Curiosities of dress were much sought after, especially in the early

[1] Henslowe's *Diary* (ed. Greg), pp. 188, 189.

period, when for instance Peele's Edward I appears in a "suit of glass". Later, exactitude conquered novelty, and for *The White Devil* the collars of six noble orders were copied.

Although there were no attempts at historic accuracy, Cleopatra appearing in a farthingale and Cassius in a doublet, there was some geographic differentiation. In *Hoffman* the lovers are disguised as Greeks; in *Caesar and Pompey* Pompey as a Thessalian. Most countries had peculiarities of dress: Englishmen, according to the Lady of Belmont, wore them all in turn. It is probable that a Dutchman's slops or a Spaniard's cloak would be given them on the stage. There was certainly a Turkish costume (*A Very Woman*, 4. 1).

Costume was also conventional. There were "robes to go invisible"[1] and Faustus would need one at the Papal court. Ghosts could wear leather, though some wore armour; but Snuffe in *The Atheist's Tragedy* disguises as a ghost in "a sheet, a hair, and a beard". The ghost's face, according to *The Rebellion*, 5. 1, was whitened with flour.

The Prologue wore a long black cloak, but no distinctive costume was given to the Epilogue, who was usually one of the dramatis personae. It caused a sensation, however, when spoken in armour at the end of the comedy of *Antonio and Mellida*.

Costume might indicate character, if Lodge may be taken seriously, when in his *Defence of Plays* he observes:

The Romans had also gay clothing and every man's apparel was applicable to his part and person. The old men in white, the rich men in purple, the parasite disguisedly, the young men in gorgeous colours, there wanted no device nor good judgment of the comedy, whence I suppose our players both drew their plays and forms of garments.

In *The Gentleman Usher*, 2. 1. 109, there is the direction "Sarpego puts on his parasite's costume".

---

[1] Henslowe's *Diary* (ed. Greg), p. 123. On the modern Japanese stage, black is used for invisibility.

The symbolic use of black and white is very noticeable. The fiendish ancestors of *The Courageous Turk* appear "all in black", and the doomed favourite in *The Raging Turk* is condemned by the Sultan "casting a gown of black velvet upon him, called the mantle of death". The stage was hung with black for tragedies: it was used for mourning and funerals, and, in *The Custom of the Country*, I. 2, there is a bride-bed in black for the tyrant who claims the *droit de seigneur*.

White symbolised innocence and purity; it was worn by angels and good spirits: there are funerals in white in *Mulleasses the Turk*, I. 2, and *The Broken Heart*, 5. 3, when a bride and bridegroom are buried.

Perhaps the most interesting use of black and white colour is in the final scene of *The Devil's Law Case*. The chaste heroine Jolenta enters with her face "coloured like a Moor" and the wanton nun Angelica in the white robes of a Poor Clare. There are also two doctors, one in the robes of his merciful calling, the other disguised as the typical figure of cruelty, a Jew. Jolenta says:

> Like or dislike me, choose you whether.
> The down upon the raven's feather
> Is as gentle and as sleek
> As the mole on Venus' cheek.
> Hence, vain shows: I only care
> To preserve my soul most fair.
> Never mind the outward skin,
> But the jewel that's within,
> And though I want the crimson blood
> Angels boast my sisterhood....

It is like a scene from a morality play. The tradition was probably helped by the vogue of the masque: in Middleton's *Masque of the Inner Temple* there is a direction for three Good Days to appear in white, three Bad Days in black, and three Indifferent Days with striped clothes and streaked faces. In

A Game at Chess Middleton produced the only play where all the characters were dressed in black or white with morals to correspond.

Disguise was so popular in both comedy and tragedy that there are very few plays without at least one instance of it. Sometimes it was donned on the stage: a false beard was enough. When the characters were not assuming any particular rôle but just disguised, like Malevole or Vindice, they probably wore a long cloak and a slouch hat.

Disguise was sometimes used allegorically, as when Bosola brings the news of her death to the Duchess of Malfi in the guise of an old man. It was fully recognised by the sophisticated as an ingenious device. Chapman, who was very prone to it himself, writes in *May Day*, 2. 4, of

those miserable poets (who try) by change of a hat or a cloak to alter the whole state of a comedy, so as the father must not know his own child forsooth, nor the wife her husband, yet you must not think they do it in earnest to carry it away so....If I am able to see your face I am able to say This is Signior Lorenzo, and therefore unless your disguise be such as your face may bear as great a part in it as the rest, the rest is nothing.

When one character disguises as another, it is only the garments which are copied: this happens in Chapman's own *Bussy D'Ambois*. Sometimes in the later drama the face was scarred or stained; in *The London Prodigal* the father has only to "pull off his scar" to reveal himself.

Stage effects were mainly spectacular. Since there was no scenic background, they were of necessity intermittent and striking. The earliest were different kinds of shows and conjuring: trees which shot up through trap doors and signs in the Heavens, particularly the Blazing Star. The effect could not have been natural; by the time the Blazing Star had appeared for the seventh or eighth time the audience must have grown familiar with it and accepted it as a conventional stage property. The properties of spectacle were in fact so limited that its value would soon cease to be purely spectacular, though the groundlings still demanded it, as the well-known passage in the Induction to *Every Man in His Humour* testifies.

Pageants and dumb shows depended more upon the rest of the play, and could be very subtly co-ordinated. The later and more complex uses of the play within the play and the treacherous revels are discussed elsewhere, but they would always have their decorative appeal also.

The most powerful stage effects were connected with the ghost, at least in the early plays. It rose from the cellerage or cried from it: in *Antonio's Revenge* the ghosts cried in chorus from above and beneath; in other plays it rose from a tomb. Unlike the devil, it was always a serious character.

There was a dumb show of particular horror known as "the bloody banquet" (*The Battle of Alcazar*, Act 4, Prologue; *A Warning for Fair Women*, Act 2, Prologue; *The Bloody Banquet*, Act 5, Prologue). It was rather like the Thyestean feast: the table was set with black candles, drink set out in skulls and the Furies served it up. The tradition of these diabolical suppers might be behind the cauldron scene in *Macbeth*. A great deal of painstaking and elaborate work went to the staging of atrocities. The realism of the mutilations was helped by bladders of red ink and the use of animal's blood. The property head was very overworked: Henslowe also had property hands which would be required in *Selimus*, *Titus Andronicus* and *The Duchess of Malfi*. Executions were first staged about 1610, according to Dr W. J. Lawrence, and became very popular. The private theatres were not behind the public ones in this respect: *The Insatiate Countess*, a Whitefriars' play, is almost entirely given up to unpleasant spectacle, though the record for murders is held by *Selimus* with eleven. Vindice's words "When the bad bleed, then is the tragedy good" might have more than one interpretation. It has to be recognised that a great many scenes were on the level of Madame Tussaud's: the horridly realistic murders in *Two Lamentable Tragedies* were staged only six years before Shakespeare wrote *King Lear*. In this respect, as in others, Shakespeare was not absolutely independent of his age but so modified what it gave that he is often judged in isolation from it.

Small details, which could be given with exactitude, had great attention: Belimperia's letter, written in her blood, was in "red incke". The company were ready to utilise any piece of suitable property, and so when, in *Believe as You List*, 2. 2, the records of State are called for, there is a prompter's note, "the great book of accompt", which Dr Greg explains as the company's ledger. This anxious ingenuity suggests how popular realism was. The players were prepared to endure some discomfort as the frequent directions "Enter wet" after shipwrecks will testify.

Noises of all kinds were most important. The directly stimulating effect of music must have been much greater than at present, to judge from the way in which characters responded, a way quite reminiscent of Dryden's Alexander. It regularly charmed and controlled the insane; it accompanied all the most emotional passages, solemn meditations, religious ceremonies, dumb shows, tableaux, love scenes. This is a typical funeral procession:

Enter at one door, recorders dolefully playing, the coffin of Touchwood Junior...at the other door the coffin of Moll.... While all the company seem to weep and moan there is a sad song in the music room. (*A Chaste Maid in Cheapside*, 4. 5)

The descent of the gods was commonly indicated by music or by thunder. Thunder also accompanied their judgments and had always an effect of the supernatural.

A feeling of suspense is often heightened by the striking of a clock or a bell. The clock at the end of *Faustus* is similar to the "little bell" which, in *Macbeth*, summons Duncan "to Heaven or to Hell" and Macbeth to a living hell of the mind, while the alarum bell which Macduff commands to ring at the discovery is a "dreadful trumpet" which rouses up the speakers "as from their graves" to see "the great doom's image" itself.

The alarum bell in *Othello* gives a feeling of horror when it is heard, which is supported by Othello's speech:

> Silence that dreadful bell, it frights the isle....

It is the signal that the tragedy has begun, for Cassio is doomed by it, and it breaks in on Othello's marriage night like a tocsin.

There was some specially diabolical arrangement of bells which is referred to in *The Battle of Alcazar*, 1. 1. 115, *Edward II*, 4. 6. 88 ("Let Pluto's bells ring out my fatal knell"), *A Warning for Fair Women*, Act 2, Prologue ("Strange solemn music like bells" accompanies the Furies) and the Induction to *The Merry Devil of Edmonton*. Bosola brings her coffin to the Duchess of Malfi to the sound of the bell rung for condemned prisoners at Newgate.

IV. GESTURE AND DELIVERY

The conditions of scenic production in Elizabethan theatres have been reconstructed by stage historians, but the nature of Elizabethan acting has never been considered in any detail. Yet sufficient evidence may be gathered from the plays themselves to give some small idea of it.

The London companies were well known to their audience, and Kempe, Burbage and the rest were public figures. There was more lamenting for Burbage's death than for Anne of Denmark's. Even the tireman was a familiar figure: Jonson put him into the Induction to *Bartholomew Fair*.

In a repertory company, which played with spectators on the stage and in broad daylight, it would be very difficult to sink the actor in his part, especially if he were alone on the forestage and soliloquising. The audience's eyes would not be concentrated automatically as they are in a darkened theatre, and hearing would be more difficult in the open air. To maintain attention it would be necessary to exaggerate movement or statuesqueness, to use inflated delivery and conventional posture. The Miracle plays had been very sensationally acted, and a tradition of some strength established. At all events, the acting was probably nearer to that of the modern political platform or revivalist pulpit than that of the modern stage.

There are many references to the actor's strut. Shakespeare speaks of the

> strutting player, whose conceit
> Lies in his hamstring and does think it rich
> To hear the wooden dialogue and sound
> 'Twixt his stretched footing and the scaffoldage—
>
> (*Troilus and Cressida*, 1. 3. 153–6)

Middleton of spiders "stalking over the ceiling" like Tamburlaine.[1]

Facial distortion was practised to an extreme degree. Dekker called Jonson "a poor honest face-maker", i.e. actor. In *Cynthia's Revels*, 2. 2, there is an exhibition of facemaking. "Your courtier theoric is he that hath arrived at his furthest and doth now know the court by speculation rather than practice, this is his face: a fastidious and oblique face, that looks as it went with a vice and were screwed thus."

Kempe's powers of making scurvy faces through a curtain was one of his principal accomplishments, and he gives an exhibition of it in *The Return from Parnassus*, 4. 3. But the tragic hero had equally mobile features. Hamlet's "Pox, leave thy damnable faces and begin" and Lady Macbeth's "Why do you make such faces?" are suggestive of much.

The "eagle eye" was also well known. In *The Spanish Tragedy*, 3. 13, there is the direction "Bazulto remains till

[1] Dyce's *Middleton*, v, p. 526.

Hieronimo enters again, who, staring him in the face, speaks". In *Antonio's Revenge*, 2. 3, there is the direction "Piero, going out, looks back" evidently for a prolonged and malignant stare at the hero. As late as Shirley, the noble soldier, confronted by the villain, "stares upon him in his exit" (*The Cardinal*, 4. 2). The nature of this glance of defiance is easily deduced.

The method of expressing grief which seems most common is for the actor to throw himself to the ground, or in milder cases to sit there. Again, in *Antonio's Revenge*, the hero has a lengthy soliloquy lying on his back. Romeo's behaviour in Friar Lawrence's cell was not extravagant by the standards of the time. In *The English Traveller*, 3. 1, a respectable old gentleman does as much.

Joy was expressed by cutting capers. In *Charlemagne*, when Ganelon the Senecal man is banished, he receives the news with a caper to show how little it affects him. Two more messages of unfortunate news are brought and each one elicits another caper. The tradition of such violent action is behind the most celebrated scene of *The Broken Heart*.

When natural action is required in early plays it is mentioned as though it could not be taken for granted. In *Alphonsus of Aragon*, 5. 3, "Albinus spies Alphonsus and shows him to Belimus....Laelius gazes upon Alphonsus.... Alphonsus talks to Albinus". A play of Chapman suggests the development of the action, where one of the characters speaks scornfully of behaving

like a king in an old fashioned play, having his wife, his council, his children and his fool about him, to whom he will sit and point very learnedly, as followeth,

> "My council grave, and you, my noble peers,
> My tender wife, and you, my children dear,
> And thou, my fool"

thus will I sit as it were and point out all my humorous acquaintance. (*A Humorous Day's Mirth*, 1. 1)

This presumably refers to something of Greene's period. Later, however, the same character enters with his arm in a sling, and when he is asked to recount something, he says:

Bear with my rudeness in telling it then, for alas, you see, I can but act it with the left hand: this is my gesture now.

It is like the "lamentable action of old Titus with his one arm".[1]

The torture scenes would need to be acted very violently. In early plays characters were flayed; in later ones they were racked or scourged. Henslowe paid for a sheep's gather for *The Battle of Alcazar*, and it is disquieting to reflect what an audience accustomed to bear-baiting might have got from *The Virgin Martyr*.

The individual actor had to be something of a gymnast. Leaps from the walls or into the trap were not easy. He had also to be a swordsman, for duels were popular and the audience critical. There is a direction in *The Devil's Law Case*, 5. 2, for continuing a duel "a good length".

On the other hand long speeches required no action at all. It is impossible to play the Nuntius. The other actors could not engage in business while a long speech was given; they would remain stiffly grouped. They could not drop into the background for there was no background in the Elizabethan theatre.

The actors' chief difficulty was to maintain their statuesque pose, particularly since they might be the object of very audible jesting or ridicule. Nashe has a passage which lists their shortcomings:

Actors, you rogues, come away, cleanse your throats, blow your noses, and wipe your mouths ere you enter that you may have no occasion to spit or cough when you are non-plus. And this I bar, over and besides, that none of you stroke your beards to make action, play with your cod-piece points or stand fumbling

[1] Dyce's *Middleton*, v, p. 590.

on your buttons when you know not how to bestow yourself: serve God, and act cleanly.

(Prologue, *Summer's Last Will and Testament*)

The delivery must have been stentorian. It was Burbage's enunciation which made lines like "A horse, a horse, my kingdom for a horse" into catchwords. Lodge compared the ghost which "cried so miserably: Hamlet, Revenge" to an oyster wife, which hints at its pitch and volume. Of course there were different fashions in this: Alleyn was fonder of Ercles' vein than Burbage, and nothing of the sort could have happened in the children's companies. There is much more opportunity for tearing a passion to tatters in soliloquy than in dialogue: the necessity for exchange produces an inevitable modulation. It may therefore be possible to relate the decline of rant to the decline of the soliloquy and the long speech, as well as to the movement into the roofed private theatres.

Very violent action would, however, imply violence of delivery even in dialogue. It would be impossible for Montsurry, haling Tamyra up and down the forestage by her hair, to deliver his lines in anything less than a roar. In battle scenes also the speech would have to be shouted above the din of the drums, trumpets and cannon. The blank verse had not at first a speech cadence, though later writers used a more colloquial movement, and presumably the enunciation changed in consequence. Perhaps the modification of blank verse was the most important controlling factor of the delivery.

It has always to be remembered that in real life action was so much more violent, that the kick bestowed upon the patient wife, or a frenzied foaming at the mouth, might only mean that the actor was holding the mirror up to nature. Elizabeth's manners are well known to have had as many shades as her vocabulary. Also the English actors were apparently considered very natural in Germany when they toured there: there were no standards of comparison, and what appears formal now was then capable of producing the illusion of reality in the simple.

V. GROUPING

The individual actor had large opportunities on the Elizabethan stage, through the popularity of the soliloquy, but the kind of team work expected of him was correspondingly strenuous, and demanded a high degree of self effacement.

The battle scenes of the chronicle plays were often staged formally. The "army" marched round the stage and went off; the principals came on and fought a series of single combats. The trumpets sounded from the side supposed to have the victory, or, as in Goffe's *Courageous Turk*, "a token of victory on the Turk's side" was hung out.

The sieges to the music room also allowed of a conventional grouping: the actual attack was often of less importance than the parleys where insults were bandied and defiances hurled.

The processional entries of princes were made as formal as possible, though sometimes their suite was not much greater than the Duke of Plaza-Toro's. In *Antonio and Mellida* the fool is pressed into the guard of honour who form a rank for Piero. The procession merges into the dumb show and the tableau. In *Every Man out of His Humour*, 3. 1, there is a scene in Paul's walk with

Orange and Clove: Puntavolo and Carlo: Fastidioso, Deliro and Matalente: Sogliano. They walk up and down and salute as they meet in the walk. They shift: Fastidioso mixes with Puntavolo: Carlo with Sogliano: Deliro and Matalente: Clove and Orange: four couple.

This sounds almost like the direction for a dance.

The Revengers especially used patterned action. They go off the stage linked together, "If not to Heaven, then hand in hand to Hell",[1] or they come on with joined hands. It is usual to swear revenge in some very ceremonious manner: in *Hoffman* they circle round one of the group who kneels in the middle; in *Antonio's Revenge* they swear on the body of the murdered Feliche, but this body is laid across the chest of the hero who has just finished his soliloquy on his back.

The movements of the Revengers are always remarkably simultaneous. In *Antonio's Revenge* "they offer to run all at Piero (with their daggers drawn) and on a sudden stop" to prolong his agony. Before which "they pluck out his tongue and triumph over him" in dumb show, which must have been a bloody and fantastic spectacle.

The dance was often used significantly. During the changes of the dance in *Satiromastix* the king reveals his love for the bride: the common end of the Revenge play was a dance by masked Revengers who suddenly threw off their vizards and ended the revels with a murder. Their hidden excitement must have been conveyed through the rapid movement most effectively. The ghosts also danced in a sinister way in Revenge plays; so did the Furies.[2]

A formal grouping was especially necessary at the end of a play. Tragedies often ended with the funeral march; comedies with a dance. Kempe, in *The Return from Parnassus*, speaks on the necessity of breaking the lengthy walk down-stage:

It is good sport in a part to see them never speak in their walk but at the end of the stage, just as though in walking with a fellow we should never speak but at a stile, a gate or a ditch where a man can go no further. (4. 3)

[1] *Richard III*, 5. 3. 314. Cf. *Titus Andronicus*, 3. 2; the triple oath in *Hamlet*; *Hoffman*, ll. 2085–3102.

[2] *A Warning for Fair Women*, Act 2, Prologue; *Tancred and Gismonda*, 4. 1; *The Revenge of Bussy D'Ambois*, 5. 2; *The Jews' Tragedy*, ll. 2380ff.; *The Raging Turk*, 5. 8; *The Courageous Turk*, 5. 3; why this should be thought comic it is hard to see. These dances were clearly descended from the *danse macabre*; but Chapman in particular is often sneered at for his dancing ghosts.

This kind of formality was the result of the stage conditions; but the drama of the treacherous revels and other patterned movements affected the quality of the feeling in the action, making it nearer to the impersonal feeling of ballet.

Plays seem to divide into passages of declaimed speech, and passages of action of a violent and conventional kind. The effect of this is to underline action where it does occur and to make it portentous. This is especially so with allegorical persons, who are not separated from ordinary characters. Tamyra and her sons, disguised as Revenge, Rapine and Murder, move among the characters of *Titus Andronicus* and, in the dumb shows of *A Warning for Fair Women*, Chastity and Lust appear with Mrs Saunders and Browne. Whether the action of these figures was formalised it is impossible to decide.

The action in the dumb shows must certainly have been inflated. At its worst it was purely spectacular, and this use persisted. In *The Revenge of Bussy D'Ambois*, 3. 2, there is the direction "Enter a gentleman usher before Clermont, Renal and Charlotte, two women attendants and others: shows having passed within". These quite irrelevant shows might have taken up many minutes' action.

By this time, however, the dumb show had also become an integral part of the play, just as the songs had. The famous "Helen passes over the stage" in *Faustus* meant that such an effect must have been expected that Faust's speech would seem inevitable. The duel in *Friar Bacon and Friar Bungay* is the most tragic action in the play, and it is given in dumb show so that it can be shadowed by another duel. The effect is parallel to the double pathos of "Enter a father that has killed his son" and "a son that has killed his father" (*Henry VI, Part III*, 2. 5; imitated in *Caesar's Revenge*), which in turn is linked to the use of similar plots and subplots, as in *King Lear*.

The action is often symbolic in these shows. Thus in *Antonio's Revenge*, when Piero woos Maria, she "flies to the tomb of Andrugio, kneeleth by it and kisseth it". In the dumb show in *The White Devil* the direction "Sorrow expressed in Giovanni and Lodovico" probably meant that they tore their hair and wrung their hands.

A tableau may provide the setting for a long lyrical monologue; as it does in *The Devil's Law Case*, where Romelio, having been presented with his own coffin in the manner of the Duchess of Malfi, recites a long set meditation on death, a friar kneeling on one side, the bellman and his mother telling her beads on the other. Sometimes the stage was set for a solemn meditation with a table bearing a death's head, a book and a candle.

Darkness had a suggestion of evil and of the supernatural: it might be directly used in tragedy, as in *Macbeth*, or slightly even in comedies like *A Midsummer Night's Dream*, *The Faithful Shepherdess* and other nocturnals.

The audiences were trained by their whole dramatic tradition to feel an allegorical significance behind a formal or rhythmic grouping. The influence of the masque and of shows helped to support it; and such passages as those between the Painter and Hieronimo in *The Spanish Tragedy* are sufficient reminder that the paintings of the period were often allegorical too.

CHAPTER III

Conventions of Action

FOR critical convenience the drama may be divided into presentation, action and speech. The presentation covers all that pertains to any actual performance, and has been discussed in the preceding chapter. The speech, which will be considered in the following chapters, covers the whole of the dialogue seen as a poem, or as literature. From these two halves rises the action, which is the plot in the Aristotelian sense, or narrative and character taken together. It is only for critical convenience that a play may be taken to pieces in this manner, but if the arbitrary nature of the division is recognised, there should be little danger of considering the results as anything but equipment for the final critical judgment.

In this chapter the action will be isolated for analysis: it would seem simpler to deal first with narrative and then with character. There seems at present to be some danger that the action should be quite disregarded; in Shakespearean criticism, at all events, there has been such a violent reaction from the nineteenth-century point of view that it is customary to refer to the play as though "the pattern of the imagery" or some other kindred abstraction were the axis of it. This is, of course, as absurd as its antithesis; it will hardly work for tragedy and is quite impossible in comedy, where there is no "pattern of imagery" at all. It is only necessary to realise that, for the Elizabethans, action had a different status from that which it has at present, a fact sufficiently obvious to any reader of the dramatic or non-dramatic fiction of the period.

The story of most Elizabethan tragedies is either too simple, or too complex, judging by modern standards. In

Tamburlaine, the Byron plays, *Sejanus* and *Catiline*, there is little action, and what there is seems monotonous: in *The Revenger's Tragedy* and *Women, Beware Women* there is so much that the reader can hardly grasp it at first reading. The minor plays of the period go further to one or the other extreme; on the one hand there are the classical tragedies of Daniel and Stirling and, on the other, *The Jews' Tragedy* or *Mulleasses the Turk*. There is a similar division in the novel, between the courtly romances of Sidney and the University Wits, and the tales of Deloney and Beard.

The commonest complaint against the Elizabethan drama is that the action is illogical, or overcrowded. When it is excused, it is the fashion to call it episodic, with the derogatory association of Aristotle's condemnation of the episodic plot. Middleton is sometimes praised for his construction (with serious reservations about his subplots), and Jonson is usually applauded for dexterity and reproved for lack of seriousness.

The first and most essential thing to be realised is that consecutive or causal succession of events is not of the first importance. It is difficult to rid the mind of the preconception that this is an essential requirement of any narrative: some of the lower forms of modern fiction depend upon it entirely. It is perhaps connected with the infection of all mental processes by the scientific method, so that even crossword puzzles and other mental relaxations depend upon clues and the sifting of evidence. The demand for a logical narrative is far deeper than the demand for realism, as the expressionist drama or the detective story will testify. It is this logical development of the narrative which made the nineteenth century consider itself so superior in dramaturgy to any preceding period, and which produced the "marvels of construction" admired by William Archer. They were simply the result of putting two and two together on a large scale. The last thing which occurred to the Elizabethan was to put two and two together in this way. Dramatists often carelessly assumed that the answer was three or five; in consequence the nineteenth century was confronted by all the problems of double time in *Othello*, the age of Hamlet, and the sea-coast of Bohemia. The Elizabethans were not culpably negligent or magnificently careless, for there were simply no standards to be transgressed unless the Unities were accepted by the exceptional writer. But the very rigidity of the Unities suggests that they felt the need for a strict discipline.

The neutral background of the Elizabethan stage meant that the succession of events was not clearly defined. It has been shown in the preceding chapter that time and space could both be neglected, telescoped or expanded. It was not likely therefore that causality would be very important. Effects existed with their causes (as in the repentance of villains, or the sudden jealousy of husbands); causes were not always followed by their usual effects (the cruelty of the prodigals to their wives and parents being repaid by an increasing devotion). Murder and suicide were committed on the slightest provocation. At the end of a tragedy, in particular, there was no need to discriminate the causes of slaughter. In *Selimus* the physician Abraham takes some of the poison he has administered to the king in a cup of wine, only because

> Faith: I am old as well as Bajazet
> And have not many months to live on earth:
> I care not much to end my life with him—
>
> (ll. 1829–31)

and in the last act of Rowley's *All's Lost by Lust*, one of Antonio's two wives stabs herself with the reflection

> I must die sometime
> And as good die this day as another.

The consequence was the Elizabethan dramatist could not

rely on his causal sequence of events, which is the principal means of controlling the emphasis in the modern drama, and in most prose. In *The Old Drama and the New* (Lecture 5), William Archer describes how a shopgirl, finding her lover already married, comments "You might have mentioned it before, you might have mentioned it". Here, Archer says, "one can feel the sickening drop from hope to despair", and therefore the phrase is "of the essence of dramatic poetry". What happens, of course, as Archer's words imply, is that the reader supplies all the feeling from his knowledge of events. Archer prefers this method as more subtle: a little later he says

for instance, after the parting in *Romeo and Juliet*, what could be more natural, one might almost say inevitable, than that Juliet should throw herself down on her bed in tears? But it does not occur to Shakespeare—

though something like it occurred to Stanley Houghton. The logical conclusion of the argument is that the essence of dramatic poetry might replace the cruder substantial form throughout the play: something natural might replace the Epithalamion. Feeling could always be presented, and never defined.

Shakespeare is not ignorant of the power of implication, but he does not use it very often. Against the shopgirl's reply may be set Ophelia's:

> *Hamlet.* I loved you not.
> *Ophelia.* I was the more deceived.

Here there is not only "the sickening drop from hope to despair", but the fineness of breed that controls reproach, together with the deeper pain that comes less from personal loss than from a recognition of the degeneration involved for the other; a feeling made explicit in the soliloquy of Ophelia which follows.

Most Elizabethans had little of Shakespeare's power of

implication. Moreover, they did not work so much through the implications of structure as through their feeling for allegory. They could put two and two together in this way in a manner which might seem as marvellous to us as our deductive powers would to them. It was "natural" to assume that ancient mythology could be interpreted as Bacon interpreted it in *The Advancement of Learning*, Book 2, chapter 13, as it was natural to put the headings to *The Song of Solomon* which survive in the Authorised Version. The feeling for allegory is one which can be developed by training: at the present it is hardly exercised at all; so that, for instance, we tend to take the inner interpretation as superseding the outer one, instead of including it.

Even when there is no question of an allegorical interpretation, plays may be affected by the habit of thought. For example, the ironic justice of Revenge tragedy, by which the characters are always hoist with their own petard, depends on the conception of an underlying pattern in their lives, of a divinity shaping them.

> Vengeance met vengeance,
> Like a set match, as if the plagues of sin
> Had been agreed to meet here altogether.
> *(Women, Beware Women, 5. 1)*

In Shakespeare's plays readers have become accustomed to making elaborate cross references, say between the murder of Duncan and the sleep-walking scene in *Macbeth*, but this kind of pattern is used by other writers as well. When Bosola says to the Duchess of Malfi, just before her death:

Riot begins to sit on thy forehead (clad in grey hairs) twenty years sooner than on a merry milkmaid's. Thou sleepest worse than if a mouse should take up her lodging in a cat's ear—

it is as an echo of the mirth of the bedchamber scene that the lines gain their keenness.

Cariola. My lord, I lie with her often, and I know
She'll much disquiet you.

Antonio. See, you are complained of.
Cariola. For she's the sprawlingest bedfellow....
Duchess. Doth not the colour of my hair begin to change?
When I wax grey, I shall have all the Court
Powder their hair with orris to be like me....

Webster's incidents have no such firm-knit texture as this,
but his verbal structure is extremely complex. Chapman also
relies a great deal on this kind of cross reference for his
emotional effects. There is a satiric one in *Bussy D'Ambois*
(2. 2. 40ff. and 3. 1. 61). Monsieur, unsuccessfully attempt-
ing to woo Tamyra, offers her a chain of pearl. She refuses
it with outraged propriety and he says:

> Horror of death! could I but please your eyes
> You would give the like e'er you would lose me.

When, later, her accepted lover Bussy is taking his leave of
her, she dismisses him by giving "this chain of pearl and
my love only" (i.e. all my love). The two chains would
probably be identical to point the irony for the audience.
Many of these parallels which are so difficult to see in
reading could easily be stressed in the acting by a gesture,
a similar grouping, or even the right tone of voice.

Chapman can use this device on a far larger scale, to construct a whole scene or a whole act. *Byron's Conspiracy*, 3. 3,
is built upon the discussion of freewill and predestination.
The conjurer's opening soliloquy gives one point of view,
to which Byron's final speech is the complement.

> O the strange difference 'twixt us and the stars!
> They work with inclination strong and fatal
> And nothing know: and we know all their working
> And nought can do or nothing can prevent.
> Rude ignorance is beastly, knowledge wretched.

Compare

> I am a nobler substance than the stars
> And shall the baser overrule the better?
> Or are they better, since they are the bigger?

I have a will and faculties of choice
To do or not to do: and reason why
I do, or not do this: the stars have none,
They know not why they shine, more than this taper.

This kind of structure is not at all dependent on the narrative. What happens between the jesting in the Duchess' bedchamber and the prison scene colours the irony in a general way; but the precise sequence of events does not matter. Neither is it of any concern in what relation the astrologer stands to Byron.

In fact, the Elizabethan dramatists could hardly have fitted all the ingredients of their play into a strictly logical framework of events. They were expected to supply so much more than a contemporary writer, and to incorporate so much non-dramatic material into their plays. There would have to be a certain amount of song and dancing, if the play were for the boys; a certain amount of swordplay and general fighting, if it were for the men's theatres. In addition, there might be some costumes or properties to be worked into the play in the manner of Mr Crummles' pump and washtubs; or a special part for an actor with a definite "line", like the quick-change artist; finally, most intractable of all, there was the bawdry and the clowning. At the same time the text had to be filled with "sentences" for the discerning courtier and the sober citizen; jests for the gull and the prentice; a strict moral code and as many topical allusions as the writer could fit in. The material was as heterogeneous as that of a revue, and the lesser writers did not achieve much more unity than the writer of revue does to-day.[1] A court performance might require a special interpolation, and revivals usually meant the additions of a few new passages.

The play was regularly followed, in the public theatres, by a "jig" or ballad sung and danced by the low comedians

---

[1] It was not merely the popular writers like Dekker who were guilty; *Histriomastix* and *Jack Drum's Entertainment* are thorough medleys.

of the troupe. This was usually indecent, and must have jarred badly with the tragedies. The clown was as intractable as possible: contemporary testimony is unanimous on the point. It is worth noting that in Shakespeare's best constructed plays, *Macbeth* and *Othello*, there is a limitation of the material. The ordinary dramatist could not hope to produce a logical unity out of his varied subject-matter.

The use of dumb shows and inductions further discomposed the narrative, by making some of the action telescoped and symbolic, and preventing consistency in the level of realism or convention on which it was presented. Action in a dumb show must be exaggerated to become intelligible, as anyone who plays in a dumb charade realises. When it was possible to contract an opening scene (such as the opening soliloquy of Faust) so that it represented a lengthy mental process in the mind of Faust himself, there was no reason why large passages of the narrative should not be dropped, why motivation should not be scamped, or ignored.

Of course it was possible for the learned writer, like Ben Jonson, to refuse the demands of the public, and to cut out dumb shows, clowning, and music. But even Jonson was well drilled in the popular methods of play-writing, and could use them if necessity drove him to collaboration or hack-writing. The majority of the writers did their best work inside the conventions of the public theatres. Webster for example, though he apparently wished to write in the manner of Jonson and Chapman, did not attempt it:

Willingly and not ignorantly in this kind have I faulted: for, should a man present to such an audience the most sententious tragedy that ever was written, observing all the critical laws as height of style and gravity of person, enrich it with the sententious Chorus and as it were, liven death in the passionate and weighty Nuntius...— (Preface to *The White Devil*)

yet the public do not like it. Of course this method was

dangerous for the poorer writers. Most of the plays which survive have little literary importance, either because the writer is really incapable of anything better, as in the case of Daborne and Goffe, or because he is deliberately writing down to his audience as Webster did in *The Devil's Law Case*. There are passages in this play which are equal to anything he wrote. As drama it is often very effective: the trial scene improves on that of *The White Devil* but, because the only true unity of an Elizabethan play was poetic, it fails, as Webster acknowledges:

A great part of the grace of this (I confess) lay in the Action: yet can no action ever be gracious, where the decency of the Language and ingenious structure of the Scene arrive not to make up a perfect Harmony.

The dramatists were too ready to disregard their own consciences in this fashion. Sequels were written for plays for which no sequel was really possible, if they had been a great success. There are also theatrical accidents to be considered, such as the necessity to alter a play for the censor, as Massinger altered *Believe as You List*. When all allowances have been made, it must still be admitted that the dramatists were not faithful to their own standards, though this was made easier by the fact that these standards had no other authority than their own conscience. Sometimes by changing the ending a play was turned from tragedy into comedy. *The Yorkshire Tragedy* is evidently an alternative fifth act to *The Miseries of Enforced Marriage*. The last acts of *The Tragedy of Valentinian* and of *The Duke of Milan* appear to be afterthoughts; the whole structure of the play is reversed, the hero becoming a villain.

Chronicle and adventure plays were frankly spectacular and non-literary, and their shapelessness proves how far all order in Elizabethan plays was a literary and poetic order. This is not to suggest that a chronicle play may not be well written of its kind, and so superior to plays like *The Devil's*

Law Case which are of no kind at all. It is only an indication that lesser writers could not disguise their lack of literary power by careful construction, because there was no alternative to construction through literary methods. The unity of a good Elizabethan tragedy cannot be imitated, because it is the personal possession of the dramatist and depends on his power as a poet. It is only the poet's power which could digest the heterogeneous elements of the Elizabethan play: no other solvent would be powerful enough. The nineteenth century's "marvels of construction" deal with relatively limited material. If Pinero had had to add parts for Dan Lupino, Madame Melba and Sandow, the construction would have had to go.

The Elizabethans did achieve a true unity, not merely a *tour de force* of "yoking the most heterogeneous ideas by violence together". They could see good and evil in their extremist forms combined in a single person (Byron, Vindice, Vittoria), or they could see hornpipes and funerals not merely in juxtaposition but in relation to each other. The relation could only be established, however, by means of a convention.

For conventions imply a limitation of interests, and the Elizabethans achieved the unification of their plays by leaving out the interconnections between the different kinds of material. Just as the kinds of feeling are limited and of an extravagant kind and these are kept sharply distinct and yet are so juxtaposed that criticism is implicit; so the events of the narrative are deliberately exaggerated, the action unnaturally rapid and farcical.[1] The value of this lies in the fashion in which it allows the inter-relation of things

[1] For instance, the villain's trick of shielding himself from the hero in fight by holding the heroine before him depends on the absolutely rigid characterisation for its effectiveness (*The Love Sick King*, Act 5; *All's Lost by Lust*, Act 5; *The Courageous Turk*, Act 5; *Alphonsus of Germany*, Act 5; *Rollo, Duke of Normandy* (twice); *Revenge for Honour*, Act 5. Cf. *The Faery Queene*, 4. 7).

normally separated: murders do not usually happen on a wedding night, but the fact that they do in *Women, Beware Women* allows Middleton to stress the sharp, naked contrast between splendour and death, which is such a constant theme of tragedy.

Of course it was not acknowledged that narrative might be deliberately strained and illogical. But, besides the Elizabethan disregard of deduction, there were several other factors which disguised the situation.

First, the narrative might be historical. It was, in fact, a general critical requirement that all tragedy should be based on incidents taken from life; and this was one of the main distinctions between it and comedy, where the plots were feigned. The reason was that tragedy would have a more powerful moral effect if the spectators were convinced that the story was not invented to improve them, but a true "example". Granted, however, that a story was true, the dramatist was under no obligation to make it dramatically convincing. What had happened was clearly possible, as Aristotle said. The dramatist could therefore use astounding coincidences, leave action unmotivated, or mix time and place; since the story was true, such actions would not affect its credibility.

There was, of course, the alternative doctrine that poetry is a higher thing than history:[1] critics and dramatists used whichever suited them. Chapman, for instance, defends *The Revenge of Bussy D'Ambois*, which, while including some real characters (even living persons), was entirely fictitious in its plot. "And for the authentical truth of either person or action, who (worth the respecting) will expect it in a poem whose subject is not truth but things like truth? Poor envious souls they are that cavil at truth's want in these natural fictions." The opposition was, however, to judge from Chapman's protest, of some strength. Jonson puts

[1] Derived from *Poetics*, IX. 3.

"truth of argument" first in his list of requirements in the address to the reader prefixed to *Sejanus*: he adds that he has given his sources not from affectation of learning, but "to show my integrity in the story". Most of the more reputable dramatists based their tragedies on a chronicle, or on contemporary happenings.

Secondly, there were those old and familiar stories which relied on folk-traditions. The kind of realism which these tales have is not dependent on the plausibility of the incidents, but upon the fact that they are woven into the people's very ways of thinking and feeling. The sleeping potion, for example, is accepted automatically, as people will accept the fact that they have ten fingers and two eyes. A legend has no particular need to be like life: it *is* life to the people who created it and to whom it belongs. Coleridge justified the story of King Lear in this way: "Improbable as the conduct of Lear is, in the first scene, yet it was an old story rooted in the popular faith—a thing taken for granted already and consequently without any of the effects of improbability".[1]

Thirdly, there were the stock stories, which acquired the incontestibility of legend by their frequent use. The Revenge plays had a fixed narrative and fixed characters; consequently the speed of the intrigue steadily accelerated, yet the people would not feel the incidents to be incredible, though their effectiveness depended on their being extraordinary. The action is rapid and complicated but not orderly; it is conventionally representative of what Englishmen believed Italian court life to be. But the tradition was so definite that Tourneur could retain the revenge-for-a-father in *The Revenger's Tragedy* as an auxiliary motive to explain the presence of Hippolito; though, actually, of course it has no "weight" in the play—Vindice's only real motive is the revenge for his mistress.

By these methods the dramatists were able to use im-

[1] Raynor, *Coleridge's Shakespearean Criticism*, I, p. 59.

probable narratives "without any of the effects of improbability". Their systems of plotting were very simple; the most popular were the cumulative and that based upon peripeteia.

The cumulative plot was used by Marlowe in *Tamburlaine* and *Faustus*, by some writers of domestic tragedy (especially the author of *Arden of Feversham*) and by the writers of some Machiavellian plays and of the plays of the Senecal hero. The plot involving peripeteia was used in Revenge tragedy, in some of the plays of the Machiavel and by most writers after 1616.

In the cumulative plot, the same type of incident was repeated again and again, in a crescendo and with quickening tempo, up to the catastrophe. Tamburlaine goes from one conquest to another; the only advance is numerical. Alice Arden makes six unsuccessful attempts to kill her husband (until the spectator feels positively irritated that she should not succeed), and the Senecal heroes endure one trial after another. *Macbeth* is the supreme example of this kind of plot.

This kind of action allows of only a single direction. There can be no side issues: clowning and subplots are excrescences because there should be no slackening of the main interest. It is very difficult to keep the tension sustained for five acts. Even Marlowe, when faced by a second part of *Tamburlaine*, could not produce a real continuation, but only a series of digressions and one or two fine scenes.

The cumulative plot, as imitated by the lesser writers, became even more shapeless, for it lost the crescendo. *Lust's Dominion*, or the adventure plays, run in an even fashion from beginning to end.

The plots involving peripeteia are much more complex. In this case the order of events is of great importance, although it does not (at first) require much piecing of evidence from the reader. The play moves forward in a series of jumps: each small action is ironically constructed. This method derived from Kyd and *The Jew of Malta*, but it was not uninfluenced by the plots of comedy. The later Revenge tragedy depended on rapid and trivial intrigue; but the irony of the action is only supplementary to the irony of the writing (particularly in the comments of the Malcontents). The narrative depends upon strained coincidences and extraordinary uses of the *quiproquo*: the more ingeniously complex it is, the better. This does not prevent very careful work on the detail, such as, for instance, Tourneur gives in *The Revenger's Tragedy*. The final result is not very different from that of *Wuthering Heights* or one of Hardy's novels. Emily Brontë and Hardy use coincidence and symmetry in the arrangement of characters and events which make their stories quite unrealistic: yet because the irony of narrative is dominated by a sufficiently powerful irony in the texture of the novels themselves, the action can be taken as serious and not fantastic. Again, the detail is precise, and of course the narrative is much more orderly and the characters are more fully drawn in the novels than in a play.

Many of the misconceptions as to the function of the drama seem to have arisen from the confusion between the methods of drama and those of the novel. During the nineteenth century the novel was the predominant literary form, and most dramatists relied upon the work of novelists. The closet drama was generally a novel in dialogue: few writers realised that a novel in dialogue was not a drama. The novel, owing to the fuller and more leisurely form, can allow logical development of action, interaction and development of character. In the drama these can at best be indicated in a summary manner, so that by rapidity of presentation they appear to be complete, as different colours painted on a wheel merge into each other when the wheel is revolved. Drama can only give the appearance of those developments possible in the novel, by the retrospective method, which makes the play cover by implication a larger amount of time than is actually presented, and so gives the illusion of character development. (For instance, in *Rosmersholm*, neither Rebecca nor Rosmer develop much in the play; they only discover how much they had been changed from their old selves, as the play proceeds.)

Again, because in a novel comment is possible, it does not impoverish the feelings to reduce the language of the characters to that of ordinary speech. Their feelings can still be defined by description so that they are seen to be delicate and not coarse, precise and not vague. Whereas the drama, where the dialogue has to define as well as to present the feeling, if the language of real life is adopted for the characters, has no other means of defining their feeling—for action cannot define but only present them.[1] It was a common practice in the nineteenth century to define the feelings by stage directions: but that is an essentially undramatic method. The actor can only translate the stage direction into action of the ordinary kind; his contribution will be the same for Pinero and Shakespeare. The Elizabethans hardly used stage directions at all, because the action, though important, was not intended to define the feelings, but to reflect those defined in the verse: and so must be the case in any literary drama. Realistic narrative, characterisation and speech starve the drama, because it is already too concentrated a form to accept the limitations of the novel in addition: it must be more selective, and selection is only possible through a convention.

In addition to the conventional narrative and its formal arrangement the Elizabethans relied upon their "feeling for allegory". On the level of the presentation this was developed in different kinds of representation, such as the dumb show, and conjuring; and on the level of the action by the

---

[1] For instance Juliet's weeping in Shakespeare would not produce a different effect from Flo's weeping in Mr Stanley Houghton's play.

contrast between different moods (almost different genus) of drama in the plot and subplot.[1]

The early dumb shows were allegorical, and the later ones have a special atmosphere of portentousness which easily becomes allegorical. Silent movement is always doubly significant on the stage. For example, when the Cardinal puts on the soldier's armour in *The Duchess of Malfi*, before he has banished her, there is a feeling that he is arming against her, though of course this is not so; but the effect is akin to the effect of Lady Macbeth's "Come all ye spirits that tend on mortal thoughts". At other times, of course, the dumb show might be only an economic and more vivid way of giving events than by a conversation between First and Second Gentlemen.

The dumb show almost disappears after 1620. It decayed with the other conventions of the great tragic period.

The induction was at first an even more primitive device than the dumb show. The presenter merely introduced the characters or expounded the moral, acting as an undisguised author's mouthpiece and sometimes pretending to be the author of the play. Sometimes particular personages were used to cast a "tone" over the rest of the play, to tinge it with their peculiar personality.[2] The Witches in *Macbeth* might be considered as an induction to the play. The debates between several allegorical personages was a clear survival of the morality;[3] it affords auxiliary evidence for the way in which plays were written around a moral.

The Spanish Tragedy's induction, with its mixture of allegorical and supernatural, stands half-way between these moral inductions and those which dealt with a different

[1] Miss Enid Welsford, in *The Court Masque*, chapter x, expresses a view similar to that developed in the following pages.

[2] Machiavelli (*Jew of Malta*); Guicciardine (*The Devil's Charter*); Sylla's Ghost (*Catiline*).

[3] *Soliman and Perseda, A Warning for Fair Women, True Tragedy of Richard III, Two Lamentable Tragedies.*

group of human characters. In this case, the play proper became a play-within-the-play on a gigantic scale.[1] There is the most curious confusion between the different levels: in *James IV* Bohun is a character in the induction, but his sons are characters in the play and have no life apart from the play, which their father controls and directs like a god, predicting the action. The introduction of several figures into the induction made it quite a different thing from an isolated presenter. The point about all these characters was that they remained on the stage the whole time and commented on the action, and so the two planes of action were felt simultaneously.

Jonson, however, invented a new kind of induction. It was a vehicle for direct social criticism or satire, or for a conscious appeal to the artificiality of the play by showing the actors as their real selves. The boys, even the bookkeeper, come on and discuss the play, their parts and the audience. Marston adopted Jonson's method and used the short introductory scene for social criticism and a discussion of the "humours" of the different characters. Jonson regularly used the induction in his comedies for social criticism of a general kind, but more directly related to his audience than that of the body of the play.

The flexibility which these different levels of acting gave to the drama is of the greatest importance. The difference between this and a dead-level play of the nineteenth century is the difference between a bicycle with three-speed gear and one without it. The dramatists were able to adjust their narrative so as to throw stress in exactly the right place.

The play-within-the-play was the most useful of all these modifications of the action. It allowed for shadow work and ironic interplay in a more complex way than the induction; for the characters who acted in it could be given parts which

[1] *James IV, Taming of a Shrew, Old Wives' Tale, Summer's Last Will and Testament.*

reflected upon their rôles within the play proper. The play in *The Spanish Tragedy* is a simple parallel to the main action, and so is *The Murder of Gonzago*. But the masque in *Women, Beware Women* is more elaborately ironical. Livia, the procuress, plays the part of Juno Pronuba; and her niece Isabella, whose incestuous love and prudential marriage form the subplot, a nymph wooed by her two swains. The colourless chastity of the masque and the lewdness of the true situation are violently opposed to each other. The masque in *The Maid's Tragedy* with its description of the "sudden storm" rising on the marriage night, is not entirely irrelevant.

The transition from the play-within-the-play to the subplot is easy, for their functions were similar. The subplot is a device which the nineteenth century rejected, as loose and untidy, and even Sheridan observed that the "subplot should have as little to do with the main plot as possible". It is true that the Elizabethans sometimes built a play from two quite unconnected stories, but this happens far less frequently than it is usual to suppose. For the subplot was contrasted and not interwoven with the main action: it reflected upon it, either as a criticism or a contrast, or a parallel illustration of the same moral worked out in another manner, a kind of echo or metaphor of the tragedy.

The *Two Lamentable Tragedies* of Yarrington are a simple example. One of these tragedies is an Italian version of *The Babes in the Wood*; the other a local murder, wherein a shopkeeper, Beech, and his apprentice were murdered by another shopkeeper named Merry. On the surface there is no possible connection between these stories. But the murderer's motive is the same in both (avarice), the methods of hiding the crime similar: both murderers are sheltered by their kinsfolk and both are repentant. The two stories are presented in alternating scenes which correspond to each other: thus the discovery of the Italian murder is followed by the discovery of the English murder; the apprehension of one murderer by the apprehension of the other, and so on. The characters in the induction, who are Truth, Falsehood and Homicide, enter at the end of each act and comment on both the actions; that is, their statements are generalisations and apply equally to both stories.

This is a very simple case of unification through the moral. It is not defensible from the results here (Yarrington was a very poor writer) but it shows that the method of contrasting plot and subplot was quite conscious.

The plot and subplot of *A Woman Killed with Kindness* are contrasted in the same way. In the main plot, Wendoll betrays his friend Frankford, to whom he is under the deepest obligation, by seducing Mistress Frankford. She, having yielded, afterwards repents and finds that the only way to regain her honour is by dying.[1] In the subplot Sir Charles Mountford contracts a debt of gratitude to his enemy; rather than not repay it, he offers the enemy the possession of a sister, whom he has long solicited. The sister, to pay her brother's debt, agrees to this, but adds that she will kill herself and so preserve her chastity with her life, which so works upon the enemy that he becomes reconciled and marries her.

These two actions are therefore antithetical in respect both of gratitude and ingratitude, and chastity and unchasteness. But also there is an overt connection,[2] and no felt fusion of the one with the other, as there was between masque and play in *The Maid's Tragedy* and *Women, Beware Women*.

The commonest division in tragedy is between the life

---

[1] *Vide* Frankford's speech:

"Though thy rash offence
Divorced our bodies, thy repentant tears unite our souls...
My wife, the mother to my pretty babes.
Both these lost names I do restore thee back,
And with this kiss I wed thee once again".

[2] Mistress Frankford is sister to Acton: they appear together in the opening and the closing scenes.

of kings and princes and that of the common people. Most of the non-literary drama of the period has a subplot of the heartiest comedy in which the common people are seen pursuing their life quite undisturbed by the tragedy of the "higher" characters, as the Gravedigger does in *Hamlet*, the Porter in *Macbeth* and the Clown in *Antony and Cleopatra*. Again, the lesser writers used the device very clumsily; but the justification lies in what *could* be made of it, not what too frequently was.

By this means the dramatist could master the most potentially intractable element, the clowning. Sometimes his intentions are better than his performance; for example, in *Antonio's Revenge*, Marston evidently means the clown Balurdo to contrast, in his careless, impregnable stupidity, with the anguish of the main characters. Antonio adopts the rôle of a fool; he even wishes really to be a fool, because the fool, who cannot sense the miseries of the world, is always happy. But Balurdo's clowning does not produce the right results; at least, not in reading. He is so bawdy that the modern taste cannot consider him quite dispassionately.

On the other hand, the clowning in *The Atheist's Tragedy* seems to me to succeed. Unless Tourneur's own disgust is felt behind the treatment of Langbeau Snuffe, Cataplasma and Soquette, the force of the subplot is lost. The obscenity is not there for its own sake; it is placed in a definite relationship to the main plot, as in the contrast between Levidulcia and Castabella in 2. 3.

There is a similar subplot in *The Second Maiden's Tragedy*. The strictly implicit relation of two plots may seem a very far-fetched notion, but it is related to the feeling for the allegorical which has been discussed earlier, and depended on the Elizabethans' training in seeing the world divided into sheep and goats: the Morality tradition, the contemporary sermon, and the permanent tendency of the simple minded assisting here. It also depended on seeing varieties of "examples" related to a central moral precept. This is the method of *Four Plays in One*, with its curious induction and its grouping of quite heterogeneous stories. (It is probable that *The Yorkshire Tragedy* formed part of a series of this kind,[1] like Yarrington's *Two Lamentable Tragedies*.) *Four Plays in One* seems a most convincing piece of documentary evidence, though it is certainly not normal. But the study of the Elizabethan stage can be helped by adopting a pathological technique.

The plots and subplots of Middleton's two tragedies have hitherto received nothing but abuse. By this method it is quite possible to find an orderly arrangement in *The Changeling* and *Women, Beware Women*, but as this requires to be proved at length, it is postponed although it is the culmination of this particular argument.

Beaumont and Fletcher show a much closer approximation to modern methods of construction than their predecessors do. They took over from Jonsonian comedy the method of keeping the audience in the dark. Hints of dark designs are thrown out, to stimulate curiosity: inexplicable behaviour (obviously dictated by some obscure policy) is followed by the sudden revelation of unsuspected new factors. This method throws a great deal more weight upon the narrative; the audience become more interested in the way in which things are worked out than in the speed of the action, or in a series of reversals and recoils. The subplot loses its significance; the clowns of *The Bloody Brother* are as irrelevant as any early ones.

. . . . .

To turn from narrative to characterisation is to find that the difference between Elizabethan and contemporary fiction

[1] There was a certain *Five Plays in One* (Henslowe's *Diary*, p. 51) which has not survived: also *Three Plays in One* (*Extracts from the Accounts of the Revels*, p. 189).

is reversed. Elizabethan narrative was fluid compared with the logical stories of to-day; on the other hand, Elizabethan characters were preternaturally rigid.

It is only during the last dozen years that there has been any attempt to discover the conventions behind Shakespeare's characterisation. The other Elizabethan dramatists have hardly been considered at all, for the "rediscovery" of Elizabethan drama coincided with the rise of the nineteenth-century school of Shakespearean criticism, which interpreted the plays entirely through narrative and character. It was inevitable that the lesser writers should be judged by the same standards, which, if they distorted Shakespeare, annihilated Chapman.

The eighteenth century had considered it the excellence of Shakespeare's characters to be typical.

The Parasite and Vainglorious in Parolles in *All's Well that Ends Well* is as good as anything of the kind in Plautus and Terence...and I believe Thersites in *Troilus and Cressida* and Apemantus in *Timon of Athens* will be allowed to be masterpieces of ill nature and satyrical snarling.

This was Rowe's judgment; and Johnson's was that "In the writings of other poets a character is too often an individual: in Shakespeare it is commonly a species". The eighteenth century knew nothing of Shakespeare's contemporaries; even Malone could dismiss all his predecessors as unworthy of consideration.

When Coleridge, Hazlitt and Lamb began to write critically of the lesser Elizabethans, Johnson's attitude was obsolete. Had the plays ever been staged it would have been obvious enough that they could not be approached by those methods which Morgann and Warton had used to interpret Shakespeare. Even Shakespeare himself was becoming divorced from the stage at least for critical purposes. Lamb's essay reflected the general opinion. As Hazlitt observed "some of his more obscure contemporaries have the *advantage* over Shakespeare himself in so much as we have never seen their works represented on the stage...".[1] The plays were read as poetic romances rather than as drama, and this meant that the action became altogether subordinated to the character. For in a novel action may be described; in drama it is presented and if the plays are not acted (or read as if they were being seen) the action will cease to be considered, because it is not part of the text.

Coleridge, Hazlitt and Lamb were interested almost exclusively in characterisation. Coleridge's psychological bent and Lamb's gregariousness turned all the characters into real human beings. The dramatists also became personal friends. Heywood has "generosity, courtesy, temperance in the depths of passion, sweetness in a word and gentleness: Christianism: and true hearty Anglicism of feeling shaping that Christianism....His plots are almost invariably English. I am sometimes jealous that Shakespeare laid so few of his scenes at home....I love them both equally...".[2] Hazlitt on Orlando Friscobaldo is even more revealing. "I only lately became acquainted with this last named character, but the bargain between us is, I trust, for life...", and later, "I can take mine ease in mine inn with Signor Orlando Friscobaldo as the oldest acquaintance I have. Ben Jonson, learned Chapman, Master Webster and Master Heywood are there".[3] (It is tempting to juxtapose a modern equivalent, the feelings of an undergraduate towards a minor Victorian poet, "Curious the way it immediately suggests great intimacy with the author. FRIENDSHIP. A room at night, roaring log fire, curtains drawn, chimney corner, author musing, old inns, you and him alone".[4]) This attitude towards the author and his characters persisted. Swinburne's

---

[1] *Elizabethan Literature*, Lecture III (*Works*, ed. P. A. Howe, VI, p. 246).
[2] Note to "Fortunes by Sea and Land" *Specimens*.
[3] *Works*, ed. P. A. Howe, VI, pp. 235, 247.
[4] I. A. Richards, *Practical Criticism*, p. 29.

viewpoint was virtually the same. "Many friends we have
of Shakespeare's giving whom we love deeply and well, if
hardly with such love as could weep for them all the tears
of the body and all the blood of the heart: but there is none
we love like Othello."[1]

There was another way in which these plays were used
as substitutes for living. Their bold obscenities and their
blood-and-thunder horrors were very refreshing to a re-
pressed and respectable age. Lamb's unfortunate choice of
the more mechanical and subsidiary features of the fourth
act of *The Duchess of Malfi* and his astonishing comments
upon *The Fair Quarrel* and *The Broken Heart* are the earliest
examples of a mood that found the latest expression in
Rupert Brooke's admiration for the "clean fineness of the
Elizabethans". A simple inversion of their attitude produces
the delighted recognition of their wickedness which is so
noticeable in the criticism of Symonds. Vindice, for example,

emerges from the tainted crew... with a kind of blasted splendour.
They are curling and engendering, a brood of flat-headed asps,
in the slime of their filthy appetites and gross ambitions. He
treads and tramples on them all. But he bears on his own brow
the brands of Lucifer the rebel and Cain the assassin.[2]

It was this kind of criticism which encouraged Shaw to
call Webster "Tussaud Laureate". But so long as Tourneur
and Webster are read as if their characters were drawn from
the life, this attitude is inevitable.

The Romantics ignored the drama and concentrated on
the poetry. Shaw and William Archer ignored the poetry
and could not see the drama in consequence. Happily the
persistence of criticism solely in terms of the characters is not
likely. The advance of psychology has made it plain that
even Shakespeare's characters leave much to be desired.
A modern writer has rediscovered Johnson's dictum that

---

[1] *A Study in Shakespeare*, pp. 184–5.
[2] Introduction to the Mermaid Edition, p. xiv.

each of Shakespeare's characters is not an individual but a species.

The consciousness of one's own individuality, which is a common characteristic of ordinary plain men and women of to-day, is rare in the subtlest and rarest minds of antiquity.... The psychological difference is in the individual's relation to and representation of other people. In the whole of literature before 1700, there are hardly any characters, which, if you compare them with fictional characters of the nineteenth century, are not types rather than individuals. In the drama, which before the eighteenth century was almost the only form of fiction, the audience is invited to watch the tragedy and comedy not of individual characters but of personified general human beings.[1]

Mr Woolf illustrates his point from Shakespeare's plays, and concludes that only Hamlet and Falstaff are individuals. He joins forces, consciously or not, with Stoll and Schucking. The critics of last century had not approached any kind of unity; for instance, it would not be true to say that Swinburne's reading was affected by work on the Elizabethan stage which the pioneers of the New Shakespeare Society were doing. It is only because of the labours of several generations that it is now possible to apply the results of scholarship to the criticism of the texts.

Nineteenth-century critics were therefore obliged to judge the lesser Elizabethans by the standards of their own time. They were influenced by the current dramatic theory, which was Realism; and the dominant literary form which was the novel.

The doctrine of Realism in the drama was bound up with the development of representational scenery, which had driven Shakespeare from the stage for the literary critics. "Dramatic literature" became something quite different from "drama". It would be hard to say whether closet

[1] Leonard Woolf, *After the Deluge, A Study in Communal Psychology*, p. 244.

drama had a more pernicious effect upon the later Elizabethans or the later Elizabethans upon closet drama. The writers of the sixteenth century had touched the academical Senecal drama on one hand, but also they had touched the *Commedia dell' Arte* on the other.[1]

It was easy to show that by nineteenth-century standards they were deficient in characterisation. Jonson's arbitrary system put him under a cloud for the last half of the century. Chapman had not even a visible system to recommend him. The writers of the decadence were far more popular, especially Massinger and Ford.

At the beginning of this century it became clear that even Shakespeare's characters could not stand the test of modern dramatic construction, especially in comedy. There was Bassanio who behaved like a fortune-hunter and was obviously a hero; there was Helena of Narbonne who behaved like a minx and was obviously a heroine. If the lesser Elizabethans had ever been subjected to the same kind of scrutiny they would appear much worse than Shakespeare. Nothing would have been made of Orlando Friscobaldo or Mistress Frankford; and the question of "How many children had Lady Macbeth?" pales beside that of "How many children had the Duchess of Malfi?".

The modern conception of character has therefore been granted inappropriate to Shakespeare, and so presumably to his contemporaries. There has, however, been less attempt to realise what positive standards of characterisation the Elizabethans possessed. There were roughly three: the superhuman nature of heroes, the definition of character by decorum, and the theory of Humours. There were various conventions which belonged to the drama, such as the credibility of slander, the impenetrability of disguise (which had important consequences in the characters of the villain heroes) and the limitation of motives.

[1] *Vide* Miss K. M. Lea, *Italian Popular Comedy*, II, chapter VI.

The tragic hero (quite apart from modern theories of his origin) was not thought of as a human being, on the same level as the other characters in the play. If he were a king, his royalty invested him with special powers; and the difference between comedy and tragedy was often defined in this way, that comedy dealt with common people and tragedy with kings and princes: the distinction persisted till the end of the eighteenth century.

Shakespeare describes the popular attitude to rulers in *Henry V*, 4. 1, but though he did not accept it uncritically he relied upon it to a certain extent.

> A sight too pitiful in the meanest wretch,
> Past speaking of in a *king*.

This was partly the distinction between a man and his office on which half the pathos of Edward II and Richard II depends. The Fletcherian theory of divine right is not really very different from an attitude implicit in the earlier plays, for kings were never thought of on the level of their subjects. The conclusion of a tragedy usually emphasises the superiority of the ruler. Vittoria says:

> I will be waited on in death: my maid
> Shall never go before me—

and Cleopatra is served by Charmian and Iras. It is the distance between them which makes the identity of their common end so significant:

> Sceptre and crown
> Must tumble down
> And in the dust be equal laid
> With the poor crooked scythe and spade.

The crown itself is sometimes used as symbolic of the powers conferred by the royal office.

This division between the tragic hero and common humanity is sometimes emphasised by a subplot which deals with the lower classes. In the Revenge plays the rulers exercise their power in a kind of vacuum; there is no hint of ordinary daily life outside the court. In other plays the mob are used as foils for the heroic characters, as in Jonson's *Sejanus* and Fletcher's romances. In the histories the contrast is all-important, and in some comedies the king appears as a *deus ex machina* to solve the plot; though he fraternises with his people, he is not of them.[1]

The possible range of motives was very much narrowed by this attitude toward the hero. Ambition and lust (which may be called a special form of ambition or possessiveness) are practically the only two which are admitted, and these in most narrowed and specialised forms. In the Machiavellian plays, ambition is the mainspring of the action; in Revenge tragedy, lust. There are, of course, the perpetual motives of tragedy; what is particular to the Elizabethan drama is that they are not only predominantly but almost exclusively so.

The motives and behaviour of the characters were also limited by the laws of decorum. This applied to comedy rather than to tragedy, where the tyrant was the only figure who had any relation to classical precept and example. The idea that all characters could be classified into "types" and their correct behaviour deduced from their type was due to the confusion of poetical and rhetorical theory which has been described so often. The sixteenth-century ideas of decorum were derived from Aristotle's *Rhetoric* and the *Characters* of Theophrastus; according to current interpretation it was wrong for a character to behave in any other manner than that proper to his type. Whetstone's famous precept, "To work a comeddie kindly, grave old men should instruct, young men should shew imperfections of youth, strumpets should be lascivious, Boyes unhappe and clowns should speak disorderlye", is behind a good deal of con-

[1] *Friar Bacon and Friar Bungay, The Shoemaker's Holiday, Mayor of Queensborough*, etc.

ventional motivation. "Young men should shew imperfections of youth", for instance, accounts for the lack of
any moral judgment on the prodigals like Bertram of
Rousillon.

There was no blurring or running together of these
sharply divided classes. Age and youth were kept so rigidly
distinct that the young are nearly all adolescents and the old
quite senile. Parents and children are separated by such a
gap that they seem more like grandparents and grand-
children. This is so even in Shakespeare's tragedies, while
in his later plays it is made very clear that all the population
not under twenty-one is over fifty (fifty being quite a ripe
old age by Elizabethan standards).

Most of the villains are given some kind of defect which
embitters them and cuts them off from humanity. This is no
justification for their behaviour, for the Elizabethan mind
was not accustomed to distinguish between crimes which
were the result of choice and those which were the result
of heredity. Barabas is a Jew; Aaron and Muly Mohamet
are Moors; Richard III is a cripple and Edmund a bastard.
Extreme poverty drives Flaminio, Bosola and a good many
minor villains to crime, and this makes them less villainous
as a rule. In early tragedy most of the heroes are tyrants;
even the "good" heroes like Hieronimo or Titus Andronicus
are forced to commit shocking murders and are reinforced
by several deep-dyed villains. This is partly due to imitation
of the Senecal tyrant, and partly to the fact that a villain
hero greatly simplified the business of pointing a moral.
The death of a good man could not be made into a
moral at all, unless it were more of an apotheosis than a
defeat.

The blackest kind of villain is the lustful tyrant, and he
persists from the beginnings of the drama up to the closing
of the theatres. Sometimes he was ferocious, sometimes
cunning and Machiavellian, sometimes cowardly, but, except

for the Machiavels, these villains are hardly ever interesting. Their business was to complicate the action and produce the tragic situation.

Their feminine counterpart, the noble harlot, was at first something of a Machiavel and rather an interesting figure. But, like the tyrant, she was much overworked by Fletcher and Massinger. The women of Elizabethan drama may be divided into the chaste and the unchaste. It was a masculine drama, as befitted the predominantly masculine audience. The noble harlot only occupies the chief rôle in a few plays (*The Insatiate Countess*, *The White Devil*, and *Women, Beware Women*), and wherever she is accompanied by a Machiavel she only plays a small part in the intrigue.[1]

There are very few purely ambitious women (Evadne in *The Maid's Tragedy* is the most notable exception).

The villainess is opposed to the chaste heroine. A set defence of chastity was very popular: nearly sixty examples have been recorded.[2] These (occasionally rather truculent) virgins are, apart from their chastity, quite colourless and might have appeared with that single qualification in Whetstone's catalogue.

There are a number of stock subsidiary characters, such as the cheated tool villain, the bluff soldier[3] and the pathetic child.[4] The tool villain's rôle depended upon the narrative rather than upon his character. It was usual to have several villains who were played off against one another, but the minor villains were simply there to cause this imbroglio, and consequently they exist only as counters of the intrigue. For there was no attempt to make the minor characters "human". First and second gentlemen were used as channels for conveying information to the audience; there was

---

[1] *Vide* R. S. Forsythe, *The Relation of Shirley's Plays to the Elizabethan Drama*, pp. 98–9.
[2] *Ibid.* pp. 69–70.　　　　　　[3] *Ibid.* pp. 101–2.
[4] *Vide* E. E. Stoll, *John Webster*, pp. 145–50.

no effort to disguise the fact by making one of them into a comic clergyman and the other into a maiden aunt.

The bluff soldier was a comparatively late comer in tragedy; his rôle was half humorous and half pathetic. He is shown as a kind of innocent, cheated by courtiers and perhaps by his ruler, touchingly inclined to choler, though extremely tender-hearted. The audience is meant to feel a kind of condescending affection for him: it is extremely flattering to think that those capable of prodigies of valour are so inferior to ourselves in insight and wit. The bluff soldier is the first and perhaps the most successful of "sympathetic" characters.

The pathetic child, as noted by Stoll, is precocious, lively, and usually with martial ambitions. His rôle is not very different in its effect on the audience from that of the bluff soldier.

The typical characters never present any difficulty except where their actions are at variance with their characters. In this case, the action has simply to be ignored in so far as it might affect the judgment of the character. For example in *Bonduca*, Petillus' betrayal of Poenius is quite dissociated from his rôle of bluff soldier. If the Elizabethan audience were told that a man was honest, they did not alter their mind because he happened to be caught picking a pocket. "Character" was fixed (grave old men should instruct) and action need have no effect on it.[1]

The most difficult case of dissociation is that of the prodigals. They are comic types and in comedy the rogue has a licence to go far. But these young men behave in a way which, if taken seriously, would be quite criminal. It would be perfectly easy to take it as knockabout farce if their long-suffering wives and parents were not held up as models of patient affection. But it is very difficult for a modern reader to enjoy both Mathias and Orlando Friscobaldo's daughter. Either he should be condemned or she

---

[1] Compare the attitude of the Censor, *infra* p. 126.

should be as callous as Judy in a Punch and Judy show. But this is a problem of comedy and not of tragedy.

Such old tricks as the substitution of one woman for another (which Shakespeare used twice) had no moral valency at all. The opposite device occurs in *All's Lost by Lust*. A husband, Antonio, who wishes to get rid of his wife, persuades his friend to disguise in his clothes and sleep with her. In this way his wife, though quite involuntarily, commits adultery and he is "justified" in divorcing her. The letter and not the spirit of the action was the important thing. A sudden repentance of the villain is on a similar level. It is never convincing, but it is never to be questioned.

This attitude is comparable with the great stress which Elizabethans laid on the sense rather than the intention of words, so that equivocations could be a serious matter. Very often the whole plot of a play turns on a verbal quibble, and an action will be the height of wickedness or the height of goodness according to which way the quibble is resolved.[1]

Quibbles and equivocations are of no particular significance when they are kept to the level of the narrative and do not imply any juggling with the feelings of the play. But sometimes they permit a kind of double emotional response by which the spectator or reader is allowed to indulge a feeling which does not lead anywhere, and is contradicted later on. For example, there are several reports of deaths,[2] described in speeches of great pathos so that the full emotional implications of such a death are felt; but afterwards the reports are disproved and the feeling counts for nothing. In *Hoffman*, Lucibel and her lover are mortally

---

[1] It was encouraged by all kinds of public arrangements: by the Act of Conformity, for instance, which compelled attendance at church but did not examine beliefs.

[2] *Antonio's Revenge* (twice), *The Malcontent*, *The Atheist's Tragedy*, *Thierry and Theodoret*, *Satiromastix*, *The Honest Whore*.

wounded and they have a final dialogue (a kind of "positive-ly last appearance") in which they describe their hopes of Heaven and how they will ascend together, and so on. But Lucibel is required later in the play, so that her "death" turns out only to be a swoon and she recovers.

Granted the system of rigidly defined types, of stock motivation and fixed plot, the dramatist was bound to observe the limits which he had so defined for himself.

Whole ranges of possible action were cut off by the use of types. For instance, characters could neither interact upon each other, nor develop, for the type was sharply defined and could not be modified. There is no mental interplay; the nearest approach to it is the villain's handling of his dupes (Sejanus' wooing of Livia or his courtesy to Macro, for example). Shakespeare is the exception: there is a good deal of modification of one mind by another in *Hamlet*.

Again, characters did not develop. They might be sud-denly reversed by love-at-first-sight, or repentance, but these complete changes of heart are not natural at all. The character is instantaneously swung from one attitude to its opposite, and always to its opposite. Kings become beggars (they are never reduced to genteel poverty), mothers kill their children, whores become immovably chaste, and misers incredibly generous. The process is never graduated, and the change is never less than from black to white, from wrong to right.

Moreover, there is no attempt to disguise its violent and arbitrary nature. The characters flatly describe what they feel on these occasions, and even underline its miraculous suddenness and completeness.

Again, Shakespeare is the exception. Lear, Macbeth and Lady Macbeth may be said in some sense to develop. But their development is never brought forward for open dis-cussion, or isolated from the general movement of the play, as, say, the development of Rebecca in *Rosmersholm*. Outside Shakespeare character-development is very rare: the Duchess of Malfi and Beatrice-Joanna in *The Changeling* are outstanding cases.

This method of writing affects the characterisation by blurring motives or reversing the whole nature of the person. The complete reversal of character is fairly common in tragedy.[1] It is less credible when brought about by the persuasion of another character than when it is purely self-effected: for in the first case the efficient cause is displayed in all its inefficiency, and in the other the forces at work, such as conscience, ambition or love, are left to the imagination. The exhortations of the virtuous are set pieces of moralising, like those in *The Honest Whore*, which are not adopted to persuasion. Hippolito hurls a few platitudes at the whore; Vindice has only to browbeat his mother with trite generalisations to convert her from a model of propriety to a model of wickedness and back again, when she is ready to reproduce the generalisations to her daughter.

These reversals are, however, so frankly artificial that there is no point in dwelling on their lack of verisimilitude. They are closely related to other conventions, such as the dissociation of character in disguise; and in the case of Vindice's mother, there may be another explanation.[2]

The fixed type made such reversals of character the only possible form of character-development: each type was like a mask which could only be replaced by another mask and not modified in itself. (Compare the implications of characterisation behind the masking games in *Much Ado About Nothing* and *Love's Labour's Lost*.)

---

[1] *Vide* Eugenia (*Lust's Dominion*), Piero (*Antonio's Revenge*), Aurelia and Pietro (*The Malcontent*), Lorrique (*Hoffman*), Bosola (*The Duchess of Malfi*), Evadne (*The Maid's Tragedy*), Helvetius (*The Second Maiden's Tragedy*), the Mother (*Women, Beware Women*), the daughters of Theophilus (*The Virgin Martyr*).

[2] *Vide infra*, p. 174.

Credibility of slander was a most useful convention for complicating the action. The elaborate attempts to "justify" Othello, and the criticism of Claudio or Posthumus are equally ill-founded. All three belong to the same type as Philaster, of whose "justification" by Elizabethan standards there can be no doubt. *Othello* is perhaps the most brilliantly constructed of all Elizabethan plays. Here, if anywhere, slander is made credible, and the movement of the hero's mind from security through doubt to a conviction by the slander is adequately shown. Yet even here there is a moment at which Shakespeare deliberately underlines the arbitrary nature of Othello's belief.

> Now I do see 'tis true. Look here, Iago.
> All my fond love thus do I blow to Heaven.
> 'Tis gone.
> Arise, black vengeance, from the hollow hell!
> Yield up, O love, thy crown and hearted throne
> To tyrannous hate. (3. 3. 445 ff.)

There is a memory here of such scenes as the "discovery" of heaven and hell in the ultimate hour of Faustus. "Heaven" and "hell" were definite parts of the stage, associated with their appropriate inhabitants. Othello dismissed love (with a gesture in the right direction) which he recognises as "heavenly" and receives hate, which he knows to be hellish. It is almost like Faustus' selling of his soul (and perhaps, to carry the fancy a little further, it was emphasised by Othello's kneeling to take this vow, and by Iago swearing afterwards to do him service "what bloody deed soever").

A telescoping of the time of action is inevitable in drama and unnoticed in acting or in reading (the difficulties only arise when the critic begins to analyse after his reading). A violent reversal from love to hatred would be the expected, and obvious, thing to the audience. The difficulty in Shakespeare's case arises from the difference between the realism with which he presents his characters and the conventional manner in which he motivates them. Leontes is perhaps the most striking example.[1]

A character who is behaving "according to type" will need no motivation at all. In the same way, the "motiveless malignity" of Iago is not proof that he was a monster. The Elizabethans did not expect every character to produce one rational explanation for every given action; consequently they did not think that characters who offered "inadequate" explanations were monstrous. Ferdinand of Aragon, in *The Duchess of Malfi*, describes his motive for persecuting his sister

> I hoped...to get
> An infinite mass of treasure by her death.

This has not only the fault of being incompatible with the facts of the case (he could not inherit), but the much more serious fault of being incompatible with his tone and temper. Ferdinand has not behaved like a cheated miser, but like one whose moral sense has been outraged by the Duchess' conduct. He plans vengeance:

> I would have their bodies
> Burnt in a coal pit and the ventage stopped
> That their cursed smoke might not ascend to Heaven.

His anger is almost like Othello's. Compare

> I will chop her into messes. Cuckold me!

His explanation is simply put there (and it is a delayed explanation, as usual in Webster) in case anyone requires a motive. It is so unashamedly counterfeit that to object to it shows an almost painful lack of tact. One might as

[1] Other cases of the credibility of slander are the Viceroy of Portugal (*The Spanish Tragedy*, I. 3); the princes in *Alphonsus of Germany*; Pietro believes Mendoza (*The Malcontent*); Brachiano believes Florence's letter (*The White Devil*); Mendoza believes the Queen (*Lust's Dominion*); Bajazet believes Selimus (*Selimus*); Philaster is suspicious with no evidence at all.

well object to Portia's bland refusal to explain the inexplicable news that Antonio's wealth is all restored (at the end of *The Merchant of Venice*):

> You shall not know by what strange accident
> I chanced on this letter.

To return to Iago: he is plainly a villain, as he is at pains to expound in soliloquy. Villains are villains; there is no need to ask why. "They are as they are." Besides, he is an Italian, and therefore it goes without saying that he is treacherous, jealous and Machiavellian. If, in addition, he likes to explain that he is jealous of Othello and Cassio, that he resents losing the lieutenancy, and that he is in love with Desdemona himself, his explanations must plainly be accepted; for what matters is not in the very least why he feels as he does, but how he behaves, what he says, and what he accomplishes.

The villains are particularly difficult to motivate, because the heroes are always so blameless that only natural malignance could attack them. That was why the Machiavel was so particularly useful. In Elizabethan tragedy the villain is usually the most important figure; and tragedies of the villain hero are as common as tragedies of the virtuous hero.

The villain hero grew out of the conqueror, whose cruelties were a necessary part of his triumph and were hardly judged by moral standards at all. *Tamburlaine* is the culmination (as well as the starting-point) for the conqueror plays, and in Marlowe's play the feelings towards the conquered are completely anaesthetised, so that they only serve as material to demonstrate the power of the hero. The triumph is not spoilt by any consciousness of the pain on which it is built.

This attitude was partly helped, of course, by the extreme callousness of the audience. They were used to seeing atrocities in daily life, and their senses seem to have been so blunted that, like Barabas, they "had no feeling of another's pain". It was not deliberate cruelty, but that lack of the development of sympathetic powers, which is found sometimes among highly cultivated and sensitive races (e.g. the Chinese).

Barabas, Selimus, Richard III and the early Machiavels are more complicated figures. Here the audience could, in a strictly limited fashion, identify themselves with the hero. His daring, his intelligence, his successful plotting against odds and his bitter wit were qualities which the audience enjoyed and approved. They even enjoyed jeering and deliberate cruelty, as the long and insulting triumphs of the good characters in Revenge tragedy show. Hieronimo, Titus Andronicus and Antonio, when their enemies are within their power, spend a long time in gloating over them before proceeding to business. But these were justified, whereas when a bad character was overthrown at the end, the audience, who had been thrilled by their successful daring all through, would turn round and get an equal satisfaction out of their unrepentent deaths and the tirades of triumphant virtue.

This kind of adjustment was familiar to the audience through the popularity of disguise, which enabled one character to play two parts. The stage conventions did not attempt to make it convincing, but it had simply to be accepted. The perfunctory make-up has already been discussed: occasionally the dramatist plays on the sketchiness of the disguise, as when Piero in *Antonio and Mellida*, or Julianus in *All's Lost by Lust* think their disguised daughters "something like" themselves. The same trick was much more delicately used by Shakespeare in *Cymbeline* and *Pericles*, where natural sympathy draws the kings toward their unknown children, and Ford copied Shakespeare in his early play, *The Lover's Melancholy*.

Moreover (and this is of far greater importance) a character in disguise need not retain the feelings of his other self. He is like a pathological case of alternating personality, a Doctor Jekyll and Mr Hyde. Orlando Friscobaldo, in *The Honest Whore*, though his feelings show through his disguise, allows his daughter to be roughly handled by her husband before his face, and only intervenes when he draws a dagger on her. No suggestions of self-control are adequate to meet the case. The fathers in *The Fleir* and *Englishmen for My Money* act as panders to their daughters, who are professed courtesans. Malevole in disguise plays the pander to his wife, and this is common in comedy, the most extraordinary case being in *Westward Hoe*. Disguised husbands, disguised fathers and disguised rulers were stock figures; in almost every case the motive is quite inadequate, but the character is enabled to become the marionette man of the play: he controls the intrigue and deputises for the author. The Duke in *Measure for Measure* belongs to this class.[1]

These characters are depersonalised for the sake of the intrigue; but in tragedy the effect was more often to add to the complexity of the emotional structure of the play. Such is the purpose of Edgar's disguise in *King Lear*. There is no reason for his elaborate practising of his disguise when he is alone with the mad Lear or his blind father. But a madman is needed in the storm scenes, and though the audience's knowledge that Edgar is really not mad adds to the horror, that is, as it were, one of the calculations in the margin.

A more simple example of dissociation, which does not involve disguise, is seen in Antonio's attitude to Julio, whom he loved for his own sake, but hated as the son of Piero. He kills him, but asks pardon of the "spirit of Julio" even while he is horribly mangling the body, which is "all

[1] *Vide* V. O. Freeburg, *Disguise Plots in Elizabethan Drama*, for a detailed discussion of this type.

Piero". Othello would kill Desdemona and love her after.
Chapman's Byron is seen simultaneously as a hero and a
traitor. His lying and bragging are sharply differentiated
from his noble self; therefore it is not right to slur over the
one or the other aspect.

Chapman states the problem quite explicitly:

> O of what contraries consists a man
> Of what impossible mixtures! Vice and virtue
> Corruption and eternesse at one time
> And in one subject let together loose!
> We have not any strength but weakens us,
> No greatness but doth crush us into air.
> Our knowledges do light us but to err,
> Our ornaments are burthens, our delights
> Are our tormenters, fiends that, raised in fears,
> At parting shake our roofs about our ears.
>
> *(Byron's Tragedy,* 5. 3. 189 ff.)

This kind of double personality is only made possible by
the very simple and rigid moral framework of the plays
(the clear-cut distinction between black and white, wrong
and right which were often symbolised directly), and by the
limitation of the "types". The different types were hard,
isolated units of character which were all of a piece (rather
like the atoms of nineteenth-century Atomic Theory). It
was this which made these violent juxtapositions so effective.
When Malcolm assumes all the wickedness he can, it means
the audience have to make a quick readjustment and see the
problem from that hypothetic angle. "I am worse than
Macbeth", is Malcolm's suggestion: this suggestion of other
possible points of view is characteristic of the Shakespearean
drama.

Sometimes the sense of dual personality is used in a perfectly natural manner, yet it can be felt that the convention
colours the attitude of the speaker. Troilus, disillusioned in
Cressida, cannot immediately see (as Othello could not) that

his image of her is false: instead it seems as though there are two persons.

> This she? No, this is Diomede's Cressida.
> If beauty have a soul, this is not she.
> If souls guide vows, if vows be sanctimony,
> If sanctimony be the gods' delight...
> This is not she.... This is and is not Cressida.
> Within my soul there doth conduce a fight
> Of this strange nature, that a thing inseparate
> Divides more wider than the sky and earth;
> And yet the spacious breadth of this division
> Admits no orifex for a point as subtle
> As Ariachne's broken woof to enter.
>
> (*Troilus and Cressida*, 5. 2. 134 ff.)

Such violent and complete reversals of characters are at one, therefore, with the "double characters" of the villain hero. There is not a single mixed response but two powerful and opposed ones. The boldest form of this convention is that of the disguised villain hero, Malevole, Vindice, Bosola; Edgar, disguised as Mad Tom, is a similar character. All through the storm scenes he talks of nothing but the foul fiends that inhabit him. Practically every sentence contains a reference to a devil. It seems therefore that the grotesque vision of the devil which he describes at Dover Cliff may not be quite irrelevant, or intended solely to work on Gloucester's superstitions. For after this point the devils are cast out of Edgar and he refers to them no more.

Malevole and Vindice's disguises are even more impossible, but they are simplified characters, and the juxtaposition of pander and husband or pander and brother is only a development from the earlier villain heroes of the school of Marlowe. The tenseness of the situation lies precisely in the fact that these characters are incompatible, dramatically opposed to each other. If Vindice were less than a brother to Castiza (that is, if the situation were, from the naturalist point of view, less than impossible), it would not be tragic; and Tourneur would not be able to get the sharp impact of his "sentences", and his retorts and his clear, concentrated imagery.

> There's a cold curse laid upon all maids
> While others clip the sun, they clasp the shades.
> Nine coaches waiting—hurry, hurry, hurry—
> Ay, to the devil.
> Your tongues have struck hot irons on my face.
> O angels, clap your wings upon the skies
> And give this virgin crystal plaudities.

The characters of these last two plays (*The Malcontent* and *The Revenger's Tragedy*) are Humours and arranged in the Jonsonian mould. The minor figures of *The Revenger's Tragedy* (Lussurioso, Ambitioso, Supervacuo, Spurio) like the minor figures of *Volpone* (Corvino, Corbaccio, Voltore) are not complete persons, but constituent parts of a single impression. The generic Italian names indicate, in both Marston's and Tourneur's (as in Jonson's) plays, that the characters are deliberately made inhuman. Jonson himself was probably relying upon the Morality tradition; at all events, the Humorous treatment of characters allowed for an organisation of typical characters. The heavy father, the braggart captain, and the shrew have no interconnection and no necessary relationship to one another, but the different kinds of fools and knaves of Jonson, Marston and Tourneur can only be considered as a group. Castiza (like Celia in *Volpone*) is of no interest beyond providing the ingredient of unblemished chastity necessary to complement the black lust of the villain. The malcontent replaces the Jonsonian commentor (Crites-Asper-Horace) and his sardonic accent is precisely the same. There is something very reminiscent of the morality in this interlocking of characters through a moral schema. It is not found in Webster, whose characters are definitely more human and complicated, but whose narrative remains formalised.

In the Humorous system of characterisation, a play became much more than the sum of its parts: indeed, the parts, detached from the play, were of little interest. The Humorous characters of Jonson (and also the characters of Chapman) are not motivated at all. Catiline, for instance, is the lust for destruction embodied. He is "not a man but a public ruin". It is not that his reasons for burning Rome will not square with his conduct or that they are not historically correct. It is that the Catiline of history is something less than Jonson's Catiline.

> It is decreed: nor shall thy fate, O Rome,
> Resist my vow. Though hills were set on hills,
> And seas met seas to guard thee, I would through,
> Ay, plough up rocks, steep as the Alps, in dust,
> And lave the Tyrrhene waters into clouds,
> But I would reach thy head, thy head, proud city!

Sylla's ghost, the supernatural force of destruction and hate, has symbolised this abstract and motiveless power. Shakespeare's Timon is a similar figure, whose feelings soar above the small particular causes of it, the petty ingratitudes of the petty Athenians. Lear's passion on the heath is so great and impersonal compared with its immediate cause, the behaviour of Goneril and Regan, that the latter is quite lost to sight. Or, to put it philosophically, the situation is determined teleologically rather than causally; the characters are self-determined, and not products of circumstance.

Chapman's characters can also be separated into two halves: the given motive, and the passions for which the motives act only as a scaffolding. The action in his plays seems to be carried on two or three levels: the level of the intrigue, which is relatively unimportant; that of social criticism and satire akin to the Jonsonian (for instance, the excellent handling of Tamyra in Act 3 of *Bussy D'Ambois*, which is entirely in the tone of *The Widow's Tears*); and finally that of the passions, growing out of and away from events, in the long-soaring speeches of Bussy, Clermont and Byron, which are the core of the play. So that characterisation in Chapman is never more than incidental, and often most perfunctory; for the vital parts of his plays are, like the soliloquies of Catiline or Timon, quite impersonal.

The later dramatists, Fletcher, Massinger, Ford and Shirley, used quite a different system of characterisation. Though some of their types (the lustful tyrant, the wicked queen or the bluff soldier) might seem to be the same as those of the early writers, they were used for other purposes. Instead of a juxtaposition of the tragic and the comic or the good and the evil, there was a blurring of them. *The Revenger's Tragedy* depends upon Tourneur being quite clear about the distinction between black and white, wrong and right. The two halves of Vindice's character are kept sharply distinct: it would be possible to draw a line separating them off. But plays like *A King and No King*, *A Fair Quarrel*, *The Duke of Milan*, or *Love's Sacrifice* depend upon smudging the issues between wrong and right. The dramatists are consciously playing upon the distinction between behaviour and character which has been already noted. Instead of a naïve simplification of feelings, there is a sophisticated perversion of them. Vindice acting as a pander to his sister is an incredible figure, but the horror of it is quite clearly recognised; whereas in *A King and No King* the incestuous love of Arbaces for Panthea is treated as something pathetic and touching. Arbaces is a "bluff soldier": his helplessness in the grip of his feelings is meant to raise a kind of indulgent sympathy in the audience; at times it is half-comic, in any case it is attractive "human weakness" to the superior spectator. His accent is always that of the simple soldier; it is as pathetic as that of the forsaken maids, Aspatia or Bellario. His physical prowess only serves to heighten the pathos of his simplicity.

"How dost thou do?"

"Better than you, I fear."

"I hope thou art, for to be plain with thee
Thou art in hell else. Secret scorching flames,
That far transcend earthly material fires,
Are crept into me, and there is no cure:
Is it not strange, Mardonius, there's no cure?"

The *dénouement* at the end of the play is a kind of moral peripeteia: sin becomes virtue. In *Love's Sacrifice* there is even more flagrant juggling with moral values. There is no serious morality in these plays at all; they do not depend upon a code of any kind, but simply upon exploiting the feelings and combining the pathetic and the pornographic. The essential coarseness of the writers comes out in their use of comic relief (Bessus, for instance, in *A King and No King*, 3. 3).

Sometimes the whole set of accepted values will be changed for the last act. In Fletcher's *Valentinian* and Massinger's *The Duke of Milan*[1] the hero becomes a villain, and the whole direction of the action is changed. This is only the logical development from the arbitrary repentance of the villain in Act 5, but that had not really affected the structure of the play; whereas in the later plays one set of character types is replaced by another and quite incompatible set. It is a further example of the Elizabethan taste for the maximum emotional response, a greedy desire to eat their cake and have it.

The characters of Fletcher and Massinger are based primarily on an emotional scale and not a moral one. Their chaste heroines (Urania, Ordella, Cleora, Marcella) are not neutral

---

[1] T. W. Baldwin in the introduction to his edition of this play has some sensible remarks on Massinger's types, on the villains who "shift from good to bad when the exigencies of the plot demand it", and on the characters who speak more than their rôle in comments—"their knowledge is not their own but Massinger's". (This is particularly well illustrated in 2. 1.)

figures like Castiza and Celia, but their chastity is held up as something requiring an emotional response; it is made personal and "naturalist". The change is connected with the change from the impersonality of direct speech to a uniform level of rhetorical persuasion.

CHAPTER IV

Elizabethan Habits of Reading, Writing and Listening

THE title of this chapter may suggest something very remote from tragic conventions, but the main purpose of the last chapter has been to show that the Elizabethans did not rely upon narrative and characterisation to the same extent as the modern author. They were much more interested in direct moral instruction on the one hand, and in the play of words or images on the other. These interests, like the "feeling for allegory" (which is their offspring), were cultivated by education and canalised by habits. It will be necessary, therefore, to consider these habits before going on to the Conventions of Dramatic Speech, which are to be considered in the next chapter.

The different orientation of Elizabethan writing is, of course, generally recognised. It is a commonplace that the aim of writers was primarily moral and their methods primarily rhetorical. The close connection of these two habits and their effect upon the importance of narrative and character has not, however, been so widely acknowledged.

Without some preliminary investigation of the kind attempted in this chapter, it might seem very unlikely that the audience could give that kind of attention to a play which the subsequent chapters imply. There can be no certainty as to how far they were conscious of what they were doing, or of what the author had been doing when he wrote; but it seems clear that they read and listened to poetry with a different kind of attention from that of to-day.

In the first place, the drama had not only a general moral purpose; immediate results were expected. If it did not bring murderers to repentance, convert rakes, induce misers to lean up against the wall and grow generous, and prostitutes to purge and live cleanly, it was not fulfilling its function. Stories of these miracles were common: sometimes a woman "of Linne in Norfolk" would be brought to confess a murder, sometimes a Dutchman.[1] Hamlet is referring to these anecdotes when he says:

> I have heard
> That guilty creatures sitting at a play
> Have by the very cunning of the scene
> Been so struck to the soul that presently
> They have proclaimed their malefactions.
>
> (2. 2. 625–9)

In *The Roman Actor* a play is staged for the sake of curing an old miser by "example" and he is forced to witness it by the emperor.

The audience were prepared to see the whole play related to a moral precept. It was not a *drame à thèse*, in the modern sense, for the situations did not always reflect real life (though they did in domestic tragedy). Chapman, for instance, wrote *Caesar and Pompey* upon the text "Only a just man is a free man", just as a divine might write a sermon on a Biblical text. The debates and soliloquies expounded this text, which was repeated at the crisis of the play; and the audience (to whom listening to sermons and legal pleadings offered a recreation as well as an edification or a duty), would follow the argument with interest.

There was a general recognition that "excitation of virtue and deflection from her contrary are the soul, body and limbs of an authentical tragedy",[2] and therefore the moral had to be summed up in an incisive fashion. For this purpose the "sentences" of the Ancients were the most proper, as they were the most elegant, expressions; or, if the moral

---

[1] *Vide* Heywood's *Apology for Actors* (Shak. Soc. Pub. VII, p. 57).
[2] Chapman, dedication *The Revenge of Bussy D'Ambois*.

were in English, it was stated in a pithy "sententious couplet" which the audience could remember afterwards.

The critics also recognised, however, that the moral had to be made palatable for the unsuspecting murderers, rakes, misers and prostitutes. It was the justification of drama that the pill was coated in jam.

With a tale forsooth he cometh to you, with a tale which holdeth children from the fire and old men from the chimney corner. And pretending no more, doth intend the winning of the mind from wickedness to virtue, even as the child is often brought to take most wholesome things by hiding them in such others as have a pleasant taste.

This meant that, in practice, the style was thought of as something apart from, and imposed upon the material. It was something to be learnt; for the less intelligent, something which could be learnt by rules. The poet sought for "gravity and height of elocution, fullness and frequency of sentence", "climbing to the height of *Seneca* his style".

The rules of "style" were largely derived from classical theories of rhetoric. The manner in which rhetoric and poetry were inter-related meant that both the methods and the instruments of the orator were borrowed for poetry. Puttenham has a passage which contains by implication much of Renaissance critical theory.

Now, if our presuppoal be true that the poet is of all the most ancient orator as he that by good and pleasant persuasion first reduced the wild and beastly people to public societies and civilities of life, insinuating into them, under fictions with sweet and coloured speeches, many wholesome reasons and doctrines, then no doubt there is nothing so fit for him as to be furnished with all the figures that be rhetorical and such as do most beautify the language with eloquence and sentences.

The "persuasive" and "insinuating" methods of the writer imply that his "sweet and coloured speeches" are so many protective disguises by which he can conceal himself from the prey he stalks. In the drama bloody and violent action served the same purpose. In *The Spanish Tragedy* and *Titus Andronicus* the atrocities are quite cut off from the sober and sententious speeches of the characters; there is no vital connection between the bloody acts and the moral dialogue, but as tragedy developed, the language became "warmed up", as it were, grew less formal, and "coloured" in a different sense from the rhetorical one. Nevertheless, Ben Jonson, though his views on the "figures" were extraordinarily sane and balanced, believed that "verses stood by sense alone, without either colour or accent", and "writ all his poetry first in prose for so his master Camden had taught him".[1]

Practice enabled the later playwrights to go beyond critical theory: the use which Chapman, Jonson and Tourneur made of the rhetorical influence was far subtler than that advocated by the critics, or practised by Kyd. But they built on the earlier foundations; and they also relied upon the training in rhetoric which their audience possessed.

This was largely a matter of education. Jonson's master Camden was one of the most illustrious of the Elizabethan schoolmasters who inculcated the rhetorical theory of poetry into their pupils. Rhetoric was a most important subject in the school curriculum. The children learnt the names of many "figures", with examples: they had to compose examples themselves, and they wrote themes in given styles, imitating different classical authors. They translated passages across from several languages, "out of Hebrew into Greek, out of Greek into Latin, out of Latin into French and out of French into English".

School children were required to memorise and repeat the substance of the sermons which they heard on Sundays. Their more advanced studies consisted of detailed exegesis and comment upon set texts which they were often required

[1] *Conversations with Drummond of Hawthornden*, xv.

to know by heart. This induced habits of exact memorising and close concentration upon the actual phrasing of the text; its fruits are seen in the frequency of direct quotation and repetition in the drama of the period.[1]

The serious-minded reader, realising that short cuts to the moral were possible, read in a staccato manner, making a commonplace book into which he copied the digested matter. For his convenience, the "sentences" were printed in inverted commas or italics, or a hand pointed to them in the margin. The controversial habits of the age meant that the classics and the Bible were treated in the same way: King James, scouring the scriptures for references to witchcraft, must have read like this.

Some of the dramatists kept commonplace books themselves, into which they copied useful passages for their plays. Jonson has an interesting discussion on reading methods in *Discoveries*,[2] in which he shows a lively awareness of the dangers of this habit. He describes first the indiscriminate borrower; then the man who "feigns whole books", i.e. makes up his references so as to appear learned; then those who have "whole passages together usurped from an author: their necessities compelling them to read for present use, which could not be in many books and so come forth ridiculously and palpably guilty".

This habit of incorporating indigested passages is very common in plays. Even Marlowe did so occasionally, and it was the common practice of the vulgar.

Jonson then describes those who "presuming on their own naturals (which perhaps are excellent) dare deride all diligence and seem to mock at the terms when they understand not the things: thinking to get off that way wittily with their ignorance". Consequently their style is not even, "for their

---

[1] *Vide* Professor Foster Watson, *The English Grammar Schools to 1660*, and W. F. Mitchell, *English Pulpit Oratory*, chapters II–IV.

[2] *Timber or Discoveries*: Ingeniorum Discrimina.

jests and sentences (which they only and ambitiously seek for) stick out and are more eminent: because all is vile and sordid about them". This is the result of the author's bad reading habits.

Jonson's method of imitation is described in the section headed *Poesis* (cap. III).

Not as a creature that swallows what it takes in crude and raw or indigested: but that feeds with an appetite and hath a stomach to concoct, divide, and turn all into nourishment...turn all into honey, work it into one relish and savour.

Or, to paraphrase, the original works are like the elements in a chemical compound: the new substance has different physical and chemical qualities although it is composed only of the elements and can be resolved into them. The writer who imitates well creates something new, however literal his borrowings.

The literal reproduction of sources is, in fact, a measure of his power. To transform with the minimum of alteration is the sign of the great artist. Shakespeare's use of North is the obvious example: a lesser man would have had to alter North to get his effects. Jonson, Chapman and Webster are the three playwrights most obviously indebted to their commonplace books. It is odd that the discovery of their method led to their work being called "imitative" and their sense of construction questioned. Legouis describes Chapman as of "imagination assez pauvre, vite à sec, mais qui aspirait au grandiose et affectait le mystère. Il y a un amalgame de pédantisme et de paresse intellectuelle. *Il ne reste qu'à examiner* la qualité des vers en laquelle Chapman traduit le latin des humanistes et cette qualité est bien médiocre".[1]

Since Chapman himself believed in "holding all learning but an art to live well", the direct connection between his reading and his poetry may, after all, be not merely a matter

[1] Preface to *L'Humanisme Continental en Angleterre*, by Frank Schoell.

of intellectual sloth; and, in the age of North's *Plutarch* and the Authorised Version of the Bible, the "quality of the writing" should hardly have been the last subject for consideration.

It may be granted that in Chapman's case there is some excuse, for he had a rather childlike pleasure in displaying his knowledge. His habit of quoting commentators as though he were quoting originals should not, however, have horrified M. Legouis, for the scientific conscience in the matter of verification of references had hardly been developed, and the greatest writers of the Renaissance were as guilty as Chapman.

In addition to his borrowings Chapman had also a set of favourite tags, which he repeats from play to play. Such phrases as

> A virtuous man is subject to no prince
> But to his soul and honour
> > (*The Gentleman Usher*, 5. 4. 59–60)

will recur, just as the writers of Revenge plays repeated their proverbs (*vide Bussy D'Ambois*, 2. 1. 203–4; *Byron's Conspiracy*, 3. 3. 140–5; *Caesar and Pompey*, 5. 2. 8–10).[1]

Webster's methods were much like Chapman's[2] except that his reading was narrower: Jonson's, on the contrary, was wider, but he prided himself on his translations and appropriations and made no effort to disguise them. Very often a passage which is a direct translation from the classics will also show the influence of an English writer. In *Sejanus*, 5. 1, the lines

> My roof receives me not: 'tis air I tread
> And at each step I feel my advanced head
> Knock out a star in Heaven...

---

[1] See Parott's edition (Routledge). It is the number of these phrases which is so striking, as well as the exactitude with which they are repeated.

[2] *Vide* note on "Webster's Imitation" in F. L. Lucas' edition of the *Works*.

may be Jonson's version of Seneca:

> Aequalis astris gradior et cunctos super
> Altum superbo vertice attingens polum—
>
> (*Thyestes*, ll. 888–9)

but they are not unaffected by the hyperboles of *Tamburlaine*.

The method of Jonson and Chapman was more individualistic than that of the writers of Revenge plays. They depended on their own reading to supply a body of "sentences", just as their methods of construction were more personal. Webster stands half way between the learned and the popular writers; his borrowings are individualistic, but he relies upon the public conventions of the Revenge play, though this is for tone and atmosphere far more than for verbal formulae. Since his borrowings were not from the classics they would not have the same standing as those of Chapman and Jonson.

The imitation of the classics did not mean that they were accepted as infallible (unless, possibly, Chapman's deification of Homer is excepted). Jonson has a very temperate note on the authority of the Ancients and his attitude to Aristotle is reverent but not servile.[1] "He denied figures to be invented but for aid", and objected to the uniformly dignified style of Sidney.[2]

There was more similarity between the methods of the learned and the popular writers than might at first appear. The same problems of the English language confronted both. Elizabethan English was above all fluid, and its difficulties were those of a tongue in a state of rapid development. The vocabulary was expanding at a prodigious rate; the "inkhorne terms" were only the extreme manifestation of this. The interest of the age lay in the coinage of words rather than in the structure of sentences; prose was still

[1] *Timber or Discoveries:* Non nimium credendum antiquitati and Sophocles–Demosthenes–Aristotle.

[2] *Conversation with Drummond of Hawthornden*, III.

immature and consequently rather inflexible; experiments in different kinds of sentences were common. There were many recognised games to be played with language, most of which involved the use of elaborate patterns. Poems were written in the shape of eggs or triangles and verses which could be read backwards or forwards, anagrams, riddles, and acrostics were as popular as "perspective pictures" or distorting mirrors.

Serious experiments like Euphuism were therefore suited to the popular as well as the learned taste; and Kyd's use of "figures" would please those who had no knowledge of the classics. Alliteration, doublets and parallel clauses were a ready means of controlling the sentence, which was one of the more difficult problems confronting the sixteenth century. Almost every writer had personal tricks of construction or private uses of words.[1]

Marston's coinages, which Jonson so ridiculed, could be easily paralleled. Shakespeare invented many words, and modified or extended the usage of many more. Words had powerful secondary and tertiary meanings, which encouraged not only the grosser kinds of ambiguity and pun, but the finer sorts which are characteristic of great poetry.[2]

There was a widespread interest in dialect and the canting language of thieves. Middleton, Dekker and Fletcher made capital out of their knowledge of the beggars' argot, and Jonson took pleasure in learning the technical terms of alchemy and physic.

There was a widespread interest in modern languages, and this is shown in the drama by a frequent introduction of foreigners who talk either broken English or their own tongue. The groundlings might not be able to understand

[1] Such as Chapman's "manless" meaning "lacking in the essentially human qualities" and "circular" meaning "complete, fulfilled, perfect".

[2] For an account of Shakespeare's influence on vocabulary, *vide* Owen Barfield's *History in English Words*, pp. 136–40, and G. H. McKnight's *Modern English in the Making*.

them, but they were interested to hear the sound of a strange language. The play-within-the-play in *The Spanish Tragedy* may really have been given in the "sundry languages on the stage", though considering Kyd's reputation, it would be unlikely. This exploitation of foreign tongues is not so noticeable in the later drama of Fletcher or Massinger. This may represent a growing lack of interest among the people for language as language.

During the Elizabethan period a whole series of aids to learning and politeness existed for the contemporary Samuel Smiles. Complete letter writers, collections of similes, anecdotes, or riddles, and conversation manuals were as common as books of conduct and specific guides for the studious apprentice or the industrious housewife. At the end of Nicholas Breton's *A Mad World, my Masters*, there is a mocking passage which illustrates what happened as a result.

Lor. If I can requite you, I will not forget you: and let this suffice you: shortly I will see you, I shall always love you and wish I could be ever with you.

Dor. What? Shall we have old adverbs? "As in absence you may see me, so in silence you may hear me. I pray you bear me company home and I will bring you half way back again."

Lor. Indeed, figures are good among ciphers: but honest minds have plain tongues, and therefore, not to detract your time, I am at your service.

Dor. I thank you, let us go.

Conversation was an art deliberately cultivated but, as Breton's "ciphers" suggest, it was often considered the mark of the gull. The interest in speech, however, was alive among all classes. For instance, it is not always realised that Shakespeare's fondness for Whetstone's precept that clowns should speak disorderly was quite compatible with holding the mirror up to Nature. Elbow, Dogberry and their like were more than a literary convention. The common people tried hard to pick up the words which were being coined so rapidly by the learned, with the result that such forms as "allicholly" for "melancholy" were usual; for, being illiterate, the working man would have to depend on his ear and would have of course no etymological guidance. This habit of the clowns is therefore a symptom of the general interest in the expansion of the vocabulary.

The courtier's attention to his exquisite phrases, his choice of "silken terms precise" led him, as it led the Rev. Mr Collins, to prepare compliments. Jonson ridicules rehearsed jests (*Every Man out of His Humour*, 3. 1; *Cynthia's Revels*, 2. 1). Those who could not invent terms of courtship, or stinging repartees, were driven to borrowing them: there seemed to have been a habit of repeating a complimentary phrase exactly, for it is ridiculed in Balurdo (*Antonio and Mellida*), Blanuel (*Humorous Day's Mirth*) and other fools. Plays were used as quarries for *bons mots*, and Dekker advised his gull to note them down for use in courtly bouts of wit: "Hoard up the finest play scraps you can get: upon which your lean wit may most savourily feed, for want of other stuff, when the Arcadian and Euphuised gentlewomen have their tongues sharpened to set upon you".[1] In the induction to *The Malcontent*, the gull says: "I am one of those that have seen this play often and can give them intelligence for their action. I have most of the jests here in my table book".

In *The Scourge of Villanie* Marston also describes one of these filchers:

> Lucius, what's played to-day? faith, now I know.
> I set thy lips abroach, from whence doth flow
> Nought but pure Juliet and Romeo.
> H'ath made a commonplace book out of plays
> And speaks in print at least; whate'er he says
> Is warranted by *Curtain* plaudites;
> If ere you heard him courting Lesbia's eyes
> Say (courteous Sir) speaks he not movingly
> From out some new pathetic tragedy?

[1] Grosart, *Works*, II, p. 304.

> He writes, he rails, he jests, he courts, what not
> And all from out his huge, long-scraped stock
> Of well-penned plays. (Satire 10)

This habit must have affected the playwrights, although they disliked it. Those whose jests and sentences "stick out" as Jonson observed were probably catering for a known demand. This is especially so with the epigrammatic style of later Revenge tragedy, that is, of Marston, Tourneur and Webster.

The playwrights had their revenge upon the audience by inserting scraps of real conversation into their plays. It was a stock accusation against Jonson that he reported the conversations of his friends and one which he in turn retorted upon others.

> Besides, they could wish you poets could leave to be purveyors of other men's jests and to waylay all the stale apothegms or old books they can hear of (in print or otherwise) to farce their scenes withal. That they would not so penuriously glean wit from every laundress or hackney man or derive their best grace with servile invitation from common stages or observation of the company they converse with: as if their invention lived wholly upon another man's trencher.
>
> (Induction to *Cynthia's Revels*, ll. 176 ff.)

All these habits meant that the audience would follow the dialogue as poetry, and not merely as the speech of a given character. Repetition of a word or a phrase would be noted instinctively as a reader picks up clues in a detective story to-day. The signals of the way the play was moving were as likely to be in words as in action; and though writer and spectators might be indifferent to the sequence of events they were alive to the sequence of words.

The relationship between the spoken and the written language was very close; the movement of blank verse, after Shakespeare had reshaped it in the middle nineties, was colloquial. The vocabulary of the literary man was only different from that of the ordinary man in being wider, and even the groundling was prepared to listen to a good many high-sounding terms which he could not understand and to be pleased by the sound and the fury. He also demanded clowning, however, and consequently the playwrights who had to please both courtier and 'prentice developed extraordinarily wide vocabularies. Jonson was equally at home in the language of the schools, the jargon of the alchemist, and the Billingsgate of London servingmen. Shakespeare's vocabulary was wider than that of any other English writer and "'The tongue which Shakespeare spake' was the tongue which he wrote".[1]

If the interest in words made for wider vocabularies in this way, it also made for "common form". The moral end of writing and the note-book method of composition alike encouraged the standardisation of the moral code in a series of recognisable "sentences". A study of the ethics of Elizabethan drama resolves itself into a study of apophthegms, and of their transmission and modification.

Elizabethan drama depends for its moral code upon several sources; its ethics were ostensibly Christian, but since the direct treatment of religious questions was prohibited, the language of the drama is not coloured by the language of the Church. The classics provided the learned writers with a philosophy: owing to the general ignorance of Greek and the comparative inaccessibility of the Greek dramatists, Seneca was the model dramatist, and his stoicism affected the whole of the Elizabethan drama. The "sentences" of the Ancients had a kind of special authority and sanctity; the

---

[1] H. C. Wyld, *History of Modern Colloquial English*, chapter IV, p. 101. Professor Wyld says: "We must be convinced that the literary language is not a phenomenon apart having an existence independent of the spoken language, but that the former is identical with the latter and reflects its various and changing character. This intimate relation between the highest type of colloquial English and the English of literature cannot be too strongly insisted upon".

epigrams and sentences of Seneca became axiomatic, and provided the playwrights with a body of common belief fixed in particular formulae—with a liturgy as well as a creed.

In the third place, popular beliefs furnished a number of tags and proverbs, often parallel to Senecal precept, or at least congruent with it. The sixteenth century was particularly rich in these bright little, tight little sayings which passed current for a decade or two and were forgotten, as well as in the old folk-sayings which persist for generations. The playwrights were equally ready to use the "sentences" of their own language; the less-educated writers knew no others. Domestic tragedy depends upon a number of these adages (such as "Blood will have blood" and "Murder will out"), and these by their constant usage acquired the same axiomatic values as the sentences of Seneca.

These classical or popular precepts provided the moral framework of the drama. The dramatist used them to clinch a scene, or to underline the moral of the whole play. This method did not encourage an organised moral framework, but it allowed of so many different combinations and nuances of belief that writers as different as Kyd and Chapman were able to use the same material.

The earliest borrowings were from the classics, though not always directly. Nashe could give the double-edged thrust at Kyd that "English Seneca read by candlelight yields many fine speeches, as *Blood is a beggar* and so forth". These borrowings took the form of sentences; that is, they were meant to stand out from the text of the play, to sound sententious and not dramatic. The more learned writers would not translate them; the rest would put them into a pithy couplet which could be delivered with special emphasis. They are almost inevitable at the end of scenes.

The work of Cunliffe gives an exhaustive list of these Senecal borrowings. There is a definite development in the

way they are handled. At first they are quoted literally,
and isolated by the couplet form or some other device. Often
a hand pointed to them in the margin of the printed play.
Then they became used as effective pieces of dramatic
speech, brought to life by relating them closely to the general
tone of the scene, or adding vivid metaphors, or by extension, and were definitely related to their context. Finally,
they became worn-out and were quoted without the sententious dignity of the early plays or the vividness of those
of the middle period. They were old lines, sure of their
recognition, and of applause, but really dead parts of language, like proverbs which by debasement become meaningless.

The Virgilian "Mille viae mortis" will serve as an example.
In *The Misfortunes of Arthur* it appears as

> A thousand ways do guide us to our graves,

which is simple enough, but calls attention to itself by
alliteration. In *Antonio and Mellida*, 3. 2, it is greatly expanded:

> Each man takes life hence but no man death.
> He's a good fellow and keeps open house.
> A thousand, thousand ways lead to his gate,
> To his wide mouthed porch, where niggard life
> Hath but one little, little wicket through.

The pathos is heightened by the contrast of the "wide
mouthed porch" and "little, little wicket", but it is still
quite simply done (by the straightforward action of the
adjectives). Still the passage gives Antonio's feelings, and
is not a "sentence" but an emotional outburst. In *The
Duchess of Malfi*, 4. 2, it is

> I know death hath ten thousand several doors
> For men to take their exits: and 'tis found
> They go on such strange geometric hinges
> You may open them both ways: any way, for Heaven's sake,
> So I were out of your whispering.

Marston's two gates are obviously in Webster's mind, but that curious topical detail about "geometric hinges" is in his own manner entirely. It is a reference back to the Duchess' own words about being smothered in cassia and shot to death with pearls, or perhaps there is also a reflection of Ferdinand's threat to kill her in her marriage bed, like Desdemona. The last line and a half gains its half-diabolical colouring through the extraordinarily sinister associations of the word "whisper", which seem, according to the *New English Dictionary*, to have been very prominent in Elizabethan usage.

The tag is a favourite with Fletcher and other later dramatists, but in every case it is used quite flatly and literally.

His many thousand ways to let out life.
(Bonduca, 3. 5)

Alas, old man, death hath more doors than one,
And I will find him. *(Cupid's Revenge,* 1. 1)

Death hath so many doors to let out life,
I will not long survive them.
(The Custom of the Country, 2. 2)

There are a thousand doors to let out life.
(The Parliament of Love, 4. 2)

Besides were I now in another's power
There are so many ways to let out life
I would not live for one short minute his.
(The Duke of Milan, 1. 3)

A thousand ways there are to let out life.
(Love's Cruelty, 5. 1)

During the early period (up to 1598) it was important that the audience should recognise the quotation as a quotation; during the middle period (1598–1612) its origin was lost to sight, and during the later period it was used mechanically.

The earlier versification was stiff and uncolloquial, and

consequently the "sentences" did not stand out from the body of the play because of their rhetorical formulation. But after 1598 the blank verse had become more flexible, so that an antithetical couplet is sharply cut off from the rest of the speech and would need to be spoken quite differently.

> Come, you shall leave those childish 'haviours,
> And understand your time. Fortunes flow to you;
> What, will you be a girl?
> If all feared drowning that spied waves ashore
> Gold would grow rich and all the merchants poor.
>
> (*The Revenger's Tragedy*, 2. 1. 189–93)

The last two lines demand enunciation *à haute voix*; the first three have a speech movement. Marston began this alternation of looser flowing verse and tight-knit couplet. Such lines as

> Then urge no more: O leave to love at all.
> 'Tis less disgraceful not to mount than fall,

or

> 'Tis done, and now my soul shall sleep in rest:
> Sons that revenge their father's blood are blest,

alternate with hysterical and incoherent "passions".

In the first period, the tags provided a moral framework for the play; its unity depended upon convictions about right and wrong, sin and justice (this is especially plain in *The Spanish Tragedy*). In the second period, the unity was more emotional, that of the sardonic attitude embodied in *The Malcontent*. The tags were closely related to the imagery of the play. In the third period they expressed opinions rather than beliefs and did not provide a framework for the play in any sense.

The same process may be observed in the borrowings from contemporary writers. At first they often depend on the audience having known the early play. In those passages which rely on the effect of the last scene of Marlowe's *Faustus*, the audience would have their effect ready-made;

they would carry over the emotional response into the new context.

A case in point occurs in *The Looking Glass for London and England*:

> Hell gapes for me, heaven will not hold my soul
> You mountaines, shrowd me from the god of truth
> Methinks I see him set to judge the earth
> And now he blots me from the book of life.
> O burthen more than Aetna that I beare,
> Cover me, hills, and hide me from the Lord.
> In life no peace, each murmuring that I feel
> Methinks the sentence of damnation stands.
> Die reprobate and hie thee hence to hell.... (5. 2. 1948 ff.)

This is a very expanded form of Faustus' appeal, 5. 2. 160 ff., but the context is not sufficiently like the older play for a shorter passage to serve. *The Merry Devil of Edmonton*, which is comparatively late (1601), has an induction which is entirely dependent on *Faustus*. The "fatal Chime" sounds at the beginning: the doomed scholar Fabell is seized by the devil.

> Didst thou not write thy name in thine own blood
> And draw the formal deed 'twixt thee and me
> And is it not recorded now in hell? (*Induction,* 27–9)

The scene ends, of course, in pure farce.

There is the repentant speech of Ward in *A Christian Turned Turk*:

> Wink wink thou day star, hide my guilty shame
> Make me as if I ne'er had been....
> To die I dare not, the jaws of hell do gape
> To swallow me.
> Could I but call back one seven years,
> Though all my life were servile after,
> Were my soul but free.... (ll. 1630 ff.)

Compare also the end of *The Devil's Charter*.

During the middle period, the borrowing did not rely

upon taking over the effect of the source: yet the context is often significant. In the trial scene of *The White Devil* Webster has some reminiscences of *Sejanus*.[1]

> Is he my accuser
> And must he be my judge? (*Sejanus*, 4. 1. 200–1)

> If you be my accuser
> Pray cease to be my judge.
> (*The White Devil*, 3. 2. 233–4)

> Had Sejanus both his ears as long
> As to my inmost closet: I would hate
> To whisper any thought or change an act.
> (*Sejanus*, 2. 4. 453–5)

> My lord Cardinal
> Were your intelligencing ears as long
> As to my thought, had you an honest tongue
> I would not care though you proclaimed them all.
> (*The White Devil*, 3. 2. 236–9)

> You must have patience, royall Agrippina.
> —I must have vengeance first: that were nectar
> Unto my famished spirit. (*Sejanus*, 4. 1. 1–3)

> You must have patience.
> —I must first have vengeance.
> (*The White Devil*, 3. 2. 280–1)

The fact that Vittoria is given speeches of the wronged Agrippina and of Silius is perhaps an indication of Webster's attitude to her at this point. But he has sharpened the retorts (they are parts of long speeches in Jonson) and the wording ("to my *closet*"—"to my *thought*"), and made the passages much more epigrammatic in their force. The borrowings are thoroughly digested into the play.

The later writers simply echo an effective phrase; if anything, they lessen its force. There is no essential connection between the two contexts: it is a peculiarly fruitless form of plagiarism.

[1] Only one of these is noted by Lucas, the second.

> I found not Cassio's kisses on her lips.
>> (*Othello*, 3. 3. 342)

> Kiss me. I find no Caesar here: these lips
> Taste not of ravisher in my opinion.
>> (*Valentinian*, 3. 1. 174–5)

> Methinks I find Paulinus on her lips,
> And the fresh nectar that I drew from thence
> Is on the sudden palled.
>> (*Emperor of the East*, 4. 5. 105–7)

The sharp phrase is quite blunted by the absurd "in my opinion" and the affected "fresh nectar". Massinger's methods are well known, and have been commented on.

Often it is simply the vividness of the phrase that caught the later writer's eye.

> Eating the bitter bread of banishment.
>> (*Richard II*, 3. 1. 21)

> Shall I decline,
> Eating the bitter bread of banishment,
> The course of justice to draw out a life?
>> (*The Lover's Progress*, 5. 1. 82–4)

Here the line has been thrust into the text, dislocating the grammatical order, because it seemed striking. Fletcher "collects" lines like a magpie collecting bright stones.

Of course, throughout the period the poorer writers borrowed in a shameless fashion. The passages from *Tamburlaine* in *The Taming of a Shrew* have been simply copied out of the one text into the other. (They occur in large clumps at the beginnings of the first three acts and are not evenly distributed through the play.) This is only similar to the way in which the clown repeats jests, by which Mr Sykes identified the author as Samuel Rowley and traced his connection with *Henry V* (the *Famous Victories*) and the amended *Faustus*.[1] It is only the practice of the more important dramatists that matters: the poor writers are always

[1] See H. D. Sykes, *Sidelights on the Elizabethan Drama*.

with us. Sometimes the borrowing is not verbal, but depends upon the arrangement of the speech. Thus Hieronimo, discovering Horatio's body, says

> Alas, it is Horatio, my sweet son
> —O no, but he that whilom was my son.
> *(The Spanish Tragedy,* 2. 5. 14–15)

Shakespeare at first thought the trick fit for parody only:

> Which is—no, no, which was the fairest dame
> That lived, that loved, that liked, that looked with cheer.
> *(Midsummer Night's Dream,* 5. 1. 300–1)

But later he used it seriously:

> What's best to do?
> If she come in she'll sure speak to my wife,
> My wife! My wife! what wife? I have no wife.
> *(Othello,* 5. 2. 94–6)

A good many of the more bombastic phrases were famous only in parody, such as "Feed then and faint not, fair Calipolis"; "Have we not Hiren here?"; "A horse, a horse, my kingdom for a horse"; or "Holla, ye pampered jades of Asia". Yet others, like "I hold the fates bound fast in iron chains", became the basis of the Conqueror play, since they summed up the hero's essential characteristic, his superhuman success.

> I hold the fates bound fast in iron chains
> And with my hand turn Fortune's wheel about.
> *(1st Tamburlaine,* 1. 2. 173–4)

> I clap up Fortune in a chain of gold
> To make her turn her wheel as I think best.
> *(Alphonsus of Aragon,* 4. 3. 131–2)

> Pompey, the man that made the world to stoop
> And fettered Fortune in a chain of power.
> *(Wounds of Civil War,* 4. ll. 586–7)

> Thou hast not Fortune tied in a chain.
> *(Selimus,* 2. 2420)

> Teach them that the Scythian Emperor
> Leads Fortune tied in a chain of gold
> Constraining her to yield unto his will.
>
> > (*Locrine*, 2. 1. 14–16)
>
> I have stood upon the top of Fortune's wheel
> And backward turned the iron screw of Fate.
>
> > (*Lust's Dominion*, 5. 1. 27–8)
>
> He's only worthy state,
> From Fortune's wheel plucks boldly his own fate.
>
> > (*A Christian Turned Turk*, ll. 314–15)

It is very difficult to separate "common form" from the use of rhetorical figures with which it was so closely bound up. Both formed part of the verbal framework, and this again was directly related to the conventions of presentation, so that the "conqueror" defined by these speeches might also have a whole set of gestures and bits of business which defined him at the level of the action, such as the entry of Tamburlaine drawn by the captive kings, a scene taken from *Jocasta* and surviving for parody as late as *Believe As You List*, 3. 2.

It is surprising to see how completely the system of the verbal framework collapses in the work of Fletcher and Massinger. Their echoes of older writers are literary reminiscences, casual and quite detached from the moral framework of the play or the structure of the incidents. Massinger's habit of repeating himself does not imply a body of "sentences" like Chapman's, for he repeats the dramatically striking or highly coloured phrase only. In other words, his "common form" does not express a "criticism of life". Massinger or Fletcher borrowed only for immediate effect; they are, in Chapman's phrase, without

> a soul diffused quite through
> To make them of a piece.

CHAPTER V

Conventions of Speech

THE habits of reading and of writing which have been discussed in the previous chapter produced a very different attitude towards dramatic speech from that of the present day. The Elizabethan drama was frankly rhetorical; that is generally admitted. It was because so many of the speeches were based upon public property of one kind or another—common tags or common situations—that this rhetorical speech became possible. It is manifested in two ways: by variations in the level of the speech, and by variations in its direction. I shall discuss first the formal ordering of the speech (that is, its pattern), and then the direction of the speech, or its relevance to the character speaking and the character spoken to.

Modern drama is usually written entirely upon one speech level; that is, the play is wholly in prose or wholly in verse, the language is uniformly close to or removed from the language of real life, and the characters either address each other directly, or, as in the asides of expressionist plays, speak their thoughts aloud.

The Elizabethan drama is not consistent in this respect. The variation of pattern between prose and blank verse is not the only one; the verse may be formalised into couplet, stanza or lyric interlude.

Patterned speech may be defined as verse which, by an elaborate use of alliteration, assonance, balance of epithets and clauses, parallelism and repetition or the use of rhyme, stands out from the rest of the play. Patterned dialogue occurs where speech is symmetrically allotted to several characters. The most complete contemporary account of the fashionable "figures" is to be found in Puttenham's *Art of Poesy* (Book 3, chapter 19).

Patterned speech became especially attached to Revenge tragedy through Kyd's fondness for it. It became associated with the Revenge story so firmly that when a play only contained episodes in this manner they would be written in a patterned style. *Locrine* develops a Revenge action after Act 4: the hero, owing to his infidelity, becomes a villain, and in these scenes patterned speech is frequent, while there is very little in the rest of the play.

In *Alphonsus of Germany* the story of the revenging villain hero, Alexander de Toledo, is written in patterned speech.[1]

In a study of the patterned speech of early plays[2] Mr F. G. Hubbard has calculated ten kinds of figures, culminating in the one which the Elizabethans called "tracers".

> First in his hand he brandished a sword
> And with that sword he fiercely waged war
> And in that war he gave me deadly wounds, etc.
> (*The Spanish Tragedy*, 2. 2. 119 ff.)

Mr Hubbard's tables show that Greene and Marlowe used these figures very sparingly. Peele has a large variety of figures, but not a great number of them. Kyd has a great many, both in *The Spanish Tragedy* and in *Soliman and Perseda*.

It is in this matter of texture that a difference can be felt between plays like *Selimus* and *Locrine* or *Titus Andronicus* and *Lust's Dominion*, so often lumped together by the critics.

Titus Andronicus is a Senecal exercise; the horrors are all classical and quite unfelt, so that the violent tragedy is contradicted by the decorous imagery (which is not in

---

[1] 1. 1, 2. 2. 205–20, 300–45 5. 1. 175–200, 300–15. I should like to suggest some connection between this part of the play and Chettle's *Hoffman*. Both incidents and style are very similar. There might be some material of Chettle's lost *Orphan's Tragedy* incorporated here: the ascription of the play to Chapman is generally rejected.

[2] "Repetition and parallelism in early Elizabethan drama", *Modern Philology*, XI.

"patterned speech"). The tone is cool and cultured in its effect.

> Fair Philomela she but lost her tongue
> And in a tedious sampler sewed her mind....
> O had the monster seen those lily hands
> Tremble like aspen leaves upon a lute
> And make the silken strings delight to kiss them,
> He would not then have touched them for his life.
>
> (2. 4. 38 ff.)

The patterned speech represents an attempt to impose tragedy by heightening this pastoral style.[1]

Lust's Dominion is a brawling vigorous play written in headlong blank verse. The serious action is interspersed with wild farce and the whole is as popular as *Titus Andronicus* is learned. Eleazar and Philip are often quite incoherent in their "passions": on the other hand the atrocities are much less violent, and there is a maturer stage sense.

There was probably a utilitarian purpose behind the pattern. An actor could speak rapidly and vociferously and yet be understood, and such lines would be as easy to learn as to follow. Consequently soliloquies in "Ercles' vein" are often written in patterned speech, such as Richard's soliloquy in *The True Tragedy of Richard III*, which Shakespeare enjoyed so much as to recall it in *Hamlet*. It is probably the most prodigious piece of epiphora in the English drama.

> Thus sleep I, wake I, whatsoe'er I do
> Methinks their ghosts come gaping for revenge....
> My nephew's blood Revenge, Revenge doth cry,
> The headless peers come pressing for revenge
> And every one cries, Let the tyrant die.
> The sun by day shines hotly for revenge,
> The moon by night eclipseth for revenge,
> The stars are turned to comets for revenge,
> The planets change their courses for revenge,
> The birds sing not but sorrow for revenge,

[1] Of course the problem of *Titus Andronicus* is complicated by the possibility of collaboration.

> The shrieking raven sits croaking for revenge,
> The silly lambs sit bleating for revenge,
> Whole herds of beasts come bellowing for revenge,
> And all, yea, all the world I think
> Cries for Revenge and nothing but Revenge.
> But to conclude, I have deserved revenge.

This is a part to tear a cat in and worth the delay in the action.

Repetition leads to tautology, especially in Peele, who exhausted every other means of emphasis, "Cursed be her charms, damned be her cursed charms", "casts such a heat, yea, such a scorching heat", "Accursed stars, damned and accursed stars" are typical lines. Repetition also encouraged the pun, though often the results were lamentable:

> Feed then and faint not, fair Calipolis,
> Meat of a princess, for a princess meet.

But the pun had also ironic possibilities, which were developed in the asides of the Machiavel:

> The diamond that I speak of ne'er was foiled
> (But when he touches it, will be foiled).

Marlowe used a kind of repetitive retort in *Edward II*, where there is, for the first time in his work, a good deal of pattern:

> No more than I would answer were he slain.
>
> Yea, more than thou shalt answer, though he live.
>
> My lord, he is my uncle and shall live.
>
> My lord, he is your enemy and shall die.
>
> What means your highness to distrust me thus?
>
> What meanest thou to dissemble with me thus?

There are many other "figures" in *Edward II*: it suggests that Marlowe was becoming interested in quite different uses of language from those of *Tamburlaine* or even *Faustus*. The lines are more dramatic in the modern sense; there is a consciousness of the theatrical value of setting one voice against another and of raising suspense, but there is a loss of flexibility in the language. *Edward II* has a good deal of tautology worthy of Peele:

> Successful battle gives the God of Kings
> To them that fight in right and fear his wrath.
> Since then successfully we have prevailed...
> Deal you, my lords, in this, my loving lords,
> As to your wisdom fittest seems in all.
>
> (4. 5. 28 ff.)

Shakespeare, in his early plays, developed the use of the pun, which freed repetition from the danger of tautology, and provided an excellent gymnastic apparatus on which to exercise his control of words:

> Deposing thee before thou wert possessed,
> Who art possessed now to depose thyself.
>
> (*Richard II*, 2. 1. 107–8)

It also became fashionable to affect a kind of Euphuism in verse:

> Not dallying with a brace of courtesans,
> But meditating with two deep divines,
> Not sleeping to engross his idle body,
> But praying to enrich his watchful soul.
>
> (*Richard III*, 3. 7. 73–6)

No sooner had Shakespeare released from its stiffness the blank verse of the earlier writers than he swung into the prose of the later comedies. But the plays of *Richard III* and *Richard II* in particular are primarily experiments in the use of language, necessary for the development of Shakespeare's uniquely rich, allotropic vocabulary. The first of the two is particularly interesting: it has not many figures but it makes a more structural use of patterned speech than any other play except *The Spanish Tragedy*; the second depends rather on the conceit, as in Richard's speech on Time.

In *Richard III* whole scenes are built up on the visual and verbal pattern. The laments in 2. 2 and 4. 4. 26–38 are perhaps the most striking examples. The figures sit grouped in a tableau, and each speaks in turn:

Queen Eliz. Ah, for my husband, for my dear lord Edward!
Children.   Ah, for our father, for our dear lord Clarence!
Duchess.   Alas for both, both mine, Edward and Clarence!
Queen.   What stay had I but Edward? and he's gone.
Children.   What stay had we but Clarence? and he's gone.
Duchess.   What stays had I but they? and they are gone.

The pattern changes and becomes more elaborate: in the second scene of lament there is yet more complicated orchestration.

In other plays rhyming is used in soliloquy. *Selimus*, though it has not a great deal of repetition and parallelism, is partly written in regular stanza forms, vaguely reminiscent of the Spenserian. The opening soliloquy of Bajazet, for instance, has the form *abababcc*. It has been suggested that these parts of the play are survivals from an older source play, but as they contain the most developed statements of Machiavellian doctrine, in expressions parallel to those used in *The Spanish Tragedy* and elsewhere, this proposition does not seem feasible.

A really skilful writer could achieve very subtle effects by transition from the patterned speech to ordinary dialogue. At the end of *The Spanish Tragedy*, when the play-within-the-play is concluded,[1] Hieronimo drops to a colloquial speech as he throws off his disguise: the dramatic change of tempo is reflected in the changed movement of the verse, from formality to the nervous speech of the spectators:

Belimperia. But were she able, thus would she revenge
Thy treacheries on thee, ignoble prince (*stabs him*).
And on herself thus would she be revenged (*stabs herself*).

---

[1] This play-within-the-play is spoken in the third person throughout, an excellent and simple method of indicating that the characters are not what they seem. Of course the use of the third person was common to add dignity, especially in Greene, but it is plain that Kyd is using it for a special purpose.

King. Well said!—Old marshal, this was bravely done.
Hieronimo. But Belimperia plays Perseda well! (4. 5. 65 ff.)

Shakespeare used the patterned style in this manner, but more subtly to underline specially significant moments, such as the discovery scene in *Love's Labour's Lost*, or the first meeting of Romeo and Juliet. Here, as Mr Granville Barker has noted, the lovers are isolated from the other revellers by making them share the speaking of a sonnet. This prevents their repartee from sounding too light, too like the badinage of Benedick and Beatrice, and puts an emphasis on the occasion proper to its momentous consequences.

The Murder of Gonzago, like *Pyramus and Thisbe*, is written in patterned speech for the same reason; it is on a different dramatic level from the rest of the play. Patterned speech thus played a part in determining the degree of dramatic intensity or detachment in the dialogue; how far it was "in character" and how far a generalised comment; also how far an action was of symbolic weight and significance; and finally marked actions and speeches which, for the characters in the play, were one degree removed from real life.

Repetition was used to underline the significance of omens and prophecies. Prophecies are often of an equivocal nature, and the second repetition is necessary to make this explicit. Shakespeare uses the device extensively in his histories. The examples are usually rather trivial considered separately, but their collective effect supplies the unity of the York-Lancaster series, a feeling of a tutelary fate which, concerned chiefly with the national destiny, treats the individual with little consideration.

Some such drastic and mechanical method was the only hope of controlling the intractable material of the histories. There was too much fact and too little plot to allow an interest in the narrative, but the sinking of incidents in general movements and of personality in events gave a certain coherence to the plays.

Sometimes patterned dialogue merely acted as a stimulus. It gave speed to combats of wit (Granville Barker remarks that a retort always sounds twice as telling if it rhymes) and this is its chief use in comedy. The wit-combats had to be twanged sharply off, and rhyme helped the delivery.

Echo scenes are a very popular form of patterned speech. They usually work ironically, like the equivocal riddle of the histories.[1]

Debates and laments were the equivalents of the set of wit for tragedy. These in their turn affected the soliloquy which often took on the form of a debate. An example is the soliloquy of Balthazar after he has overheard the wooing of Belimperia by Horatio:

> Yet might she love me for my valiancy—
> Ay, but that's slandered by captivity.
> Yet might she love me to content her sire—
> Ay, but her reason masters her desire.
> Yet might she love me as her brother's friend—
> Ay, but her hopes aim at some other end.
> Yet might she love me to uprear her state—
> Ay, but perhaps she loves some other mate.
> Yet might she love me as her beauty's thrall—
> Ay, but I fear she cannot love at all.
>
> (*The Spanish Tragedy*, 2. 1. 19 ff.)

When Field parodied this passage in *A Woman is a Weather-cock*, it was in dialogue and not soliloquy, the answering half of each couplet being given to different people who in turn jeer at the lover, until in the final couplet the lady herself clinches it:

Sir Abraham. O no, she laughs at me and scorns my state
For she is wilder and more hard withal
Than beast or bird or tree or stony wall.

[1] *Vide The Wounds of Civil War*, Act 3; *The Arraignment of Paris*, 3. 2; *Old Fortunatus*, 1. 1; *Antonio and Mellida*, 3. 1; *Cynthia's Revels*, 1. 1; *The Return from Parnassus*, 2. 2; *The Duchess of Malfi*, 5. 3; *Mulleasses the Turk*, 5. 1; *Anything for a Quiet Life*, 5. 1; *The Captives*, 2. 4; *Love's Mistress*, 1. 1.

Kate. Ha! God-a-mercy, old Hieronimo!
Sir A. Yet might she love me for my lovely eyes.
Count. Ay, but perhaps your nose she doth despise.
Sir A. Yet might she love me for my dimpled chin.
Pedant. Ay, but she sees your beard is very thin.
Sir A. Yet might she love me in despight of all.
Lucida. Ay, but I fear I cannot love at all. (1. 2)

Stichomuthia and rhyming were the usual means for isolating the "sentence", but outside the Revenge code they seldom formed part of the structure of the play.

The tendency was to make the more gnomic soliloquy patterned, and the more passionate scene, such as the wooing of Lady Anne in *Richard III*. When all the verse was stiff and endstopped this was a simple matter. But during the middle nineties blank verse developed out of all recognition. This was chiefly Shakespeare's doing. It became flexible, colloquial and an adequate instrument for expressing a wide range of feelings. The time for the discipline of "figures" was past.

Yet when Marston revived Revenge tragedy he retained the figures and even added some new ones, such as Piero's amazing antistrophe:

> Fly, call, run, row, ride, cry, shout, hurry, haste,
> Haste, hurry, shout, cry, ride, row, run, call, fly,
> Backwards and forwards, every way about.
> (*Antonio and Mellida*, 3. 1)

Marston was, however, an unusually wild versifier, and passages of galloping blank verse or his rapid shambling prose alternated with artificially balanced couplets in Latin or Italian. Marston used the "figures" at crises in the approved way; the greater the emotional tension, the more balanced the speech. But owing to the greater range of contrast this practice made his purple passages seem much more artificial than it had done in the earlier drama: verse had outgrown the figures when it outgrew the endstopped line.

In *The Malcontent* therefore Marston dropped them all. There are new and less obvious sets of patterns, which were to be used by Tourneur and Webster. Some of these belong to prose, in which the greater part of the play is written.

The couplet is retained for "sentences", but these have changed their subject. They are sharp comments on the action, not generalised Senecal reflections. There are about fifty such couplets in *The Malcontent*, and most of them belong to Malevole himself. The later malcontents, Vindice, Flaminio and Bosola, have the same kind of pithy generalisations, dealing with feeling rather than principles:

> But to express the sonnet by natural reason,
> When stags grow melancholic, you'll find the season.
> We endure the strokes like anvils or hard steel
> Till pain itself makes us no pain to feel.
> 'Tis gold must such an instrument procure,
> With empty fist no man doth falcons lure.

The prose equivalent of the sententious couplet is the epigrammatic simile or metaphor. The malcontents' satiric comments are summed up by some detailed, vivid and unexpected comparison, which gives the impression of a trained observation and an alert darting intelligence. Marston began this in *Antonio and Mellida*, but it is much more frequent in *The Malcontent*.

> He is made like a tilting staff and looks for all the world like an o'er roasted pig.
> Thy voice squeaks like a dry cork shoe.
> When thou dost grin, thy face doth look like the head of a roasted rabbit.

Webster uses this manner continuously.[1] It is suited to the note-book method of composition, and to plays of

[1] *Vide* p. 30 of Lucas' Introduction.

"observation"; perhaps both Marston and Webster were modelling themselves on Jonson's style.

Is he not a courtly gentleman? When he wears white satin one would take him by his black muzzle to be no other creature but a maggot.

The trick died out after Webster, except for the curious and neglected early plays of D'Avenant. In his case it seems more exuberant than sardonic:

I cannot tipple like a duck
In a green pool....
Call for a bonesetter, for Time hath sprained his feet and goes awry.
He looks now like an alchymist that is
Broiling of red herring....

It may, however, be due to imitation of Webster, for there are some verbal parallels (e.g. "O speak ere thou dost catch an everlasting cold!" *Albovine*, 5. 1 *ad fin.*; cf. *The White Devil*, 5. 6: "I have caught an everlasting cold!").

In Webster's plays the older patterns occasionally appear at a climax:

> *Vittoria.* You did name your duchess.
> *Brachiano.* Whose death God pardon.
> *Vittoria.* Whose death God revenge!
> (4. 2. 105–7)

This is, however, a reminiscence of *Richard III* (1. 3. 135–7).

If Webster's combats of wit are compared with those of earlier writers, it will be obvious that the pattern is much more subtle. As he disguised the long reflective soliloquy (such as those of Hieronimo) under a dialogue form, so he arranged his "sets of wits" according to personal formulae and not in stichomuthia. For example, he liked the "well with two buckets",[1] a dialogue which consists of two people

[1] *Vide The White Devil*, 1. 1. 29, and compare *The Malcontent*, 3. 3. 78.

browbeating a third in alternating speeches. They may even
share the speaking of one sentence.

> *Cardinal.* We are to part from you: and your own discretion
> Must now be your director.
> *Ferdinand.* You are a widow:
> You know already what man is: and therefore
> Let no youth, high promotion, eloquence—
> *Cardinal.* No.
> Nor anything without the addition, honour,
> Sway your high blood.
> *Ferdinand.* Marry, they are most luxurious
> Will wed twice.   (*The Duchess of Malfi*, I. I. 320 ff.)

There is an artificial air about the passage, which the Duchess
comments on:

> I think this speech between you both was studied
> It came so roundly off.

This indicates that the delivery was brisk and uncolloquial,
but such an attempt to "explain" a convention which would
simply have been accepted earlier is typical of Webster's
naturalisation of detail.

Jonson also had a number of personal patterns, such as the
one in which each of a group speaks one short phrase. He
uses this for his sycophants, and as the flattery runs down
the row (like a rank of soldiers numbering off) the insincerity
is made quite plain.

> Hail, great Sejanus!
> Hail, the most honoured
> Happy
> High Sejanus.   (*Sejanus*, 5. 7)
> Sejanus trusts him well.
> Sejanus is a noble bounteous lord.
> He is so, and most valiant.
> And most wise.
> He's everything.   (*Ibid.* 5. 10)

The habit of definition which is behind the epigrammatic
simile links it to the short character sketches. Ben Jonson

had prefixed the "character of the persons" to *Every Man out of His Humour*: in the inductions to *Antonio and Mellida* and *The Malcontent*, the characters are discussed in this way. This summing up of the familiar (for the "types" were all based on neat definitions of the obvious) demanded an incisive form, so that they are usually put into rhyme, or even into the octosyllabic couplet. The best example in Shakespeare is Iago's character of a good housewife (*Othello*, 2. 1. 148 ff.). Sometimes the description is merely a list of phrases, and no character at all, as in Dekker's description of the happy man:

> He that makes gold his wife but not his whore,
> He that at noonday walks by a prison door,
> He that i' the sun is neither beam nor mote,
> He that's not mad after a petticoat,
> He for whom poor men's curses dig no grave,
> He that is neither lord's nor lawyer's slave....
>
> (2 *Honest Whore*, 1. 2)

The most successful examples are usually either satiric or farcical.[1] Sometimes a whole play seems built up of set characters, whose only purpose is to display themselves; perhaps the best example is Middleton's *Your Five Gallants*.

Octosyllabic verse is sometimes used for scenes of farce (e.g. those between the friars in *Lust's Dominion*, *Grim the Collier of Croydon* and *The Troublesome Reigne of King John*) or for "meditations" (such as Romelio's in *The Devil's Law Case*). It isolated the passages in question almost as sharply as the regular songs, and much more than the stanza forms of *Selimus*.

There are no examples of song forming a part of the

[1] *Vide Cynthia's Revels*, 2. 1, 3. 2; *Epicoene*, 1. 1; *The New Inn*, 1. 1, 4. 2; *May Day*, 2. 2; *All Fools*, 5. 1; *The Dutch Courtesan*, 1. 2; 1 *Honest Whore*, 2. 1; *The Fleir*, 1; *The White Devil*, 3. 1; *The Duchess of Malfi*, 1. 1; *Appius and Virginia*, 3. 4; *A Trick to Catch the Old One*, ad fin.; *All's Lost by Lust*, 2. 1, 5. 3; *Poor Man's Comfort*, ll. 2039–49; *Hoffman*, 2. 2; *Love's Cruelty*, 4. 3; *The Alchemist*, 1. 1.

dialogue in tragedy, but some of them are so apt for the occasion that they hardly appear to exist apart from it. Songs generally seem to be used when the emotional tone of the scene cannot be summed up in dialogue, e.g. in the dirges of Webster, Desdemona's Willow Song, the songs in *Cupid's Revenge* and *Valentinian* and the final scene of *The Broken Heart*.

In Middleton's *A Trick to Catch the Old One* the marriage of old Hoard and the Courtesan is celebrated in an improvised catch which definitely belongs to the dialogue: in *Bonduca*, the cure of Junius' love-sickness is celebrated similarly. In *A Fair Quarrel* there is a great deal of patterned speech, and the gull Chough who has sworn not to reveal that the bride, Jane Fitzallan, has had a child, lets her bridegroom know it by singing a catch with his man, beginning:

> *Chough.* Take heed in time, O man, unto thy head!
> *Trimtram.* All is not gold that glistereth in bed. (5. 1)

The same device is used in Heywood's *Rape of Lucrece*. Most of the songs there are highly irrelevant, but the clown reveals the rape in a catch because he has sworn to say nothing.

In *The Captives*, the echo scene is sung. Two women stand outside the monastery at which they have sought relief and sing:

> *Palestra.* O charity where art thou fled?
> And how long has thou bin dead?
> *Answer Within.* O many many hundred years.
> *Scribonia.* In village, borough, town or city
> Remains there yet no grace, no pity?
> *Answer Within.* Not in sighs, not in wails, not in tears.
>
> (2. 1. 84 ff.)

Later a most exciting piece of action is represented by a song within. The villains who are pursuing the women

come up to their shelter and the meeting is represented by
a "great noyce within" and a ditty:

> [1] Helpe, helpe oh helpe a wretched maid
>   Or else we are undone then.
> [2] And have I caught, and have I caught you?
>   In vayne it is to run then.   (3. 2. 46 ff.)

Such lyrics were not used in tragedy, but they indicate the
frankly artificial nature of the dialogue in comedy, and there
is reason to suppose that tragedy was still further removed
from "deeds and language such as men do use". In general
the different kinds of patterned speech and dialogue correspond to the different levels of relevance in what is said.
Prose, blank verse, patterned blank verse, couplets and stanza
forms represent an ascending scale of artificiality. It may
correspond to the difference between speeches "in character"
and general meditations, or to that between unemotional
and emotional passages, or to the division between the comic
and tragic plots of a play. In the first two instances, the
formal ordering of the speech is only a technical auxiliary
for the indication of the direction of the speech; it is "out
of character" whether addressed *ad spectatores* or not.

It is generally assumed on the modern stage that the
characters speak to one another and not to the audience.
Even the soliloquy is (or was) discouraged as unnatural.
Upon the picture stage such assumptions are necessary,
because actors and audience are sharply cut off from each
other by the proscenium arch and the footlights. Upon the
Elizabethan stage there was no such division and there was
a place for the direct address. Sometimes the dramatis
personae exchange speeches in the modern manner, where
each character has his limited rôle and remains inside it:
sometimes the character, still inside his rôle, will approach
the spectators; sometimes again a character may transcend
the limits of his special rôle and assume a kind of choric
speech, in which he states the total situation and expresses

the "moral" or central significance of the play. The speeches of King Lear on the heath are of this sort; not only do they express all "the riches of that sea, his mind", but that of the whole play (whereas in Act 5 he is limited to his rôle).

The variations between the different kinds of speech are difficult to define but easy to feel. They may be compared to the effect of the use of different formations of the verb for Oratio Obliqua. Patterned speech would correspond to such a different formation, but patterned speech is only one way of securing this enlargement of the utterance.

The uses of direct speech may be roughly divided into the expository (revelation of the intrigue and also of the thoughts and feelings of the characters) and the moral, or statement of the total situation, the core of the play. These are fused in some of the greatest speeches of the drama: the early soliloquies of Barabas, Vindice's address to the skull, Volpone's speech to Celia (*Volpone*, 3. 5).

The simpler kinds of direct speech usually recognise the presence of the audience explicitly. The habit was inherited from the moralities and interludes, where the spectators were often taken into the play (e.g. in *The Pardoner and the Frere*). It was supported by the masque and court plays, where the drama often dissolved into panegyric (e.g. *The Arraignment of Paris, ad fin.*) and also by the readiness of the audience to be directly moved by the story, as if it were a piece of real life.

The recognition of direct speech as a legitimate convention is necessary to the rehabilitation of Elizabethan methods of construction. It is true that the dramatists did not define their methods with the precision of Corneille or Racine, whose confidants (dummy figures representing the audience) kept everyone from being shocked by a "primitive technique" of direct address. Actually, the graduation between the frank appeal *ad spectatores* and the subtlest nuances of Shakespearean dramaturgy, make the dead-level of modern dialogue seem a very primitive affair.

It was easy to come out of character when neither action
nor speech was realistic. The dramatists had no hankerings
after the vocabulary of the plain man.

That were a precept no less dangerous to language than life,
if we were to speak or live after the custom of the vulgar; but
that I call custom of speech which is the consent of the learned:
as custom of life which is the consent of the good.[1]

Nor was the actor's moralising circumscribed by the presence
of drawing-room furniture. It was helped by the fact that
he was probably so well known to the audience that they
only saw the character as a transparent cover to his own
personality. It is essential to remember that the repertory
system produces a very special kind of dramatic illusion; for
not only do the audience know their actors so completely
that they cannot sink them in the part, but the actors also,
to a certain extent, know their audience. This affected
comedy more than tragedy: sometimes the clown would
make a reference to some particular person in the audience,
and at the end of a play Kempe used to improvise rhymes
on subjects suggested by the audience, which must often
have been of a personal nature.

The Elizabethans were helped by the way in which their
prologues and epilogues shaded into the body of the play.
In early plays the Chorus or the presenter who "served as
chorus to (a) tragedy" was closely linked to the story.
When a dumb show was used, choric figures might appear
to act as interpreters (e.g. the pilgrims in *The Duchess of
Malfi*, 3. 4).

In the plays of the University wits the presenters stand
in a special relation to the play; they are either the authors

---

[1] Jonson, *Timber or Discoveries*: Consuetudo.—Perspicuitas, Venustas;
cf. Dryden. "It is very clear to all that understand poetry that a serious
play ought not to imitate conversation too nearly. If nothing were
to be raised above that level the foundation of poetry would be
destroyed"—preface to *The Conquest of Granada*.

of it, or closely connected with it in some other way. They address themselves quite frankly to the audience. St Dunstan, who introduces *Grim the Collier of Croydon* is a late and interesting example of the habit. He uses the second person throughout his speech.

> Know then who list that I am English born,
> My name is Dunstan: whilst I lived with man
> Chief Primate of the Holy English Church....
> Ne will I trouble you with court and kings
> Or drive a feigned battle out of breath:
> Or keep a coil myself upon the stage.
> But think you see me in my secret cell
> Armed with my portace, bidding of my beads.
> But on a sudden I'm o'ercome with sleep.
> If aught ensue, watch you, for Dunstan dreams.

He immediately goes to sleep and a scene in Hell "ensues" on the inner stage.

In the play-within-the-play the dialogue is often spoken *at* the stage audience rather than *to* them, the ironic *doubles ententes* being directed at the real audience.

The Nuntius was used in the tragedies of Chapman and Jonson. In *Caesar and Pompey*, 2. 2, he appears on an empty stage and therefore does not address himself even theoretically to stage spectators. The Nuntius' method of description is never naturalistic; he does not give the more important facts first, but begins at the beginning of his tale and tells it orderly.

The Nuntius was, however, as Webster records, something of a luxury to the popular playwright, though the Chorus in Shakespeare's *Henry V* seems to differ only in name. In the less learned plays the dramatis personae often acted as messengers, and their speeches are also undramatic. Gertrude's account of Ophelia's death is tenderly pastoral; Maria's account of the death of Mellida in *Antonio's Revenge* is lusciously sentimental, and could moreover have betrayed the whole plot to Piero.

Messengers' speeches, or descriptive speeches of great length, were usually distinguished by a heightened vocabulary; Chapman's are grandiloquent, Tourneur's and Webster's decoratively lyrical.[1]

The presenters and the Chorus did not survive the University wits; the exposition was thereafter in an opening soliloquy of the hero.

The expository soliloquy was particularly necessary for the Machiavellian villain, and the majority of the plays listed are of this type. Occasionally a more subtle device was used: Shakespeare gave Iago the gull Roderigo to serve as a confidant, but even then a great deal is revealed by soliloquy. Marlowe uses Machiavelli as prologue to *The Jew of Malta*, and Jonson's use of Sylla's ghost casts a supernatural shadow over *Catiline*. These figures are something more than presenters; their function is nearer to that of the witches in *Macbeth*.

The conclusion of the play is often expository too. The fate of the characters may be finally summed up,[2] as the early nineteenth-century novelist reviewed all their characters in a final chapter. Occasionally dialogue slides imperceptibly into epilogue, as, at the end of *Antonio's Revenge*, the hero, mourning over his mistress' body, says:

> And oh, if ever time create a muse
> That to th' immortal frame of virgin faith
> Dares once engage his pen to write her death
> Presenting it in some black tragedy
> May it prove gracious....

More frequently, the play becomes undramatic at the end; the characters refer consciously to their rôles, or pose in them. Such are the repentances of Witgood and the Courtesan at the end of *A Trick to Catch the Old One*.

---

[1] E.g. Aumerle's speech, *The Revenge of Bussy D'Ambois*, 4. 1. 11–40. Borachio's account of Charlemont's death, *The Atheist's Tragedy*, 2.1.85 ff.

[2] E.g. *As You Like It* (5. 4. 184–90). *The Malcontent, ad fin.*

Other writers made play on the spectators' consciousness of illusion. In *Antonio and Mellida* Alberto makes his final exit saying:

> Farewell, dear friends: expect no more of me.
> Thus ends my part in this love's comedy.

Compare

> Then farewell, friends:
> Thus Thisbe ends:
> Adieu, adieu, adieu.

This kind of private epilogue was more frequent in comedy than tragedy.[1] When, as in *Antonio and Mellida*, the characters had also discussed their parts during the induction, it must have meant that the taking up and dropping of the rôle was intended to be shown to the spectators, and in a repertory company it is a useful and obvious practice.

It is also interesting to note that, in *Antonio and Mellida*, the lovers, on meeting in the marsh, greet each other in Italian. When they have left the stage, Mellida's page apologises for this to the audience.

None of these speeches is of very great importance, but they show that the awareness of the audience was acknowledged, and that there was no question of the characters "stepping out of the picture", for they were never in it.

Expository soliloquy is usually preferable to expository dialogue, for it can be stiffened up to fit in well enough with the typical characterisation. The use of dialogue implies an attempt to hide the exposition, to make it naturalistic, and if the disguise is not efficient, there is a definite sense of failure. The opening of *Richard III* is frankly conventional; the opening of *As You Like It* is an unsuccessful subterfuge. The opening scene of *Hamlet* contains some rather blatant exposition; both Horatio and Marcellus suffer from tem-

---

[1] E.g. *Patient Grissel, Greene's Tu Quoque, Westward Hoe, A Trick to Catch the Old One, The Alchemist, ad fin.*

porary amnesia of the first act, a disease which Sheridan was to diagnose:

> *Sir Walter Raleigh.* Philip, you know, is proud Iberia's king.
> *Sir Christ. Hatton.* He is....
> *Sir Walter Raleigh.* You also know—
> *Dangle.* Mr Puff, if Sir Christopher knows all this why does Sir Walter go on telling him? (*The Critic*, 2. 2)

Expository dialogue is often the refuge of the incompetent.

> *Medici.* So, 'twas well fitted, now shall we observe
> How his wished absence will give violent way
> To duke Brachiano's lust.
> *Monticelso.* Why that was it.
> To what scorned purpose else should we make use
> Of him for a sea captain?...
> It may be objected I am dishonourable
> To play thus with my kinsman: but I answer
> For my revenge I'd stake a brother's life
> That being wronged durst not avenge himself.
> (The White Devil, 2. 1. 371 ff.)

This might have been made quite plausible, as, for instance, Claudius' determination to send Hamlet to England (3. 1. 173 ff.) where the ostensible and the real reason are both given and the whole thing sounds less forced because it precedes Claudius' public action in the matter. Webster is addicted to the delayed explanation which always has an air of awkward improvisation, of being *post hoc ergo propter hoc*.

The technique of exposition is, however, one of the more mechanical parts of construction: consequently it improved in the drama of Fletcher and Massinger, and is usually indirectly given there. In the later Jacobean drama, the habit of deliberate mystification made full exposition unnecessary. The villain throws out ambiguous but sinister remarks, such as

> I will do something but I know not what—

and all explanation is reserved for the final scene.

Direct speech is also used in dialogue for debates, flytings and "sets of wit".[1] The drama had grown from debates on such subjects as "Wherein consists true honour and nobility?" (the subject of *Fulgens and Lucrece*) and in such a typical interlude as *Nobility* four characters come on in the void as it were, and begin a debate which constitutes the whole play. The debating figures of early inductions are their lineal descendants. The debate persists in *Faustus* in the exhortations of the good and evil angels and in the catechisms of Mephistopheles by Faust: in the debates of *Richard III* the characters become slightly detached from the story.

The "sets of wit" belonged to comedy, but the wooing scenes in *The Spanish Tragedy* between Belimperia and Horatio, and Belimperia and Balthazar,[2] show that they could be successfully fitted into tragedy. They became more frequent in the tragedy of the middle period, when comic types and situations were freely used. There is a very glaring case of the intrusion of a "set of wit" in *The Atheist's Tragedy*, 1. 3, where Castabella is wooed by Rousard. The heroine is given flippantly bawdy speeches, which would better fit Cataplasma or Soquette; and, as she is a carefully idealised Romantic virgin of the chaste and colourless kind, the scene is fatally incongruous. Tourneur was perhaps imitating the exchange of Hamlet and Ophelia in the play scene without realising precisely what Shakespeare had done with the conventional "set of wit" on that occasion.

This temporary sacrifice of character is quite frequent. There is the conversation between Helena and Parolles in *All's Well that Ends Well*, which is, as Professor Brander Matthews observed, "impossible to a modest-minded girl",[3] and a conversation between Jolenta and Angelica in *The*

[1] So called in *Love's Labour's Lost*, 5. 2. 29.
[2] *The Spanish Tragedy*, 2. 4. 16–49, 3. 10. 88–103.
[3] *All's Well that Ends Well*, 1. 1. 118 ff. *Shakespeare as a Playwright*, p. 224.

Devil's Law Case, in which the chaste heroine bets on the sex of her brother's unborn bastard.

In the flyting scenes of *Bussy D'Ambois* and *The Revenge of Bussy D'Ambois*[1] the combatants prepare for the fight like a pair of fencers saluting:

> A bargain, o' mine honour.
> What else, sir? Come, pay me home: I'll bide it bravely.

The speeches are straightforward invective, but they are detached from the play; for, though they are in earnest, the whole thing is *supposed* to be a jest and Monsieur drops suddenly from furious cursing to

> Why, now I see thou lovest me: come to the banquet!

The trial scene of *The White Devil* is another example of flyting. The Lawyer and Vittoria are conscious of it:

> *Lawyer.* Well then, have at you!
> *Vittoria.* I am at the mark, sir, I'll give aim to you
> And tell you how near you shoot. (3. 2. 20–8)

In Act 1, Scene 3, of *The Lover's Melancholy* there is a flyting match between a malcontent and a physician. The duelling spirit in which it is conducted is even more obvious than that of Chapman's or Webster's plays.

> *Corax* (*throws off his gown*). Do what thou darest: I'll stand thee.
> *Rhesias.* Mountibanks, empirics, quacksalvers, mineralists, wizards, alchemists, cast apothecaries, old wives and barbers are all suppositors to the right worshipful doctor, as I take it....
> *Corax.* Have at thee! Thou affectest railing only for thy health: thy miseries are so thick and lasting that thou hast not one poor denier to bestow on the opening a vein: wherefore, to avoid a pleurisy, thou'lt be sure once a month to prate thyself into a whipping, and bleed in the breech instead of the arm....
> *Rhesias.* Have at you again....
> *Corax.* Come!...

---

[1] *Bussy D'Ambois*, 3. 2; *The Revenge of Bussy D'Ambois*, 1. 1. 228–90.

Rhesias. Thou art in thy religion an atheist, in thy condition a cur, in thy diet an epicure, in thy lust a goat, in thy sleep a hog: thou takest upon thee the habit of a grave physician, but art indeed an imposterous empiric. Physicians are the cobblers, rather the botchers, of men's bodies: as the one patches our tattered clothes, so the other solders our diseased flesh. Come on.

Scenes like the malcontent railings of Flaminio and Lodovico depend on the antiphonal chant of the two characters, yet it does not matter much who speaks any particular line. Dialogue is used because the several voices make counterpoint possible; but the individuality of each speaker is not retained.

There are some comedies, such as *Humour out of Breath* and *The Fleir*, which, as their very titles suggest, consist almost entirely of debates and sets of wit. *Love's Labour's Lost* is akin to them.

Another device is the acting of a scene by someone who wishes to recount it. The characters are always dramatising themselves and their situations. These scenes are often comic, though not always so.[1] In Daborne's *The Poor Man's Comfort* the old man Gisbert, who has been refused justice by the court, puts on a bitter mood after the case is over, and plays the parts of the different senators, sits in their chairs and mimics their voices. This is perhaps a reminiscence of the farmhouse scene in *King Lear*. In comic scenes of this kind it is usual for the characters to forget themselves in their parts, and bait their masters or commit some other blunder. At the end of *Lust's Dominion* and *A Christian Turned Turk* the villain is hoist with his own petard, when, staging the death of his victims, he plays their part and is killed in earnest by a treacherous servant. This curious blurring of acting and reality may partly be explained by

[1] *Satiromastix*, 5. 1, 2; *Troilus and Cressida*, 3. 3; *A Christian Turned Turk*, ll. 1607 ff.; *The Poor Man's Comfort*, ll. 1205 ff.; *The Bondman*, 2. 2; *The Lover's Melancholy*, 3. 1; *The Traitor*, 3. 1.

the physical conditions of the playhouse (the neutral setting and the proximity of the audience), and by the views of the spectators. On the one hand the gentlemen came to criticise the speech and the songs in a spirit of complete detachment; on the other, the groundlings shared the views of the grocer and his wife in *The Knight of the Burning Pestle*, and were half inclined to raise the watch when murder was threatened. The popular comparison of life to a play and the world to a stage was at times something more than an analogy. It was evidently not only the grocer and his wife who might be directly affected by a play; for the old miser in *A Roman Actor* is not particularly unsophisticated and yet he acts in the same way.

The aside is the bridge between dialogue and soliloquy in the Elizabethan drama. Some asides are so lengthy that they are practically soliloquies. The short aside may be divided into the explanatory and the ironic varieties. The explanatory aside is often used to make the feelings of a character explicit, where the modern dramatist would rely upon the actor. Desdemona's

> I am not merry but I do beguile
> The thing I am by seeming otherwise.

or Othello's

> O hardness to dissemble!

would not be necessary with naturalist acting.

When any important part of the plot is explained in asides, the exposition at once becomes more brusque and cursory than if it were done in soliloquy. Cornelius' aside (*Cymbeline*, 1. 5. 33 ff.) disposes summarily of the old convention of a sleeping potion which appears to be a poison.[1] The writers of the middle period used the aside when they were not interested in action, but only in the situations which

---

[1] *Vide Romeo and Juliet*; *Satiromastix*; *The Honest Whore*, Part 1; *A Chaste Maid in Cheapside*; *The Malcontent*; *The Jew of Malta*.

BTC

the action produced. There is great difference in emphasis between the careful explanations of Iago's conduct which his soliloquies provide, and the brief statements thrown off by Webster's characters to give the merest covering of justification for their action (e.g. Flaminio's reasons for playing the madman).

Villains use the aside much more frequently than any other characters. In the opening scene of the *Two Lamentable Tragedies* the Italian villain, in a series of asides which are marked "To the People", makes the hypocrisy of his pretended affection plain. The Elizabethan asides, unlike those of the modern stage, were not meant simply to reveal the inner feelings of the character, but practically always showed some consciousness of the audience, to whom they were addressed.

The bitter punning aside belongs to the Machiavel. It is used by Lorenzo in *The Spanish Tragedy* and by Barabas in *The Jew of Malta*; there is an obvious connection with the punning retorts of stichomuthia.

When Marston invented the rôle of the disguised Malcontent it became of structural importance, and something more than a witty interpolation. Malevole constantly uses it, and it keeps his dual personality in the mind. When he is tempting his wife, in the disguise of Mendoza's pander, his asides reveal his "other self". Vindice uses the aside in the same way. These asides are more complicated than those of Othello and Desdemona because they imply the juxtaposition of two *incompatible* personalities, which is only possible when the characterisation is simplified. Edgar's asides, in the rôle of Mad Tom, are rather similar. In all these cases the aside is still spoken to the audience.

The Malcontents also used to comment on the action of the other stage personages, to some third person; and this constituted an aside addressed not to the audience but to another actor.

Mark her, I prithee: she simpers like the suds
A collier has been washed in.

The cardinal lifts up his nose like a foul porpoise before a storm.

These asides would be given much more confidentially and realistically.

Jonson developed from Marlowe the structural use of the stage aside.[1] In the final scene of *Volpone* a duel goes on between Mosca and Volpone in asides. Volpone is in disguise and reported dead; Mosca, who is his heir, is trying to double-cross him:

> *Volpone.* Mosca, I was almost lost.... Say I am living. [*Aside.*
> *Mosca.* What busy knave is this? Most reverend fathers
> I had the sooner attended your grave pleasures
> But that the order for the funeral
> Of my dear patron did require me—
> *Volpone.* Mosca!   [*Aside.*
> *Mosca.* Whom I intend to bury like a gentleman
> *Volpone.* Ay, quick: and cozen me of all.   [*Aside.*
> Thou shalt have half.
> *Mosca.* Whose drunkard is this same? Speak, some that
>   know him
> I never saw his face—I cannot now   [*Aside.*
> Afford it you so cheap.

Here there is no consciousness of the audience.

The scene in *The Maid's Tragedy* (4. 2) where Melantius almost drives Calianax mad by making suggestions in asides which he denies aloud was perhaps modelled on Jonson. In this case, the whole scene is built upon the asides. The aside is chiefly used in later plays for satiric exposure and comment (e.g. Bacha on the king's senile amorousness, *Cupid's Revenge*, 2. 4; the page, *The Fatal Dowry*, 4. 1, who speaks only in asides throughout the scene).

In *The Changeling* Middleton used the simple asides of Beatrice-Joanna to build up the ironic situation of Act 2.

---

[1] *Vide The Jew of Malta*, 1. 2. 331–65, 2. 3. 30–95.

Her puzzled observation of De Flores' excitement and eagerness:

> Possible his need
> Is strong upon him;

her frightened ejaculation at his persistence:

> Bless me!
> I'd fain be rid of him;

alone make possible the irony of her final outburst to him:

> Why, 'tis impossible thou canst be so wicked
> Or shelter such a cunning cruelty
> To make his death the murderer of my honour.

It is only those dramatists who made this structural use of the aside who raised it from a convenience to a convention. Even Jonson in his early plays made flagrant use of the expository aside in scenes when it was not justified, e.g. Canon Hugh's in *A Tale of a Tub*, 3. 5.

The most important form of direct speech was the soliloquy. Its expository function was comparatively negligible, and its use for the statement of the "moral" so highly developed that the soliloquies of Tamburlaine, Faustus, Barabas; of Hamlet, Othello, Iago, Lear, Macbeth and Lady Macbeth; of Bussy, Biron, Sejanus, Vindice, are the most dramatic and significant parts of the plays.

A speech which is not spoken on an empty stage may yet be nearer to soliloquy than dialogue. Vindice's second speech upon the skull is spoken in the presence of his brother, but it is essentially a soliloquy. In *The Devil's Law Case* Romelio has a "meditation" which he recites while a friar and two bellmen[1] pose by him; whilst on the other side his mother kneels telling her beads. Against this solemn tableau, Romelio speaks as follows:

> I have a certain meditation
> If I can think of 't, somewhat to this purpose.

[1] Symbols of death—cf. *The Duchess of Malfi*, 4. 2. 93.

I'll say it to you while my mother there
Numbers her beads.

You that dwell near these graves and vaults
Which oft do hide Physician's faults
Note what a small room doth suffice
T' express men's good—their vanities
Would fill more volumes of small hand
Than all the Evidence of Church Land.
Funerals hide men in civil wearing,
And are to drapers a good hearing,
Make the Heralds laugh in their black raiment,
And all die worthier, die worth payment
To the altar offerings, though their fame
And all the charter of their name
'Tween heaven and this, yield no more light
Than rotten trees that shine i' the night. (2. 3. 110ff.)

And so on for twenty lines or so more. The artificial and
wholly undramatic character of this "meditation" needs no
comment.

Romelio is, of course, something of a Malcontent, and
they usually emphasise the detachment of their railings
with a—

> Mark my meditation

or

> Observe me now—

as a warning that a satiric generalisation is to follow.

In Chapman's plays much of the dialogue consists of
meditation from the hero, the other characters inserting
admiring ejaculations or leading questions, but playing no
greater part in the scene than Romelio's mute supporters.
The trick is particularly common in *Caesar and Pompey*
and *The Revenge of Bussy D'Ambois*, especially 1. 2, 2. 1,
3. 4.

The soliloquies are the chief means of defining the
characters. A good deal has been written on Shakespeare's
use of the soliloquy for this purpose, on the "primitive

technique" of the self-descriptive soliloquy, and the flatness with which the situation is explained:

> I am determined to be a villain.
> Let them view in me
> The perfect picture of all tyranny.
> Then, Wendoll, be content,
> Thus villains, if they would, cannot repent.

This kind of statement fits in with the simplified characters like Barabas and Richard III, but not with characters like Wendoll and Prince Hal, who are thought of as complete and normal human beings.

Other characters will also be described with undramatic frankness. The villains praise the hero's noble qualities even while they are plotting against them, in a manner which cannot be explained as mere cynicism. But even then there is no consistency: Iago laughs at Othello's simplicity but he also "pays tribute" to his good qualities.

Those critics who have been interested in the plays as "realistic" or "psychological" studies have been much concerned with this self-characterisation and the characterisation of other dramatis personae; but if it is considered not in isolation but in relation to other kinds of direct speech, it appears a straightforward and unimportant device, hardly worth the discussion it has provoked.

It is worth remembering, in connection with the objective truth of soliloquy, that the Censor was apt to take up a very uncompromising attitude towards any doubtful speech, and not to regard the character of the speaker at all. It seems less unnatural that even the villain should not be allowed to question the hero's nobility, when Sir George Buc would not allow Prince Maurice of Nassau to be called "proud" by a man who is the villain of the piece.[1] His villainous character did not affect the validity of his statement.

---

[1] *Vide Sir John Van Olden Barnevelt*, l. 281; also ll. 2233 ff., 2350 ff. In *The Second Maiden's Tragedy*, Buc indignantly erased the retort to

The description of feeling and sensation is as full as the description of character and motives. Characters who suffer pain, or experience a change of heart, describe the process with scientific detachment. In this case it is not a matter of "primitive technique", for any actor can represent bodily sensations. It was simply due to the Elizabethan habit of making everything explicit and of stating everything in the verse itself, in contradistinction to the modern habit of leaving more and more to the action, and to implication.

The technique of motivation might be so undeveloped as to make the opening soliloquy of Richard III necessary, but the technique of acting could scarcely have been so neglected that the hero's dying pangs had to be analysed by himself with such unconcern as this:

> A gripping pain hath seized upon my heart
> A sudden pain, the messenger of death:
> O hold me up! my sight begins to fail:
> My sinews shrink, my brain turns upside down.
> (*The Massacre at Paris*, 1. 3)

> O Lorrique, torture!
> I feel an Aetna burn
> Within my brain and all my body else
> Is like a hell of ice: all the Baltic seas
> That now surround us cannot quench this flame.
> My sinews shrink like leaves parched in the sun.
> (*Hoffman*, 1. 1)

In the later plays the sufferer often glories in his pangs in a perverted manner (*Valentinian*, 5. 1, 2; *Love's Sacrifice*, 5. 3).[1]

"Your king's poisoned"—"The King of Heaven be praised for 't!" It might not be irrelevant to remember the exceptionally severe sentences passed by the Court of Star Chamber upon too free political speeches, even when it was certain no sedition was involved.

[1] *Vide* also 2 *Henry VI*, 3. 1, 3. 2; *King John*, 5. 1; *The Jew of Malta*, 5. 1; *The Revenger's Tragedy*, 4. 4; *The Devil's Charter*, 4. 3, 5. 1; *Alphonsus of Germany*, 4. 1; *Locrine*, 1. 1; *The White Devil*, 5. 3; *Thierry and Theodoret*, 5. 2; *The Duke of Milan*, 5. 2; *The Distracted State*, 5. 2; *'Tis Pity She's a Whore*, 5. 1.

This descriptive method is used for mental processes as well. A repentant villain will give a description of how it feels, instead of presenting the process of feeling directly.

> Believe me, countrymen, a sudden thought
> A sudden change in Sylla's mind hath wrought.
> *(Wounds of Civil War, 5. 357–8)*

> We are amazed...our spirits...numb'd...we blush.
> *(Antonio and Mellida, 5. 1)*

> On the sudden
> I feel all fires of love quenched in the water
> Of my compassion. *(The Maid of Honour, 5. 2)*

This flat statement was the only possible way of presenting conventional reversals of feeling, such as the villains' repentance, or love-at-first-sight. They could not be made "natural", and since the process is never of any importance, but only the results, a frank recognition of its arbitrary nature, such as these speeches imply, is preferable to a stumbling effort at credibility.

All these functions of the soliloquy may be classed as expository, since they are on the levels of narrative and character. But the second use of soliloquy, which is the statement of the "moral" or central significance of the play,[1] is more interesting and more important.

Marlowe used the soliloquy in *Tamburlaine* and *Faustus* for this purpose. Tamburlaine's speeches do not contain much information, either about the action or his own feelings; even when he is describing his love for Zenocrate, it is given as a general statement, not a personal one.

> What is beauty, saith my sufferings then?...
> *(1st Tamburlaine, 5. 1)*

---

[1] The moral is not always an ethical statement, though it is so in the more learned dramatists. By "the statement of the moral" I mean the complete verbal expression of the whole complex of feeling behind the play, in a manner which means that the character speaking transcends the limits of his rôle. The degraded modern equivalent is the speech of the *raisonneur*.

The play is concerned with a single and simple theme, which is most completely expressed by Tamburlaine in the speech beginning:

The thirst of reign and sweetness of a crown,... (2. 7)

The hero himself, who is the means by which this theme is stated, is of such overwhelming importance that all the other characters are either foils or supporters to him. Therefore the dialogue is hardly ever more than a means for displaying Tamburlaine; his soliloquies and long-soaring speeches are the very core of the play. But since the play depends upon the hero so completely, he does not have to transcend his rôle to state the moral.

Faustus' soliloquies are almost of equal importance, though he is more of a human being and less of an impersonal force than the Scythian. The introduction of Mephistopheles, however, makes genuine dialogue possible; the scenes between the two are more than an exchange of "sentences".

In *The Jew of Malta* and still more in *Edward II*, the soliloquies are distributed among the minor characters and are expository. The growing interest in intrigue makes it of some importance to know how characters are prepared to act, and not only how they feel. Only the last soliloquy of Edward is in Marlowe's earlier manner.

The Jew of Malta depends for the first two acts upon the soliloquies of Barabas. These soliloquies are not a means of dodging exposition, and of letting the audience know what a bogey Barabas is; they are adequate statements of his total self, which a circumscribed character is obliged to make. Such characters cannot define themselves by action, for their acts are necessarily crude and melodramatic. They must be defined in words, otherwise there is nothing to separate Barabas from Selimus.

Chapman and Jonson, who were both influenced by Marlowe, use the long-soaring speech and the soliloquy in the same way. These speeches are always to be taken straight-forwardly and not with reference to the character of the speaker. Tiberius' speech on the duties of a prince (*Sejanus*, 3. 1) is not less splendid and sincere for being spoken by a tyrant. Tamyra's appeal to her maid to tell the truth in the name of womanhood (*Bussy D'Ambois*, 4. 1. 213–24) is meant to be a genuinely moving thing in itself, and not to strike the hearer as a piece of consummate hypocrisy. Tamyra's guilt is not relevant here. Professor Parott remarks: "When Chapman has a fine speech he does not care much into whose mouth he puts it". This is not exactly the point: Chapman never thinks of the possibility of contrasting what his characters say and what they may be supposed to think, which is the commonest method of gaining concentration now.

Shakespeare is an exception. Antony's speech to the mob on Caesar, or the way in which Iago "plays" his victims, depend upon the contrast between the intention and the calculated emotionalism of the speech. Compared with this, the hypocrisy of the Machiavel or the double rôle of the disguised Revenger are kept away from their true selves, which emerge in asides: the two halves are juxtaposed, not fused. In the case of Tiberius or Tamyra there is not even any juxtaposition. The characters are temporarily mouth-pieces for the writer.

Jonson's Humours fuse exposition and moral. They display themselves, limitations and all. *Sejanus* depends very largely on the working of "policy" in the narrative, of simulation and dissimulation, and the disguising of intention behind masks of all kinds, but the characters are simple and fixed. Sejanus presents himself in soliloquy in the manner of Barabas:

> Adultery! It is the lightest ill
> I will commit: a race of wicked acts
> Shall flow out of my anger and o'erspread
> The world's wide face....

> On, then, my soul, and start not in thy course
> Though Heaven drop thunder and hell belch out fire,
> Laugh at the idle terrors: tell proud Jove
> Between his power and thine there is no odds:
> 'Twas only fear first in the world made gods. (2. 2. 12 ff.)

The criticism is implicit in the very conception of the character; he is a magnificent monster, deliberately dehumanised, who only needs presenting for a "moral" to be stated. The relationship of this speech to Tamburlaine's

> The thirst of reign and sweetness of a crown,

is plain at first sight. Sejanus, like the Scythian, is less a man than a destructive force,[1] and consequently he can be explicit, because he is not "human". (Compare the character of the moralities who, being abstractions, could do no more and no less than display themselves in this dispassionate and analytic way.)

In Revenge tragedy, the soliloquy was at first the vehicle of the moral in a very obvious sense. The sententious reflections of Hieronimo on death and judgment arise from the action of the play, but they are a comment on it, like the speech of a *raisonneur*. Marston uses the soliloquy for the same purpose in *Antonio and Mellida*. The action is rapid and melodramatic, but the stoical meditations of Andrugio and Feliche are quite detached from it.

There is a sense of timelessness about these generalised reflections when they are set against the movement of the rest of the play, which relates them to the classical chorus. Many of them are "out of character"; for example, Andrugio the man is "unkinged by passion", but Andrugio the stoic is above personal feelings of any kind.

---

[1] *Vide* the description of his death when the contrast of his physical vulnerability seems so amazing: and compare the death of Catiline who died

> "Not with the face
> Of any man but of a public ruin".

> He may of valour vaunt
> Whom fortune's loudest thunder cannot daunt...
> This heart in valour even Jove outgoes,
> Jove is without, but this 'bove sense of woes.
>
> (*Antonio's Revenge*, 1. 5)

The play is built upon contrasts between stoicism and despair; between the invulnerability of the hero and the invulnerability of the fool.

> Note a fool's beatitude:
> He is not capable of passion:
> Wanting the power of distinction
> He bears an unturned sail with every wind.
> Blow east, blow west, he steers his course alike. (4. 1)

It is chiefly in soliloquy that these ironic contrasts and comparisons are worked out.

In Tourneur the sententious and the emotional are fused through the more skilful use of the Revenge tradition. Vindice's address to the skull, which, though not technically a soliloquy, may be counted one, states the moral of the whole play in a particular complex and satisfactory way. It is the node of the play, structurally and poetically. In no other play (except *King Lear* and *The Duchess of Malfi*) is the moral summed up and stated so completely. Tourneur used a stock situation, and the usual imagery of decay and death to secure this particular concentration, as well as putting it at the centre of the action.

The third act of *King Lear* could not be adequately discussed except at great length, but the fourth act of *The Duchess of Malfi* has also this timeless quality, and this detached, generalised speech. The Duchess concentrates the whole play into herself; she sits unnaturally fixed and poised while her speeches are delivered out of a void. She herself is conscious of it.

> Who do I look like now?
> Like to your picture in the gallery,
> A deal of life in show but none in practice....
> Very proper.... (4. 2. 32 ff.)

Again, she is not speaking in soliloquy, but neither is she addressing the other characters; her speeches have a detached and impersonal character like that of Vindice's address or the great speeches of Lear. The nearest equivalent to them is the Greek scene of suffering.

This self-dramatisation is necessary for characters who are not definitely limited and Humorous, like Marlowe's and Jonson's. They see themselves as a "picture in the gallery", and because of this, they can express the total situation as though they were standing outside it. Shakespeare's characters use this self-dramatisation; sometimes they, like the Duchess of Malfi, see themselves as a picture at moments of great tension,

> Now he goes
> With no less presence, but with much more love,
> Than young Alcides when he did redeem
> The Virgin tribute paid by howling Troy
> To the sea monster: I stand for sacrifice:
> The rest aloof are the Dardanian wives
> With bleared visages come forth to view
> The issue of the exploit.
> (*The Merchant of Venice*, 3. 2. 53–60)

Compare the lighter passage:

> In such a night
> Stood Dido with a willow in her hand
> Upon the wild sea banks and waft her love
> To come again to Carthage....
>
> In such a night
> Did Jessica steal from the wealthy Jew
> And with an unthrift love did run from Venice
> As far as Belmont. (*Ibid.* 5. 1. 9–17)

In such a scene as that where Hamlet's grief is symbolised by the stiff figure of the actor, ranting about Hecuba, there is the same visual projection of the feelings.

The great "painter's scene" in *The Spanish Tragedy* used this method.

When, sir, after some violent noise, bring me forth in my shirt and my gown under my arm with my torch in my hand and my sword reared up thus and with these words

"What noise is this? who calls Hieronimo?"

Then bring me forth, bring me through alley and alley still with a distracted countenance going along and let my hair heave up my nightcap. Let the clouds scowl, make the moon dark, the stars extinct, the wind blowing, the bells tolling, the owls shrieking, the toads croaking, the minutes jarring and the clock striking twelve....

This magnificent passage is obviously similar in technique to the passion of "the mobled queen". The deliberate posturing appears artificial now, but the Elizabethans were accustomed to it in daily life. Spenser tells a story through pictures, and the frequency of masques assisted the sublimation of the spectacular; but its real justification lay in Queen Elizabeth's progresses, the pageantry of public ceremonies, and even of executions. The death of the Earl of Essex or of Mary Queen of Scots would give the dramatist a precedent for that self-dramatisation upon which a critic has remarked.[1] The last speeches of Biron, Cato, Sophonisba, Vindice, Othello, Cleopatra and Coriolanus are all dependent on the characters seeing themselves in a dramatic light. It is the same method as that of the dying speech of Thomas Stukeley, which Beaumont so justly parodied.

Stukeley. Stukeley, the story of thy life is done
　　　　　Here breathe thy last and bid thy friends farewell,
　　　　　And if thy country's kindness be so much,
　　　　　Then let thy country kindly ring thy knell.
　　　　　Now go and in that bed of honour lie
　　　　　Where brave Sebastian's breathless corse doth lie.
　　　　　Here endeth Fortune's rule and bitter rage,
　　　　　Here ends Tom Stukeley his pilgrimage.

．　　　　．　　　　．　　　　．

[1] T. S. Eliot, *Shakespeare and the Stoicism of Seneca.*

Othello. Soft you: a word or two before you go:
I have done the state some service and they know it.
No more of that. I pray you in your letters
When you shall these unlucky deeds relate
Speak of me as I am: nothing extenuate
Nor set down aught in malice....
                    Set you down this:
And say besides that in Aleppo once
Where a malignant and a turbaned Turk
Beat a Venetian and traduced the state,
I took by the throat the circumcised dog,
And smote him thus. (5. 2. 337 ff.)

The difference between these two speeches is that of a
fifth-rate versifier and the greatest English poet at his greatest:
the similarity is that both depend upon a common convention, which must not be excused as a fault of rhetoric but
judged by its possibilities and its results. The later writers
seldom used direct speech. They were concerned to argue
and persuade, not to state. Massinger is always plausible
but never convincing; he treats the feelings of his characters
as he treats their beliefs. Cleora's self-immolation in *The
Bondman* is clearly meant to produce something of the
effect of the imprisonment of the Duchess of Malfi,[1] but
Cleora's posturing is of quite a different kind

                    When like a Vestal
I show you to your shame the fire still burning
Committed to my charge by true affection,
The people joining with you in the wonder:
When by the glorious splendour of my sufferings
The prying eyes of jealousy are struck blind
The monster god that feeds on fears, e'en starved
For want of seeming matter to accuse me:
Expect, Leosthenes, a sharp reproof
From my just anger. (2. 1)

Cleora is not impersonal: she is not viewing herself with
the detachment of a feeling which has passed beyond hope

[1] There is a significant echo in Act 4, Scene 3.

or despair like the grief of the Duchess of Malfi or of Othello: therefore "the glorious splendour of my sufferings" sounds like a personal boast and not like the naïve self-characterisation of the earlier plays. This self-conscious posturing disfigures both Massinger and Fletcher; it distinguishes, for instance, the final speeches of Bonduca, and the whole character of Ford's Penthea. Only Beaumont had the right Elizabethan note, in the most splendid passage of *The Maid's Tragedy*, a passage which owes something to the speeches from *The Merchant of Venice*:

> Suppose I stand upon the sea beach now,
> Mine arms thus and my hair blown with the wind
> Wild as that desert: and let all about me
> Tell that I am forsaken....
>   And the trees about me
> Let them be dry and leafless: let the rocks
> Groan with continual surges: and behind me
> Make all a desolation. (*The Maid's Tragedy*, 2. 2)[1]

The feeling is projected and expressed wholly in terms of imagery, as are the greater part of the Duchess of Malfi's speeches and the scene from *The Spanish Tragedy*. Massinger and Fletcher and Ford used the convention for scenes of a relatively low emotional pitch: they did not isolate and concentrate the feeling; above all, they did not transcend the limitations of the character. Cleora and the rest still speak inside their rôles; therefore their speeches are not really "direct speech" at all, but an imitation of it.

---

[1] Cf. Aurelian Townshend's *Though Regions Far Divided*:

"See then my last lamenting,   Those arms, wherein wide open
Upon a cliffe I'le sitt,   Love's fleete was wont to putt,
Rock Constancy presenting,   Shall layd acrosse betoken
Till I grow part of itt;   That haven's mouth is shutt.
My tears a quicksand feeding,   Myne eyes noe light shall cherish
Where on noe foote can rest,   For shipps at sea distrest,
My sighs a tempest breeding   But darkling let them perish,
About my stony breast.   Or splitt against my breast".

PART TWO
THE DRAMATISTS

CHAPTER VI

Christopher Marlowe

THE attempt to define the conventions of a particular dramatist is more difficult than to define those of a period. They will depend on the limitations of his interests and sensibility, which are disputable qualities: they will also involve a modification of the more general conventions which have been already considered. In the work of the greater dramatists the formulae which Chettle, Goffe or Daborne passively supported are seen to be something more than literary laziness. The degree in which the greater writers relied upon general conventions naturally increases with the development of the drama. Marlowe had the least to rely upon: he found dramatic forms, like dramatic blank verse, stiff and inflexible; the history of his development is one of growing plasticity. He was affected by his age chiefly in matters of presentation.

The two parts of *Tamburlaine*, his earliest surviving work, illustrate a temporary equilibrium of personal and general conventions and its breakdown through Marlowe's own development. It is generally conceded that *Tamburlaine*, Part 1, has a unity of the parts with the whole which *Tamburlaine*, Part 2, does not possess, and that Marlowe attempted to do twice what could only be done once.

The unity of Part 1 is supplied by Tamburlaine himself. He is hardly thought of as a man, though it is not in Part 1 that he is most frequently equated with a god or a devil. He is a dramatic figure symbolising certain qualities, and he defines himself in the famous "Nature that framed us of four elements". The most direct statement of his nature is, however, given by Meander.

> Some powers divine or else infernal mixed
> Their angry seeds at his conception:
> For he was never sprung of human race,
> Since with the spirit of his fearful pride
> He dares so doubtlessly resolve of rule
> And by profession be ambitious. (2. 6. 9 ff.)

Tamburlaine's ambition has no definite object; it exists in and for itself. His aspiring mind is drawn upward as naturally as gravitation draws a stone downward. Herein Marlowe encounters a difficulty, for Tamburlaine's immediate aims can never be the objective correlative of this divine striving. The extraordinary drop at the end of "Nature that framed us of four elements" to

> That perfect bliss and sole felicity
> The sweet fruition of an earthly crown (2. 7. 28 ff.)

has been often observed. It is in vain that Marlowe insists that Tamburlaine despises wealth and only desires rule: earthly rule is in itself no fit equivalent for his feelings (as language has no fit expression for the divine beauty of Zenocrate). Tamburlaine is god-like ("a god is not so glorious as a king") but his accomplishments are limited to human possibilities. Marlowe escaped from this difficulty by making Tamburlaine's objects as generalised as possible, and his conquests effortless; also by formalising the action which showed his mundane success and insisting on his contest with "Jove" and the fates.

To generalise Tamburlaine's aims, Marlowe uses riches in their most beautiful forms, though the "milk white harts" and "ivory sled" of Zenocrate, the "sun-bright armour", "silk and cloth of gold", are in any case only symbols of the pomp of rule, of "riding in triumph through Persepolis". Marlowe's sensuousness has the maximum of concreteness and the minimum of particularity. The dazzling pictures of gold and jewels and the use of bright, clear colours makes the impression of Tamburlaine's wealth solid enough, but it is not particularised; there are few cases where shape or outline is given to the visual image. The sonorous place-names too suggest somewhere precise; yet since they are devoid of associations for the most part, they have, as it were, a catalytic value only.

This unfocussed impressionism is helped by the firm un-colloquial movement of the "mighty line" and by Marlowe's lack of sentence structure.[1]

Tamburlaine's conquests are always quite effortless. There is no doubt in his mind, and no check in his success. He "holds the Fates bound fast in iron chains". The series of opponents are only a row of ninepins to be toppled over: there is no interest attached to them, except as necessary material upon which Tamburlaine can demonstrate his power. Hence the deaths of the virgins of Damascus or of Bajazet are not meant to excite sympathy or convey a feeling of physical suffering at all. (The natural callousness of the Elizabethans would make this perfectly possible.) They are not considered for themselves, but only as a means of displaying certain qualities of Tamburlaine, his absolute power and his superhuman inflexibility (for the fact that he can be indifferent to them, and even subdue his own re-lenting at Zenocrate's distress is a proof that he is superior to the gods).[2]

There is no hint in the verse of the physical sufferings of the virgins; they are a set of innocent white dummies, without sticky blood like Duncan's. Their death is not shocking because it is not dramatically realised. They speak in the voices of public messengers, not of terrified women:

> Pity our plights. O pity poor Damascus!
> Pity old age....
> Pity the marriage bed....

[1] E.g. in 2. 1. 7–30, 3. 2. 70–80, 5. 2. 72–128.
[2] 5. 2. 120ff.

> O then for these and such as we ourselves
> Pity, O pity, sacred Emperor. (5. 2. 17 ff.)

Their acting was probably as formal as their speech.[1]

Similarly, Bajazet's sufferings are never seen from Bajazet's point of view. His rage is a necessary proof of Tamburlaine's power, as the sufferings of the damned were popularly supposed to contribute to the glory of God: without him Tamburlaine's glory could not be demonstrated:

> Such are objects fit for Tamburlaine
> Wherein as in a mirror may be seen
> His honour, that consists in shedding blood.
>
> (5. 2. 413 ff.)

Even in his love for Zenocrate Tamburlaine scarcely descends to the human level. The one episode where he shows any feeling is in dumb show (3. 2. 65). Zenocrate is much more human, and herein contrasted with him; but she thinks of Tamburlaine as half-divine. For instance, when Agydas is persuading her not to love him, the arguments are quite shrewd and incontrovertible at a naturalist level:

> How can you fancy one that looks so fierce
> Only disposed to martial stratagems?
> Who, when he shall embrace you in his arms
> Will tell how many thousand men he slew
> And when you look for amorous discourse
> Will rattle forth his facts of war and blood....
>
> (3. 2. 40 ff.)

It is reminiscent of Falstaff upon Hotspur. But Zenocrate does not attempt to meet Agydas at the same level of dis-

---

[1] It may have been violent, of course: they would weep but not realistically. Cf. Miriam in *The Jews' Tragedy* who begins at l. 2216: "Weep, O weep, my eyes, a flood of tears"; weeps again at l. 2371, follows up at ll. 2958, 2968, 3130, 3157, 3164, 3174, 3185, 3192. The play fitly concludes: "Exeunt omnes, the lady weeping". This was the kind of action Falstaff parodied: "Weep not, sweet queen, for trickling tears are vain".

course. She soars over his argument and confutes him by a quite irrelevant reply.

> As looks the sun through Nilus' flowing stream
> Or when the morning holds him in her arms
> So looks my lordly love, fair Tamburlaine....
>
> (3. 2. 47 ff.)

This is quite a different person from Agydas' Tamburlaine: Zenocrate has dehumanised him.

Of course Tamburlaine has a human level. His irony is a personal trait. Such things as the "pretty jest" of attacking Cosroe, the jeering repetition of Bajazet's phrase: "Where are your *stout contributory kings*?" (3. 3. 214; cf. 3. 3. 93); and his remark to the caged Turk before he goes to fight the Soldan: "Pray for us, Bajazet: we are going", are not very noticeable at first reading, but they became characteristic of the Marlovian villain hero, such as Aaron and Richard III.

The same kind of mordant satire can be felt in the comic episodes. Mycetes' buffoonery criticises even the heroics of Tamburlaine himself, as later, the cynicism of Calyphas does.

> Brother Cosroe, I find myself aggrieved,
> Yet insufficient to express the same,
> For it requires a great and thundering speech. (1. 1. 1)

This is, in its minor way, a corrective to the high-astounding terms. The peevish tone of Mycetes is sustained in a kind of nagging self-importance, sometimes emphasised by a rhymed couplet:

> O where is duty and allegiance now?
> Fled to the Caspian or the Ocean main?
> What shall I call thee: brother? no, a foe,
> Monster of nature, shame unto thy stock
> That durst presume thy sovereign for to mock!
> Meander, come: I am abused, Meander. (1. 1. 101 ff.)

The whining vowels of the last line make the purpose of the passage quite unmistakable. It is in the same ironic spirit as Tamburlaine's "horseplay" or Calyphas' refusal to fight.

> Go, go, tall stripling, fight you for us both:
> And take my other toward brother there....
> Take you the honour, I will take my ease.
> My wisdom shall excuse my cowardice.
>
> (Part 2, 4. 1. 33 ff.)

Again one is reminded of Falstaff at Shrewsbury. Of course, Tamburlaine's ideal is not seriously attacked, but these minor contrasts throw it into relief, like small touches of a contrasting colour in a painting.

The other minor characters act as foils to Tamburlaine; for example, the three followers are set against him in 2. 5. Zenocrate, though she defends the superhuman Tamburlaine, often evokes personal feelings, and those connected with human frailty.

> Ah, Tamburlaine, my love, sweet Tamburlaine
> That fightest for sceptres and for slippery crowns....
> Behold the Turk and his great emperess. (5. 2. 293–5)

The dying words of Arabia are the most poignant in the play and suggest the temper of Zenocrate's own death scene in Part 2:

> Since death denies me further cause of joy
> Deprived of care, my heart with comfort dies
> Since thy desired hand shall close mine eyes.
>
> (5. 2. 367–70)

The narrative is built upon a cumulative plan: Tamburlaine's enemies appear as in a Mummer's play, one down, t'other come on. Marlowe, however, shows a growing skill in interweaving the episodes; the Soldan begins to move before Bajazet is quite finished with, so that there is not a gap between the two campaigns. Also the enemies become progressively nobler: Mycetes is a fool and Tamburlaine attacks him merely for wealth: Cosroe and Bajazet are soldiers and it is a greater triumph to overcome them; the Soldan and Arabia are fighting for the person of Zenocrate.

But the actual battles are not of any great importance in Part 1; the stage directions are comparatively short, and speech is much more stressed than action, which is mostly violent and symbolic. (It should not be forgotten that the plays are styled "The two tragicall *discourses* of Tamburlaine the Great".)

Action is formalised for the same reason that Tamburlaine's objects are left undefined; because it is an inadequate correlative to the feeling. It tends to be on another level of interest altogether. For example, the use of the crown, and the different pieces of action concerned with it have been considered horseplay or even interpolations. But as the symbol of power and rule, the crown was often used on the Elizabethan stage in purely conventional action, which on the modern stage would appear ludicrous. In the deposition scene of *Edward II* the King removes his crown saying:

> Here, take my crown: the life of Edward too.

But he cannot bring himself to resign it, and retracts, feeling that while he wears the crown he has power as a king.

> See, monsters, see, I'll wear my crown again.
> What, fear you not the fury of your king?

And after there is the stage direction: "The king rageth". He has another lengthy speech, full of hesitations.

> Here, receive my crown,
> Receive it? no, these innocent hands of mine
> Shall not be guilty of so foul a crime:
> Take it....
> Yet stay, for rather than I'll look on them
> Here, here!   [*Gives the crown.*

In the deposition scene of *Richard II* there is similar action; and the division of the coronet in the opening scene of *King*

Lear is also relevant. If the sacred power of the crown is re-membered, the struggle of Mycetes and Tamburlaine (2. 4), the similar tussle of Zabina and Zenocrate, and the final crowning of Zenocrate may be seen in a new light.

When Tamburlaine supports Cosroe, he offers him the crown which he had taken from Mycetes (at the beginning of 2. 5). Cosroe told him to keep this crown, for he had already been crowned (at 1. 1. 160) by his own followers.

Then when Tamburlaine attacks Cosroe in turn, his triumph is assured by the stage direction: "Tamburlaine takes the crown and puts it on" (2. 7. 52).

When Tamburlaine goes to fight Bajazet he gives his crown to Zenocrate to wear while he is fighting. Bajazet gives his to Zabina and the two queens have a wordy battle while the alarums are sounded within. When the fighting is over, Tamburlaine resumes his own crown, but his fol-lowers also wrench Bajazet's from Zabina and crown him with that as well.

In 3. 3 the followers enter with the crowns of Bajazet's followers, saying:

> We have their crowns: their bodies strew the field.

These crowns they deliver up to Tamburlaine. (Compare the scene in Part 2 where they deliver their crowns to Tamburlaine in token of fealty and receive them again.)

In 4. 4 there is a "course of crowns" brought into the banquet. (These were presumably sweetmeats shaped like crowns.) Tamburlaine says to his followers:

> Here are the cates you desire to finger, are they not?

But they refuse, saying that only kings should feed on them.

Zenocrate's coronation is reserved until Tamburlaine has greater honours to give her; it closes the play and marks his final triumph.

It is very striking that "crown" is often used as a synonym for "power" or "kingdom". The "golden round" must

have served as definite a part in the stage action as storming
the tiring house, or the descent of the throne. These various
incidents would obviously hang together in any stage performance and acquire a general significance.

Something similar is effected in 1. 2, where Tamburlaine
first appears in "shepherds' weeds". Zenocrate treats him
as an inferior; someone at all events who can be argued with.
But Tamburlaine throws off his shepherd's clothes and puts
on full armour, taking a curtle axe. The difference in appearance, when Alleyn played Tamburlaine, must have made
the action easily seem symbolic. Techelles comments on it:

> As princely lions when they rouse themselves
> Stretching their paws, and threatening herds of beasts,
> So in his armour, looketh Tamburlaine.
> Methinks I see kings kneeling at his feet,
> And he with frowning brows and fiery looks
> Spurning their *crowns* from off their captive heads.
>
> (1. 2. 52 ff.)

From this point Tamburlaine's accent grows even more
assured than before. There is, as Miss Ellis-Fermor has noted,
a development in his attitude towards himself. At first Jove
is his protector; later he is a rival, even a worsted rival. The
constant imagery of battle against the gods, and the relative
unimportance of Tamburlaine's actual battles, keep this
before the mind and prevent his desires "lift upward and
divine" from seeming to be fixed on "the sweet fruition
of an earthly *crown*". Consider such passages as

> Our quivering lances shaking in the air
> And bullets like Jove's dreadful thunderbolts
> Enrolled in flames and fiery smouldering mists
> Shall threat the gods more than Cyclopian wars.
>
> (2. 3. 18 ff.)

The play is full of such speeches wherein the actual enemy
is quite lost to sight. Tamburlaine's battles are fought much
more in his defiant speeches than in the "alarums and

excursions" which occasionally reproduce them at the level of the action. Hence his command to Zenocrate to "manage words" with Zabina while he fights Bajazet seems to make her really included in the contest (besides, she is wearing his crown, as has been said, and therefore has some delegated authority). So that the issue of the flyting match is a matter for serious concern. Tamburlaine's own defiance of Bajazet and of his other enemies is similar in effect.

Tamburlaine is in fact more like a pageant than the modern idea of a play. Its central theme (Tamburlaine's "thirst of reign") is highly generalised, its speech is uncolloquial, its feeling dehumanised and its action conventional. But this does not prevent its being a good play in the Elizabethan manner. Regarded simply as an artistic success, *Tamburlaine*, Part 1, is the most satisfactory thing Marlowe ever did, except *Hero and Leander*. But it could not be repeated. The sensuous intensity and emotional tenuity were only possible to an immature mind. Marlowe could not help developing, and so becoming more aware of personal feeling and of a wider range of sensuous impressions; he could not help his blank verse reflecting the increased development and becoming more varied and flexible too. So that in *Tamburlaine*, Part 2, he could not revive the conqueror of Part 1. The cumulative narrative could not be stretched any further, and the story of Part 2 is either a variation of Part 1 (the four kings being substituted for Bajazet) or a series of irrelevant incidents, such as those connected with Olympia. Marlowe's flagging interest is betrayed by the incorporation of passages from his current reading, in an undigested form (especially the speeches on military strategy, 3. 2). The characterisation is also less consistent. Marlowe is in parts capable of a new tenderness to humanity, which does not fit in with the old figures. At the death of Zenocrate, when Tamburlaine says:

> For she is dead! thy words do pierce my soul;
> Ah, sweet Theridamas, say so no more:

Though she be dead, yet let me think she lives,
And feed my mind that dies for want of her—

(2. 4. 125 ff.)

there is, as Miss Ellis-Fermor notes, a development beyond the earlier play. Even the decision to burn the town where she died is made the occasion for a conceit which would have been out of place before, because based on a natural human grief.

The houses, burnt, will look as if they mourned.

(2. 4. 139)

On the other hand the Tamburlaine of Part 2 falls below the earlier figure in some respects. His ends are more definite and less exalted. He even says:

Cooks shall have pensions to provide us cates:
And glut us with the dainties of the world. (1. 6. 92–3)

The coarsely sensuous "glut" indicates the new kind of feeling which has crept in. Marlowe cannot keep Tamburlaine's magnificence generalised any longer, nor can he keep the slaughter unreal and unmoving. There is a great deal of red, sticky blood in Part 2; it flows in the scene where Tamburlaine cuts his arm (3. 2. 115) and it is given through the verse. Battlefields are "covered with a liquid purple veil" and "sprinkled with the brains of slaughtered men" (1. 4. 80–1).

The finest passages of verse are those which point forward to *Faustus* and the later plays, or which depend on other writers—

Helen, whose beauty summoned Greece to arms
And drew a thousand ships to Tenedos— (2. 4. 87–8)

or the reminiscence of Spenser (4. 3. 119–24). Marlowe is clearly uncertain of himself, and his verse reflects the transition. It is noticeable that he sometimes tries to pull it together by a use of strophic repetition, as in the famous "To entertain divine Zenocrate" or the choric lament of the three followers (5. 3) for the death of Tamburlaine. This scene opens with an echo of the earlier play.

> Now clear the triple region of the air....
> Smile, stars that reigned at my nativity
> And dim the brightness of their neighbour lamps...
>
> (Part 1, 4. 2. 30ff.)

reappears as

> Weep, heavens and vanish into liquid tears!
> Fall, stars that govern his nativity
> And summon all the shining lamps of heaven
> To cast their bootless fires to the earth....

Each of the three kings speaks in turn, and each speech ends with a rhymed couplet. The same kind of pattern appears at the level of action in the scenes where the three kings deliver their crowns up to Tamburlaine (1. 4, 5): it is very like the entries of the lords in 3 *Henry VI*, 5. 1.

There is on the whole little symbolic action in Part 2, the particular equipoise which made it possible in Part 1 having been destroyed. In his next play, Marlowe took a different type of narrative, and constructed his play in quite another fashion.

Faustus is comparatively domestic and familiar in its setting. The University of Wittenberg is thought of in terms of Cambridge: Faustus' relations with his scholars are quite different from Tamburlaine's with the kings: the conjurors Valdes and Cornelius are invited in to dinner (1. 1. 164–5) and the clowns are fully drawn yokels. All this makes the play more naturalistic, in spite of the supernatural element, as befits the more relaxed and colloquial verse.

The Prologue makes the transition from the stately stories of "proud audacious deeds" to "the form of Faustus' fortunes, good or bad". The very use of such a folk-legend suggests that Marlowe was no longer so scornful of popular taste, and the large provisions for spectacle cannot be wholly attributed to collaborators.

Yet the story itself required some conventional handling. It was more difficult to telescope Faustus' history than Tamburlaine's, and to give a panoramic view of the twenty-four years. It was also hard to get the objective correlative for Faustus' aspiring mind, when Marlowe had come down to particulars; he only succeeded in suggesting a worthy bribe in the figure of Helen.

Finally there was the comic relief. A recollection of Mycetes and an anticipation of *The Jew of Malta* will confirm the opinion of Dr Boas that part of the comedy in *Faustus* is Marlowe's work and represents an attempt to give a burlesque subplot. The play is primarily a study of the mind of Faustus himself; his biography is arranged to show his mental development, rather than simply to present "the form of Faustus' fortunes, good or bad". For instance, the first speech of Faustus is, I think, meant to suggest in a telescoped fashion a long period of mental debate, not to represent a single occasion. The tempo is quickened beyond that of ordinary life, just as movements are speeded up sometimes in the cinema. The prologue, with its subtle and, I think, intentional confusion of tenses, prepares the spectator for a further summary presented in the form of a soliloquy.

> He *profits* in divinity....
> His waxen wings *did mount* above his reach....
> He *surfeits* upon cursed necromancy. (Prologue)

Faustus, turning from one book to the next, represents in conventionalised form his own mental history, as the prologue has given the outward events of his life. (The good and bad angels are also, I think, not tutelary spirits but projections of Faustus' own contrary impulses.) In the first speeches, the mood of Tamburlaine is sometimes recalled.

> I'll have them fly to India for gold
> Ransack the ocean for orient pearl
> And search all corners of the new found world
> For pleasant fruits and princely delicates. (I. I. 83 ff.)

But this kind of exaltation does not last: Faustus descends to "the seignory of Embden" and silk gowns for his students. The drama might have been a simple extension of the conquering power of the Scythian:

> Emperors and kings
> Are but obeyed in their several provinces
> Nor can they raise the wind or rend the clouds,
> But his dominion that exceeds in this
> Stretcheth as far as doth the mind of man—   (1. 1. 58 ff.)

but as a matter of fact Faustus' ambition falls below Tamburlaine's; and his power, if greater in extent, is more shadowy. For even in the midst of his triumphs, he "is but Faustus and a man".

His character is in fact not one of fixed determination, as is so often asserted; he constantly wavers, and his purposes change. Sometimes he sounds immovable:

> This night I'll conjure, though I die therefore....
>   (1. 1. 167)
> Had I as many souls as there be stars,
> I'd give them all for Mephistopheles....   (1. 3. 104–5)

Yet he has continually to screw up his courage, as Macbeth has. Before he begins the conjuring, he says, half apprehensively:

> Then fear not, Faustus, to be resolute—

and his soliloquy at the opening of Act 2 is full of the twists and doublings of his mind.

> Now, Faustus, must
> Thou needs be damned and canst thou not be saved
> What boots it then to think on God or heaven?
> Away with such vain fancies and despair.
> Despair in God and trust in Belzebub:
> Now go not backward: no, Faustus, be resolute.
>   (2. 1. 1 ff.)

If it takes so many negatives to stop Faustus' repentance there must be very strong forces working for it. It is after this debate with himself that the two angels again appear, as incarnations of the alternatives before him. In this speech for the first time (and it is even before the contract is signed) Faustus tells himself to "despair". The idea of despair in the theological sense (that is, a conviction of damnation such as the one from which John Bunyan suffered) runs through the play. It is the means by which the devils, from the very beginning, secure Faustus' soul, making him incapable of repentance, even though he wills with all his might to repent. "Distressed" is also used as an alternative description of this mental state. At other times, however, Faustus is determined to an extent that makes his resolution appear ludicrous. He can say to the devil himself:

> Learn thou of Faustus' manly fortitude
> And scorn those joys thou never shalt possess.
>
> (1. 3. 87–8)

His intoxication at his power to command the devil occasionally blinds him to everything else, and when Mephistopheles tells him truthfully of hell (2. 1. 116–40) he simply refuses to face it—

> I think hell's a fable.

Faustus' mind is revealed in the first two acts: it is seen swinging constantly between repentance and damnation, wavering remorse and fixed pride. In 2. 2 there is a third repentance; the two angels again appear symbolising the conflict, but their speeches are shorter and sharper, and the passage ends with the triumph of the bad angel:

> Faustus never shall repent. (2. 2. 17)

Immediately Faustus falls into "despair"—

> My heart is hardened, I cannot repent. (2. 2. 18)

And he returns to his catechising of Mephistopheles; for this is the means by which he salves his despair. At the end of this scene there is the fourth and last conflict. Faustus goes further than before: he calls upon Christ, and the devils come in to attack him. There is extraordinary irony in the juxtaposition.

> *Faustus.* O Christ, my saviour, my saviour,
> Help to save distressed Faustus' soul!
>
> *Enter Lucifer, Belzebub and Mephistopheles.* (2. 2. 85 ff.)

This kind of irony of situation is paralleled by the use of quotations with an ironic significance. Faustus, as he signs the bond, says "Consummatum est", the final words of Christ in St John's Gospel. It immediately reminds one of the masterly adaptation of Ovid:

> O lente, lente currite, noctis equi!

in the final soliloquy.

The middle part of the play contains nothing which could not be spared, even if some of the writing is Marlowe's, except the few lines before and after the horse courser's episode.

> Now Mephistopheles, the restless course
> That time does run with calm and silent foot
> Calls for the payment of my latest years: (4. 2*a*. 101 ff.)

and

> What art thou Faustus but a man condemned to die?...
> Despair doth drive distrust into my thoughts...
> Tush, Christ did call the thief upon the cross
> Then rest thee, Faustus quiet in conceit. (4. 5*a*. 29 ff.)

The stealing away of time is hardly thought of in the bustle of Faustus' conjuring, and the first speech brings up what is to be the theme of the final soliloquy, the contrast of time and eternity; after this it is impossible to forget the hour-glass. The second passage recalls Faustus' earlier repentances and despairs, and his refusal to face the consequences of his situation. But since Faustus' mind is meant to be distracted with his pleasures during the four-and-twenty years, and the tragedy is based on mental suffering, the interval could have little significance for Marlowe.

In the last act the moods of the first two acts reappear. Faustus repents (5. 1. 55 ff.) and then he "despairs" and is about to commit suicide; but his "distressed soul" is comforted by the old man. The feeling cannot exist, however, without the support of the old man's presence: as soon as he goes Faustus exclaims:

> I do repent: and yet I do despair.   (5. 1. 79)

Mephistopheles forces him to sign another bond; and Faustus drugs himself with Helen, whose embraces will extinguish "those thoughts which do dissuade me from my vows". The lovely invocation, though it is the most magnificent verse in the play, is quite cut off in style from the rest of it and is nearer to speeches of *Tamburlaine*.

The last scene begins in prose: it is simple, colloquial speech, stressing above all Faustus' humanity. His poignant feelings are shown through the repetition of phrases (compare the doubling of "lente" in the Ovidian line).

> What wonders I have done, all Germany can witness, yea, all the world: for which Faustus hath lost both Germany and the world: yea heaven itself, heaven the seat of God, the throne of the blessed, the kingdom of joy: and must remain in hell for ever—hell, ah, hell for ever! Sweet friends, what shall become of Faustus, being in hell for ever?

This repetition indicates Faustus' helplessness (he can only say the same thing over and over), and his fixation upon the single problem which at last he cannot evade. He already sounds broken: the devil's power over him is already of a physical kind, so that his despair is enforced: "I would lift up my hands—but see, they hold them, they hold them!" The repetition here has the effect of a plea; but whether mercy is asked of God or Mephistopheles does not emerge.

The scene which comes between the dialogue of the Scholars and the final soliloquy has been generally considered the addition of another hand. In any case, it offers the conventionalised version for the feeling which is poetically given in the soliloquy. The good and bad angels enter from opposite sides: heaven and the saints are disclosed to music: hell is revealed and described by the bad angel. It "exploits", as Dr Boas says, "the theatrical devices of the period".[1]

This scene is thoroughly based on the mediaeval stage, and whether Marlowe agreed to its presence or not, it suggests much about the temper of the play.

It acts as a spectacular prologue to the final soliloquy, rather as a dumb show might precede a play. The greatness of the final speech of Faustus depends not only on its poetic power, but the subtle way in which it gathers up and focusses all the feeling of the earlier scenes. For example:

> See, see where Christ's blood streams in the firmament,

besides being remodelled from *Tamburlaine*, suggests the scene where Faustus' own blood congealed, as he was about to sign the bond and he cried

> Why *streams* it not?

in his haste to sell his soul. His former moods reappear, intensified by the pressure of his feeling. He frantically denies the situation: tries to play King Canute as he had done for so long; to conjure in a more daring manner than ever.

---

[1] Introduction to the Methuen edition, p. 43. Though he seems to think the throne is a "state" or chair, and not the machine for descent from above. *Vide* Lawrence's article in *Pre-Restoration Stage Studies*. Also, it seems probable that hell was under the stage. It would not need to be described in such detail if, like the angels, it were visible. The trap might open, smoke and flames ascend, and Faustus look down into it. Cf. "Ugly hell, *gape not*" (5. 2. 193). There could not be one hell on a backcloth, as Dr Boas suggests, and another which "gaped".

> Stand still, you ever-moving spheres of heaven
> That time may cease and midnight never come;
> Fair Nature's eye, rise, rise again. . . .

The quick repetition comes because he is trying to cram as many words into his little hour as possible, and also, by repeating the same word, to give himself the illusion that time is not passing at all. He ends with desperate commands to body and soul, to God and the devils, as though by the exercise of his will he could reverse the course of events.

> Ugly hell, gape not! Come not, Lucifer!
> I'll burn my books—Ah, Mephistopheles.

The last is, of course, a scream (and so the reading proposed by Mr Empson does not stand).[1]

The treatment of Faustus in Acts 1, 2 and 5 has a particular homogeneity which could only come from the impress of a single mind. The Faustus of Acts 3 and 4 is a different figure, whether Marlowe was responsible for parts of these lines or not. There is only one scene of the comic underplot which is definitely related to the main tragedy; that is, the one singled out by Dr Boas, the debate between Wagner and the clown (1. 4 *b*) which is a parody of Faustus' compact with Lucifer. The clown is offered a shoulder of raw mutton as a bribe to take service with Wagner: then he is given his wages and told "thou art to be at an hour's warning, when-soever and wheresoever the devil shall fetch thee" (1. 4 *b*. 30; cf. "full power to carry the said John Faustus...into their habitation wheresoever"). The clown, like Faustus, repents and has to be recalled by devils; like Faustus he is contented with the promise of the power of conjuring, though he is obliged to address Wagner with humblest respect and follow him in the right attitude for a servant, as Faustus is brought to heel by the devils when he revolts.

Furthermore, the comic relief helps to elucidate that baffling play, *The Jew of Malta*. The tricks of Faustus in the

[1] *Seven Types of Ambiguity*, p. 261.

middle scenes are, in their childish malice, rather like those of the Jew, and even like those of Marlowe himself, as Kyd reports them: "Sudden privie iniuries" and unsavoury jokes about the rôle of the angel Gabriel in the Annunciation fit in well enough with Faustus' attitude to the Pope or Barabas' to Mathias and Lodowick.

The Jew of Malta is one of the most difficult of Elizabethan plays. T. S. Eliot's explanation[1] will not cover the obvious change of tone between Acts 1 and 2 and the rest of the play. The first part of the play is, like *Faustus*, concerned only with the mind of the hero: Barabas' actions are comparatively unimportant. In the last part of the play actions supply nearly all the interest: there is an attempt to make the narrative exciting in itself, to connect the various episodes causally and consecutively to produce something of a story. This is the technique of that very different play, *Edward II*. I shall indicate below the most striking parallels in constructive method.

The first part of *The Jew of Malta* has a theme similar to *Faustus* and *Tamburlaine*. Barabas' sponsor, like Faustus, says:

> I count religion but a childish toy
> And hold there is no sin but ignorance.   (Prologue)

The hypocrisy of his enemies is Machiavelli's justification: "Admired I am of those that hate me most". This is also Barabas' case as he puts it to the merchant and to Abigail (1. 1. 110–18 and 1. 2. 290–3), and as it is illustrated by Ferneze and the friars. In the opening scene the glory of his wealth is given with a precision far from the indefinite splendours of *Tamburlaine*:

> Bags of fiery opals, sapphires, amethysts,
> Jacinths, hard topaz, grass green emeralds,
> Beauteous rubies, sparkling diamonds....   (1. 1. 25 ff.)

[1] "A Note on the Blank Verse of Christopher Marlowe", in *The Sacred Wood*, reprinted in *Selected Essays*.

This elastic movement improves even on *Faustus*; and the movement of the following lines shows the same flexibility:

> Why, then, I hope my ships...
> Are gotten up by Nilus' winding banks,
> Mine argosy from Alexandria,
> Loaden with spice and silks, now under sail
> Are smoothly gliding down by Candy shore
> To Malta, through our Mediterranean Sea.
>
> (1. 1. 41 ff.)

The jerky laboured movement of the first line is set in opposition to the slurred glide of the last. So far as the action is concerned there is also a distinct advance. Barabas' asides to the other Jews should be compared with those of Faustus to the Pope and the knight.

The scene between Barabas and Ferneze (1. 2) develops a satiric tone: the Christian hypocrisy is contrasted with Barabas' open wickedness, and their greed with his. It is a development of the quarrel between Christians and infidels in *Tamburlaine*, Part 2. Ferneze does not keep faith with infidels, and though the famous invocation of Orcanes is too heroic for a wronged merchant, it is the same theme treated at a different level.

> Open, thou shining veil of Cynthia...
> That he which sits on high and never sleeps
> Nor in one place is circumscriptible
> May in his endless power and purity
> Behold and venge this traitor's perjury.
>
> (2 *Tamburlaine*, 2. 2. 47ff.)

The Christians here accuse the Jews of being responsible for the plague of the Turks (1. 2. 63 ff.) and of being doomed to misfortune (1. 2. 108–10). They end with a virtuous repudiation of any desire to shed blood and assurances to Barabas that he has had "nought but right".

In Barabas' laments there is a new and poignant note which recalls Faustus. Some of his phrases are out of all proportion

to a material loss: they express general disillusion, like that
of Job[1] from which they derive.

> Only I have toiled to inherit here
> The months of vanity and loss of time
> And painful nights have bin appointed me.
>
> (1. 2. 197–9)

The soliloquy which opens Act 2 is full of such passages:

> The incertain pleasures of *swift-footed* time
> Have ta'en their flight and left me in *despair*:
> And of my former riches rests no more
> But bare remembrance, like a soldier's scar
> That has no further comfort for his maim.
>
> (2. 1. 7–11)

It is the vocabulary of Faustus, but after this scene it appears
no more. Not only the character of Barabas but the quality
of the verse is changed; pity and human values are dropped.

What happens may be defined (but not explained, of
course) as the substitution of a technique of action for a
technique of verse. The last half of the play shows an interest
in stage situations and the manipulation of the narrative.[2]
The use of asides depends largely on stage effectiveness, and
on a close intrigue. Such effects as the sudden revival of
Barabas after he is thrown over the wall are parallel to the
reversals of meaning achieved by giving him a final word
to speak aside.

> Use him as if he were a—Philistine. (2. 3. 229)
>
> And be revenged upon the—governor. (2. 3. 145)

(He is speaking to the governor's son.)

The last three acts depend upon different kinds of reversals,
verbal or narrative. The gulling of Lodowick and Mathias

---

[1] Cf. *The Book of Job*, 7. 3.

[2] This may or may not indicate revision by another hand. *Vide* H. S.
Bennett's edition of the play, and *Thomas Heywood*, by A. M. Clark.
I have assumed single authorship, feeling personally unfitted to pro-
nounce judgment.

("slaves are but nails to drive out one another"), of the friars, and of Ithamore, and the final series of cross betrayals between Ferneze, Calymath and Barabas, are more in the style of Kyd than of anyone else. The "play of Pedringano" (with variations) is the basis of it, and the asides derive from those of Lorenzo (e.g. when he overhears Horatio's love-making) and of Hieronimo. To the influence of Kyd I think Marlowe's development of a new technique must be ascribed. It can be traced at the basic level of the versification. Marlowe uses the patterned speech of *The Spanish Tragedy* freely and depends a great deal on cut-and-thrust repartee, whereas in the earlier dramas his play on words had been of quite a different kind, and his flytings had not approached stichomuthia. The characters had flung long speeches at each other, like Marlowe's favourite simile of the giants throwing rocks at Jove.

"The hopeless daughter of a hapless Jew" (I. 2. 316) is not in *Tamburlaine's* style (as Mr Bennett suggests) but an adaptation of

> The hopeless father of a hapless son.
> (*The Spanish Tragedy*, 4. 4. 84)

Lines like

> And naught is to be looked for now but wars:
> And naught to us more welcome is than wars.
> (3. 5. 35–6)
>
> Will Barabas recover Malta's loss?
> Will Barabas be good to Christians? (5. 2. 75–6)

are quite unlike anything Marlowe had written before, but they can be found on every page of *The Spanish Tragedy*.

It is generally admitted that the stage Machiavel, as Marlowe used him, was descended from Kyd's Lorenzo, and that the earlier Marlovian plays are not Machiavellian. It is in this play that the keyword "policy" first appears.

The Christians are consistently satirised in the last part of the play for their "close hypocrisy". Ferneze, breaking his word with Selim as Sigismund had with Orcanes, uses the same kind of virtuous flourish to cover his treachery. Compare

> Take the victory our God hath given
>> (2 *Tamburlaine*, 2. 1, *ad fin.*)

and

> Proud daring Calymath, instead of gold
> We'll send thee bullets wrapt in smoke and fire:
> Claim tribute when thou wilt, we are resolved—
> *Honour is bought with blood and not with gold.*
>> (2. 2, *ad fin.*)

Since they were deciding to keep their gold and break their word, the implications of the last line are directly ironical, especially if Ferneze's protestations to Barabas are still remembered. At the end he profits by Barabas' betrayal of Calymath to the extent of getting him into his own power and murdering his soldiers, even while declaiming against the treachery of the Jew and assuring Calymath that he has saved his life. Barabas' soliloquies upon his villainy enforce the point.

> This is the life we Jews are used to lead;
> And reason too, for Christians do the like. (5. 3. 115–16)

The "two religious caterpillars" are a more broadly farcical illustration of the same theme, with their competitive attempts to secure Barabas' wealth. The ease with which he plays on them is a measure of their contemptibility.

> — O good Barabas, come to our house.
> — O no, good Barabas, come to *our* house! (4. 1. 80–1)

This satire is persistent and unmistakable, and makes limited identification with Barabas' point of view possible to the very end.

Edward II is generally acclaimed as Marlowe's greatest dramatic success; but this is only possible by ignoring Elizabethan standards, and judging purely on "construction". As poetic drama, the last speech of Edward is inferior to the last speech of Faustus or even to the early soliloquies of *The Jew of Malta*, and how it is possible to fail as poetry and succeed as drama is not easy to understand.[1]

It is clear that Marlowe is developing in the manner suggested by *The Jew of Malta*, that is, the co-ordination of intrigue and the use of patterned speech. There is a new pattern, the "retort repetitive" and a use of little connective speeches which are not always successful.

Marlowe's compression of his sources and his articulation of the plot has been much praised: it is evidence of this new preoccupation with construction; but it is not always realised that it is responsible for the decline of the soliloquy. In his early plays only the heroes soliloquise and then not for the purpose of making the narrative clear, but for the purpose of expressing the central feelings of the play. In *Edward II* there is no central feeling or theme; it is merely a history. These soliloquies are merely pointers (especially Isabella's and Kent's) indicating when they are on Edward's side and when they are not. Sometimes the change is very clumsily done: the transformation of Isabella is not at all convincing. Mortimer, before his capture, is the most reckless of the Barons; afterwards he is a Machiavel. Kent vacillates more frequently but has less of a character to lose. Edward is really a different person before and after his capture: he even becomes much older (there are frequent references to "old Edward" and "aged Edward") to heighten the pathos.

The different kinds of feeling expressed in *Edward II* seem curiously unconnected and incongruent. Mortimer's use of irony and his worship of "policy" recall Barabas, while the speech of Lightborn—

> I learnt in Naples how to poison flowers,
> To strangle with a lawn thrust down the throat... —
>
> (5. 4. 31–2)

[1] This passage was written before the publication of Charlton and Waller's edition of the play; it is very reassuring, and the more gratifying, to find that they have expressed the same opinion (pp. 53 ff.).

is the completest expression of the Machiavellian mood of
Tourneur and Webster to be found in the early drama.

There is also a new satiric observation of manners and habits,
which is very different from Marlowe's early style. It depends
on the emphasis of detail to the point of caricature, and fore-
shadows Webster's use of the epigrammatic metaphor.

> The slave looks like a hog's cheek newly singed.
>
> > (*The Jew of Malta*, 2. 3. 42)
>
> Leaning on the shoulder of the king
> He nods and scorns and smiles at those that pass.
>
> > (1. 2. 23–4)
>
> 'Tis not a black coat and a little band,
> A velvet-caped cloak faced before with serge,
> And smelling to a nosegay all the day...
> Or looking downwards with your eyelids close
> And saying "Truly, an't may please your honour"
> Can get you any favour with great men. (2. 1. 33 ff.)

This irony belongs to the "Machiavellian" attitude; it
re-entered tragedy with the figure of the Malcontent, who
was influenced by the critical heroes of Jonson. The feeling
centred in Edward himself is quite different from this ironic
Machiavellianism. The scene in which he is tortured and
murdered produces an effect similar to the last scene of
Faustus; the King knows that he is doomed, and his desperate
efforts to pretend it is not so are overshadowed by the
certainty that it will be so. The passage of time is important
because the conflict between the two moods becomes
sharper every instant. His speech at his deposition is a
definite reminiscence of the earlier play:

> Continue ever, thou celestial Sun;
> Let never silent night possess this clime:
> Stand still, you watches of the element;
> All times and seasons, rest you at a stay,
> That Edward still may be fair England's king.
>
> > (5. 1. 64 ff.)

(Compare *Faustus*, 5. 2. 140–6.)

Edward, in his refusal to face the implications of his actions and his belief that what he wants must necessarily happen, is close to that aspect of Faustus which is usually overlooked, but which seems important as a contrast to the fixed wills of Tamburlaine and Barabas. He oscillates between the lords and his favourites until, delivered up to Mortimer, he becomes simply a passive object of pity.

Throughout the play, Edward's feelings give what life there is to the verse. He seems to be describing an impersonal sorrow; his statements, that is, are always generalised. Gaveston or his ill-fortunes are only the cause, not really the subject.

> My heart is as an anvil unto sorrow.... (1. 4. 311)

The image is of a sensation rather than an emotion. When the King receives his favourite again, this note is stronger than that of joy, through the use of a comparison which professes to deny it.

> Now thy sight
> Is sweeter far than was thy parting hence
> Bitter and irksome to my sobbing heart. (2. 2. 56 ff.)

Later, when he is defeated, the King says to the abbot:

> Good father, on thy lap
> Lay I this head, laden with mickle care,
> O might I never ope these eyes again,
> Never again lift up this drooping head,
> O, never more lift up this dying heart. (4. 6. 39 ff.)

This languorous repetition, and the use of such emotively powerful words as "drooping", "dying", "care", hardly escapes sentimentality. It is a preparation for the conscious pathos of "old Edward" of "My daily diet is heart-breaking sobs". This warm, naturalistic pity is certainly the strongest feeling in the play. It may be compared with the feeling in *The Jew of Malta* (2. 1. 1 ff.). That Marlowe, who reduced the human feelings to a minimum in *Tamburlaine*, should have come to rely on them so much has caused little comment; yet it seems remarkable enough, particularly when at the same time he maintained the completely unfeeling "Machiavellian" attitude also, in the character of Mortimer.

The structure of *Edward II* shows the unevenness of a transitional work. It is evident that Marlowe was developing very rapidly, both technically and in the more important senses. It might even be hazarded that he was developing towards a more "Shakespearean" (that is, a more inclusive) style, for in *Edward II* there can be found the most formalised qualities of feeling, and the most naturally human.

CHAPTER VII

Cyril Tourneur

Tourneur's plays are easy of interpretation on the surface, because they are written in the Revenge convention, though he modified it in a manner peculiarly his own. His plays are closest to Marston's, not only in time but in temper. The temptation scenes in *The Revenger's Tragedy* are modelled very closely on those of *The Malcontent*: for this play Tourneur also used the Humorous system of characterisation, and the dual personality of the disguised villain hero, which have been discussed in Chapter II. The characters are "distorted to scale"; and Vindice is two characters in one.

The narrative is formalised as well as the characters. Hence some of the incidents which at first sight seem episodic strengthen the main structure of the play, which is an enlarged series of peripeteia. I have counted a list of twenty-two ironic reversals, but to cite them would be tedious and unimpressive. The play opens with the Duke, an old lecher, condemning his stepson for a rape; it ends with Vindice revealing his crime, and being condemned to death, not so much for the crime itself as because

> You that have murdered him would murder me.

The narrative illustrates with ingenious variety in how many ways a villain may be hoist with his own petard. This is its main purpose, and must be recognised if it is to be appreciated. In particular, the indiscriminate slaughter at the end must be seen primarily as the judgment of Heaven upon the murderers and not as a rational solution of a story. For the supernatural plays a very large part in *The Revenger's Tragedy*, though Tourneur dropped the ghost. The play might almost be called a *drame à thèse* on the contrasts between earthly and heavenly vengeance, and earthly and heavenly justice.

The purely arbitrary and dissociated nature of Vindice's different personalities can be felt most strongly in the scene where he puts one of his disguises on to the dead Duke, to pretend that that particular personality has killed the Duke and fled: it is a rôle that is of no further use to him. Moreover, as he has actually killed the Duke, and has also been hired to kill himself in this secondary rôle, he is bringing down more than two birds with one stone.

> *Vindice.* So, so, he leans well, take heed you wake him not, brother.
> *Hippolito.* I warrant you, my life for yours.
> *Vindice.* That's a good lay, for I must kill myself.
> Brother, that's I: that sits for me: do you mark it.
> And I must stand here, ready to make away myself yonder—I must sit to be killed and stand to kill myself. I could vary it yet more: it hath some eight returns, like Michaelmas Term.
> (5. 1. 1 ff.)

This is the same kind of peripeteia as that of the narrative itself. It is frankly artificial: but the whole play is made up of these *volte-faces*. For example, in the subplot of the young Princes, Spurio is instructed by Vindice that Lussurioso is seducing Castiza, and goes to take him in the act. At the same time Lussurioso is told that Spurio is seducing his step-mother the Duchess, and goes to take *him* in the act. But the Duchess is abed with her husband, Lussurioso's father; and so he is arrested for attempted parricide. His step-brothers, who hate him, pretend to plead for his life with the Duke, but really blacken the case against him by indirect hints. The Duke, realising this, pretends to accede to their pleas, to test them: they are obviously dismayed. He therefore pretends to harden himself again and condemns Lussurioso to death. The nobles come to petition him for his son's life, and he pretends again to be won over reluctantly, though actually he realises all the time that Lussurioso made a mistake and had no thoughts of parricide. The relation of this to Vindice's disguises is obvious.

All this ironic interplay happens in a couple of scenes. The play is built up of such episodes. They are always just logically possible, like a detective story, though impossible by any other standards.

The dramatis personae enjoy their own ironic effects: Lussurioso plumes himself on using Hippolito to find a pander for his own sister, unaware that the pander is a second brother in disguise. Vindice, who controls events more than the other characters, sees more of the ironies, and he frequently uses such phrases as "O rare, delectable, happy, ravishing!" or "I'm in a throng of happy apprehensions!" When he reveals his final villainy he adds: "'Twas somewhat wittily carried, though we say it". This kind of consciousness belongs rather to the author than the character: compare the speeches of Guardiano and Livia[1] in Act 2 of *Women, Beware Women*. The contrast between divine and human justice is closely bound up with this constructive system of ironies. Human justice is seen to be corrupt. This is the purpose of the old Duke's trial of his stepson, Junior. "Judgment itself would be condemned" if the ravisher were freed; but justice is as decrepit as the old Duke himself.

> If judgment have cold blood,
> Flattery and bribes will kill it. (1. 2. 104–5)

Justice is sold, either for favours or money: this is insisted on again and again in the imagery and by direct statement.

> Judgment in this age is akin to favour. (1. 4. 61)
> Judgment speaks all in gold. (1. 4. 67)
> It well becomes that judge to nod at crimes
> That does commit greater himself and live. (2. 2. 352–3)

[1] *Vide infra*, p. 228.

Faiths are bought and sold,
Oaths in these days are but the skin of gold.   (3. 1. 7–8)

The statement is always as concrete as possible: in contrast
with the formalised narrative and characters, the speech has
a bare directness of metaphor, as in the last line quoted.

"Revenge is a kind of wild justice" and therefore the
various revenge actions are seen as springing out of the cor-
ruption of earthly justice. The bastard's private revenge
is just, as he says; he cuckolds his father. Vindice advises
Lussurioso to "be revenged and marry" Castiza. Vindice,
when he is disguised, has a passage on the law's delay (4. 2.
55 ff.): it is quite irrelevant logically at this point, but its
significance in connection with the play as a whole should
be plain. There is an antithesis between "justice" and the
"gold" which buys it. Honesty is always poor. Throughout
the play there is a feeling of great bitterness against poverty:
Castiza has a soliloquy on her honesty where it is described
as her "fortune", her "child's-part" (2. 1. 1), but it is in a
strictly metaphorical sense for "grace will not suffer her to
get good clothes". Chastity is "heaven's beggar" and "lies
a-cold". It is the "sticking on her poor estate" that wins
Gratiana. Vindice, in his disguise as a poor scholar, has
"almost forgotten the look of gold". The theme of virtue
unrewarded was a commonplace: it is its place in the general
scheme of the play, and the peculiar literalness of the images
that make it a living issue here.

As wealth buys "justice" of the great, it buys honesty,
the "jewel of the soul", from the poor. As judgment is
literally transmuted into gold in the passages above, so
beauty is coined into wealth. (This is also a common
metaphor of the time.)

Oh she was able to make a usurer's son
Melt all his patrimony in a kiss.   (1. 1. 29–30)

The verb "melt", besides making the translation seem quite
literal (as in the story of Cleopatra melting a pearl in a cup

of wine), has the particular emotional intensity of Tourneur's vocabulary in it, and separates this passionate expression from such satiric reflections as

> I have seen patrimonies washed a pieces,
> Fruitfields turned into bastards. (1. 3. 57–8)

> I would count my yearly maintenance upon her cheek:
> Take coach upon her lip. (2. 1. 108–9)

> Lands that were met by the rood, that labour's spared,
> Tailors come down and measure them by the yard.
> (2. 1. 244–5)

The temptation scenes are very important: Vindice in the character of a pander tempts his mother and is himself tempted, as a poor scholar, by Lussurioso. Luxury goes to the heads of the poor. Throughout the play the momentous nature is stressed of the single "bewitching minute" in which virtue is overcome. It is a surrender which can never be retracted. Feasts are chosen frequently where virtue is off her guard. The bastard describes his mother's seduction—

> In such a whispering and withdrawing hour...—
> (1. 2. 207)

and Antonio's chaste wife was trapped and ravished

> Last revelling night
> When torches made an artificial noon...
> O vicious *minute*. (1. 4. 32 ff.)

Vindice describes midnight as the Judas of the hours

> that betrays
> Honest salvation unto sin. (1. 3. 77–8)

And when he himself, under the disguise of such a feast, has entrapped the old Duke, he cries

> Now nine years' vengeance crowds into a minute!
> (3. 5. 126)

All the betrayed women are in a sense represented by the poisoned skull of Vindice's mistress—not only she herself, but Antonio's wife, Castiza, who would have been betrayed, and the imaginary "country lady" whom the Duke thought he was about to seduce. At least the way in which these various incidents are related is very close; they are variations on the same theme. The vengeance of the skull is also, in a sense, Heaven's vengeance. Measure for measure is meted out. The imagery of beauty transmuted into land through prostitution is paralleled by the imagery of beauty transmuted into worms. Vindice addresses the skull of his mistress, who died for her chastity, as though it were that of a courtesan. The whole of the address to the skull is relevant here. It expresses what was also a common mood in Revenge tragedy, "Go, get thee to my lady's chamber, tell her, let her paint an inch thick, to this favour shall she come".

The curious connections in the Elizabethan mind between painting the face and the decaying of a corpse is of course to be explained by the habit of painting to hide disease or merely to hide dirt (as clean rushes were strewn over dirty ones). Since the flesh itself was a covering to the "very ragged bone" the decoration of living or dead flesh seems an equal horror. Vindice says that when Gloriana was alive her face shone beyond "any woman's bought complexion". Lussurioso again equates this painting with sin in general, making the whole connection explicit.

> Offences
> Gilt o'er with mercy, show like fairest women,
> Good only for their beauties, which, washed off, no sin is
> fouler. (1. 2. 32–4)

(Cf. *Hamlet*, 3. 1. 51–3.)

The painting of the skull in Act 3, Scene 5, has therefore an intimate connection with the feeling of the play, as crystallised in its imagery. The poisoning is significant too because the disfigurements of poison are like those of disease, and so it is a fitting death for a lecher. (The ghost's description of his poisoning in *Hamlet* is in the same kind of language as Hamlet's attack on his mother for her lechery.)

In this scene Vindice has the co-operation of the undying worm and is fulfilling the justice of Heaven. The actual device of painting a skull was an old one; but it had never been used with such wealth of implication before, so welded into the play. The language is extraordinarily complex.

> Doth the silk worm expend her yellow labours
> For thee? for thee doth she undo herself?
> Are lordships sold to maintain ladyships
> For the poor benefit of a bewitching minute?
> Why does yon fellow falsify highways
> And put his life between the judge's lips
> To refine such a thing? keep men and horses
> To beat their valours for her? (3. 5. 75 ff.)

The images of beauty transmuted into wealth and of the "bewitching minute" are there: "ladyships" is also used with a pejorative implication (meaning "whores"). "Falsify" had many subsidiary meanings like "adulterate", "pervert from its right use" (*vide N.E.D.*). The line may mean that the broken gallant turns highwayman; but also that he falsifies his own way to salvation, so that the "life between the judge's lips" (note the concreteness of the image!) suggests the Last Judgment. We have seen the Duchess' son with "his life between the judge's lips" for a woman already, and he is certainly a lost soul. "Refine" was also used literally (meaning "wear off" or "rub off") so that it suggests the woman's flesh is wasted by venereal disease

> to have their costly three piled flesh worn off
> As bare as this!

It also means here to pamper, of course, and perhaps to defend her name by fighting her detractors, keeping men and horses "to beat their valour for her". "Beat" has a pun on "bate" (then pronounced similarly); it could also mean "to overcome" or "to cheapen" (as in our phrase "to beat down "): the passage suggests the prostitution of the sound masculine valour of the men and horses to the defence of something foul.

This scene is the core of the whole play: it illustrates how, if earthly law is corrupt, there is "an unbribed everlasting law" which is inescapable. The sword of the just man is "a bribeless officer". And when Vindice appeals to Heaven, the thunder indicates that Heaven is on the watch with its

> eternal eye
> That sees through flesh and all.

This thunder is purely symbolic, and so its promptitude is no reason for amusement, though few of the critics have refrained. It acts like Tamburlaine's tussle for the crown, or Chapman's use of the ghost, not by realistic methods.

Tourneur's *naïveté* in this respect may seem to clash with his very complex use of language, as shown in the address to the skull. But there he only extracts the full body of the meaning by taking the words in a particularly literal manner ("refine" and "beat") and not by emotional overtones in Webster's manner. It is even compatible with certain clumsiness in the language. Tourneur's puns are the most awkward and ineffectual of all the Elizabethans, especially his obscene ones.

Such a strictly planned pattern as that of *The Revenger's Tragedy* would only be possible to a very narrow, if deep, sensibility. The naïve quality of Tourneur's feelings has been insisted on by most of his critics. His moral comments are remarkable for a kind of triteness which is expressed, at the level of versification, in jingling sententious couplets. In the scene of Gratiana's repentance there are dozens of these gems of proverbial wisdom: see especially the speech beginning

> For honest women are so seld and rare
> 'Tis good to cherish those poor few that are:
>
> (4. 4. 68 ff.)

and such lines as

> To weep is to our sex naturally given:
> But to weep truly, that's a gift from heaven. (4. 4. 62–3)

> And well remembered, joy's a subtle elf,
> I think man's happiest when he forgets himself!
>
> (4. 4. 92–3)

> she first begins with one
> That afterwards to thousands proves a whore:
> Break ice in one place, it will crack in more!
>
> (4. 2. 87–9)

To this last Gratiana admiringly replies "Most certainly applied". This habit of giving applause to another character is also common in Tourneur: it adds a further smugness to the jaunty assurance of the sententious couplet:

> Sister, y'ave sentenced most direct and true,
> The law's a woman and would she were you.
> Brother, y'have spoke that right.
> You have my voice in that, etc.

After the magnificent speech, "Now 'tis full sea abed over the world", his brother says to Vindice, "You flow well, brother", and Vindice trying to outdo himself, falls into the bathos of an appeal to the audience

> Pooh! I'm shallow yet,
> Too sparing and too modest: shall I tell thee?
> If every trick were told that's dealt by night
> There are few *here* that would not blush outright.
>
> (2. 2. 163–6)

There is a kind of incandescence about his best passages not incompatible with this *naïveté*. The metaphor of fire occurs often. Castiza is

> Cold and chaste as an unlighted taper
> Save that her mother's words
> Did blow fire on her cheeks;

and she says

> I have endured you with an ear of fire,

recalling the box on the ear she gave Vindice.

The same mixture of *naïveté* and subtlety is seen in the action. There is the "blazing star" of the old tragedy, and the skilful counterpoint of the young Princes' plots. The ingenuity of the final catastrophe can, however, hardly be called *naïveté*, Vindice's acknowledgement is too definite.

> Now I remember too here was Piato
> Brought forth a knavish sentence once—no doubt (said he) but time
> Will make the murderer bring forth himself.
>
> (5. 3. 159 ff.)

Heaven is responsible for his fall, and Heaven alone. There is one other episode which seems tinged with the supernatural; the fall and conversion of Gratiana. The imagery points to a kind of demoniacal possession. Castiza says:

> Mother, come from that poisonous woman there;

and refuses to recognise her. Later she accuses her of coiling "a black serpent" of evil counsel. The two brothers decide to

> Conjure that foul devil out of our mother;

so that their violence seems not unnatural. Gratiana herself says, "I wonder now what fury did transport me?" suggesting that she was not responsible for her speeches.

Of course this remains a suggestion only. Gratiana is not possessed as indubitably as Mother Sawyer, but then she is not a real person in the same sense as Mother Sawyer. It may indicate the way to approach her lightning conversions; and it is, after all, as plausible as the possession of the husband in *A Yorkshire Tragedy*, which has found general acceptance.

Tourneur's second play is generally considered inferior to his first, but it is built upon the same plan. *The Atheist's*

Tragedy deals with what may be called "the philosophy of Nature". "Nature" is a key word; it occurs so frequently in the speeches of D'Amville the atheist as to be noticeable to anyone (I have counted a total of thirty-two occasions). The definitions of this "Nature" is that set out by Shakespeare's Edmund in

> Thou, Nature, art my goddess.

(*King Lear* and *The Atheist's Tragedy* have many verbal connections, as Schücking has observed.) For D'Amville Nature means the world of phenomena plus the human reason. His own intelligence enables him to control his brother (as Edmund does his father), and he considers it the distinguishing mark of humanity. The only end of reason is the pursuit of happiness; and as the only values are measurable ones, happiness consists in material success. In the debate with Borachio (1. 1. 1–32) this is set forth. D'Amville concludes that a moment's extreme and violent pleasure is not so good as a lifetime of moderate enjoyment; he therefore rejects lust for ambition. His first object is to increase wealth not only for his own sake but for his children. His affection to them is looked on only as an enlarged selfishness, for through them he hopes for vicarious existence after death. (Of course he does not believe in immortality.)

> they are as near to me
> As branches to the tree on which they grow....
> There's my eternity. My life in them
> And their succession shall for ever live.   (1. 1. 59 ff.)

For this he relies upon his reason (1. 1. 142–3). He aims at a concrete result and goes about it with forethought. Images of building are constantly used.

> This work will rise and soon be perfected.   (2. 1. 137)
> My plot still rises
> According to the model of my own desires.   (2. 2. 34–5)

The villain Borachio, carrying stones to use for the murder, says:

> Such stones are used to raise a house upon
> But with these stones I go to ruin one.   (2. 4. 1–2)

When the murder is accomplished, D'Amville picks one up and says:

> Upon this ground I'll build my manor house
> And this shall be the chiefest corner stone.   (2. 4. 118–19)

The plot does work so smoothly by means of a sequence of events so specially adapted for one purpose as to imply the co-operation of external forces.

In fact, throughout the planning of the murder of his brother, D'Amville feels the assistance of Nature; that is, of the universe at large. The night is conveniently dark—

> Now Nature shows thee how it favoureth our
> Performance.... (2. 4. 179–80)
> Thus propitious Nature winked
> At our proceedings.... (2. 4. 185–6)
>   For it follows well
> That Nature, since herself decay doth hate,
> Should favour those that strengthen their estate.
>
> > (2. 4. 190–2)

There is, however, no suggestion of an overruling deity. Thunder, the sign of God's presence in *The Revenger's Tragedy*, is explained as "a mere effect of 'Nature'", the scientific explanation of which D'Amville is perfectly acquainted with.

In *The Atheist's Tragedy* thunder is, however, replaced, as a symbol of the deity, by "the stars". Wherever there is a reference to them, it has more than a merely astronomical implication (again *King Lear* will be remembered). D'Amville, like Edmund, denies the power of the stars; denies, that is, any controlling power which shapes his life, beyond himself. God is "him they call the Supreme of the stars", and there-

fore the starless night when Montferrars was murdered has
a symbolic as well as a practical value. D'Amville explains
the stars scientifically. He cannot think

> their influences are governors
> Of sublunary creatures when themselves
> Are senseless of their operations.   (2. 4. 159 ff.)

After the murder, counterfeiting a Christian grief, D'Amville
laments the starless night, calling them "viceroys to the king
of Nature", "whose constellations govern mortal birth"
(2. 4. 47 ff.). At the end of the scene he feels that Nature
has co-operated, and recapitulates his plot in a manner to
stress both its subtlety and its success. The first two acts are
a remarkably coherent and supple piece of narrative in the
Elizabethan manner, particularly the quarrel of the servants
and the use of Snuffe. During the third act Charlemont is
also entrapped by a series of ingenious manœuvres.

But D'Amville questions his own success:

> For what effect and end have I engaged
> Myself in all this blood? to leave a state
> To the succession of my proper blood.
> But how shall that succession be continued?   (4. 2. 36 ff.)

(Compare Macbeth's preoccupation with his succession.)
D'Amville doubts the lives of both his sons. But he cannot
bear that his family should decay ("Nature forbid", 4. 2. 47),
and so he attempts to seduce Castabella. In this he is pre-
vented by Charlemont in the disguise of a ghost. The
symbol of mortality is not fortuitous. D'Amville's reason,
on which he exclusively relies, is overthrown by this; he
thinks he is about to die, and, like Faustus, only desires
annihilation:

> O were my body circumscribed
> Within that cloud: that when the thunder tears
> His passage, it might scatter me
> To nothing in the air.   (4. 3. 277 ff.)

Night seems now horrible to him, not a "beauteous mistress" but a bawd. He recovers, however, from this temporary fear and in the next scene recomforts himself with gold: he equates the coins with the "stars" and reason with God.

> These are the stars whose operations make
> The fortunes and the destinies of men.…
> These are the stars, the ministers of fate,
> And man's high wisdom the superior power
> To which their forces are subordinate. (5. 1. 22 ff.)

He is again certain that

> My real wisdom has raised up a state
> That shall eternize my posterity. (5. 1. 56–7)

At this point Heaven executes its *coup de main*.

> *Enter servants with the body of his younger son,*

and simultaneously the groans of his elder son, who is dying, are heard from within. The effect is naturalistically indefensible: as a miraculous intervention of Heaven it is as appropriate as the thunder of *The Revenger's Tragedy*.

D'Amville sees the ruin of his house. The imagery marks the downfall: first he appeals to Nature—

> Dear Nature! in whose honour I have raised
> A work of glory to posterity,
> O bury not the pride of that great action
> Under the fall and ruin of itself. (5. 1. 98 ff.)

He tempts the doctor with "gold" and "honours"; he offers enough gold for the "spirit" of it to be extracted in order to revive him. But the doctor points out that gold will not restore life. The gasps of the elder son, as he is dying, sound in D'Amville's ears

>   like the falling noise
> Of some *great building* when the ground work breaks.
> On these two pillars stood the stately frame
> And architecture of my lofty house. (5. 1. 92 ff.)

When the elder son dies, he is utterly bewildered at Nature's betrayal and the doctor summarily proves that

> Of necessity there must
> Be a superior power to Nature. (5. 1. 137–8)

The argument is (intentionally I think) flat and unconvincing. D'Amville feels a grudge against the universe. And here, obliquely and by a pun, he begins to acknowledge the possibility of a superior power. He has fulfilled all his side of the contract in the pursuit of happiness: only Nature has cheated:

> Nature, thou art a traitor to my soul,
> Thou hast abused my trust. I will complain
> To a superior court to right my wrong.
> I'll prove thee a forger of false assurances.
> In yon Star Chamber thou shalt answer it. (5. 1. 140 ff.)

The stars in their courses have fought against him after all. From this point D'Amville is certainly meant to be crazed, but that is because he has suddenly seen more than he can bear. So he comes into the court in the last scene, crying "Judgment! Judgment!" with the bodies of his sons borne before him. He wants a verdict on his case. (Compare the farmhouse scene in *King Lear*.) In court he is confronted with Charlemont, the nephew whom he has disinherited, and, by a trick, caused to be condemned to death. Charlemont faces death calmly. D'Amville is puzzled; he feels that there must be something quite concrete which causes this.

> I would find out
> The efficient cause of a contented mind. (5. 2. 184–5)

He begs Charlemont's body in order that he may have it anatomised.[1] The death of his son has terrified him, so that he is afraid of death for himself and ready to give everything, even his gold, for some of Charlemont's courage.

[1] Cf. "Let them anatomize Regan".

At the end of the scene Heaven gives the judgment D'Amville had come for. He offers to behead Charlemont himself, but, as he is lifting up the axe, "strikes out his own brains". The action is almost impossible from a rational point of view, but, like the self-revelation of Vindice, it is meant to be taken as a miracle.

D'Amville is at last converted. He abjures Nature and reason, "man's wisdom" which he had assumed guided the stars, and acknowledges God's justice.

> *Judge.* God forbid!
> *D'Am.* You lie, Judge. He commanded it.
> To tell thee that man's wisdom is a fool.
> There[1] was the strength of Natural understanding.
> But Nature is a fool. There is a power
> Above her that hath overthrown the pride
> Of all my projects and posterity,
> For whose surviving blood
> I had erected a proud monument,
> And struck them dead before me: for whose deaths
> I called to thee for judgment. Thou didst want
> Discretion for the sentence. But yon power
> That struck me knew the judgment I deserved
> And gave it. (5. 2. 271 ff.)

Even the building metaphor, it will be noted, is revived in this careful speech. After the death, the moral is pointed in a further series of speeches by the survivors.

This play is as certainly D'Amville's tragedy as the other is Vindice's. The minor figures form a subsidiary pattern in themselves and serve as foils to him. Levidulcia, the harlot of the play, has a doctrine of Nature like his: lust is natural—

> 'Tis like
> That natural sympathy which e'en among
> The senseless creatures of the earth commands
> A mutual inclination and respect. (4. 5. 17 ff.)

It is in the name of Nature that she urges Castabella to

[1] I.e. in his plots.

break her troth and marry another man. Her reasons are stated a little abstractly for one who believed "the passage lies not through reason but her blood". For in this respect Levidulcia is contrasted with D'Amville, that she acts wholly upon instinct and identifies herself completely with the beasts, as in the passage quoted above.

> Our creation has no reference
> To man but in his body, being made
> Only for generation.... If Reason were
> Our counsellor we would neglect the work
> Of generation, for the prodigal
> Expense it draws us to of that which is
> The wealth of life. Wise Nature therefore hath
> Reserved for an inducement to our sense
> Our greatest pleasure in that greatest work. (1. 4. 86 ff.)

D'Amville's attempted rape of Castabella was not due to lust but simply a desire for posterity, and his arguments in favour of incest are entirely drawn from "reason", while Levidulcia's impulses are irrational. In 2. 3 she is formally contrasted with Castabella. The scene opens with a soliloquy from the latter:

> O love! thou chaste affection of the soule
> Without the adulterate mixture of the blood....
>
> (2. 3. 1–2)

It ends with Levidulcia, amazed at her coldness, exclaiming:

> My affections even with their cold bloods
> (As snow rubbed through an active hand, does make
> The flesh to burne) by agitation is
> Inflamed....

H'as set my blood o'boyling in my veins. And now (like water poured upon the ground that mixes itself with every moisture it meets) I could clasp with any man. (2. 3. 50 ff.)

Her death, like D'Amville's, provides an example of divine justice both in the manner and the means of it: she acknow-

ledges this explicitly in another of those speeches built on
the theme of "The wheel is come full circle".

Charlemont, the Senecal man, is set against D'Amville
rather as Castabella is against Levidulcia. There are no double
personalities in this play, like Vindice; the contrasts are
between character and character. Charlemont also identifies
himself with his family, but it is from a different point of
view. His love for the wars is hereditary and he feels it his
duty to distinguish himself. To his father he says:

> My affections for the wars
> Are as hereditary as my blood
> To every life of all my ancestry.
> Your predecessors were your precedents
> And you are my example. Shall I serve
> For nothing but a vain parenthesis
> I' the honoured story of your family? (1. 2. 15 ff.)

His ambitions are quite free from any mercenary taint. He
accepts D'Amville's loan as an offer of affection, though he
leaves a bond for it too, whereby D'Amville in spite of his
protest, "'Tis a witness only of my love", is enabled later
to imprison him for debt. To Langbeau Snuffe, the Puritan,
he says:

> Sir, I will take your friendship up at use
> And fear not that your profit shall be small:
> Your interest shall exceed your principal. (1. 2. 154 ff.)

This seems at the time no more than an incidental metaphor. But later D'Amville bribes Langbeau Snuffe with a
diamond ring, and Langbeau, weighing the two together,
takes D'Amville's side against his friend. "Charlemont! thy
gratuity and my promises were but words."

When later Sebastian finds that Charlemont is imprisoned
for a thousand pounds, he too weighs honesty against profit.
Charlemont had saved his life; but Charlemont was his
father's enemy. "No matter, Charlemont! thou gavest me

life and that's somewhat of a purer earth than gold, as fine as 'tis" (3. 2. 91 ff.).

Disinterestedness, however, is not Charlemont's most out-standing characteristic. His bravery is commented on by all the characters, and it is that which principally endears him to Castabella. Borachio's account of his death, though fictitious, reflects upon this side of his character. He is the most definitely soldierly of all Elizabethan heroes: in this respect, there is a contrast with D'Amville's sons, as well as with D'Amville himself, for the "honest soldier" was the recognised opposite of the politician. The two are finally contrasted in the trial scene where Charlemont's courage so baffles D'Amville; the difference between stoicism and hedonism being symbolised by Charlemont calling for a glass of water and D'Amville for a glass of wine which seems to him like the blood of his victims.

The use of omens is very frequent, especially in the early part of the play. This gives the impression of a watching providence, and, although D'Amville's schemes appear to be successful, suggests that he is only being given opportunity to damn himself more completely. Montferrars is full of foreboding before Charlemont goes to the war (1. 2. 44), and before Borachio enters with his false tale (2. 1. 52); he also foresees his own death. Castabella prophesies of her tears, comparing them to rain:

> As their showers presaged, so do my tears
> Some sad event will follow my sad fears. (1. 2. 123–4)

This is when she takes leave of Charlemont. The prophecy is recalled by her repetition when she is forced to marry Rousard:

> Now Charlemont! O, my presaging tears!
> This sad event hath followed my sad fears. (1. 4. 135–6)

Charlemont's dream of his father's death may also be classed with the omens. He has a very curious and "metaphysical" theory of the origin of dreams, but this is summarily contradicted by the reappearance of the ghost.

The omens also help to formalise the action. The narrative may be defined as a rigid pattern of incredible events conforming to a general thesis. D'Amville's scheming is very complex, and flawless from an Elizabethan point of view, but of course it is not naturalistic. The action tends to become overtly symbolical at the crises: for instance, Charlemont's climb into the charnel house, when he slips upon a skull; Charlemont and Castabella's convenient "heaviness" which leads them to sleep each with a skull for a pillow; and the glasses of water and wine in the judgment scene and D'Amville's striking out his own brain. When the characters are Humorous and the narrative formalised it is easy for particular actions to become non-naturalistic as well.

The comic relief has to be seen, I think, in the light of a Swiftian commentary on the main action. Cataplasma, Soquette and Langbeau Snuffe are yahoos, and their jokes are never meant to be less than ghastly, like the lechery of the old Duke in *The Revenger's Tragedy*.

It is true that there is a perceptible slackening of tension in *The Atheist's Tragedy*. The writing is on the whole less forcible, the vocabulary less pungent and concentrated. It is a *drame à thèse*, but less complex and more purely intellectual in its central theme. Several critics have noticed echoes of Chapman's style; there is a great deal of his type of generalised analysis of feeling. The relation of the story to *The Revenge of Bussy D'Ambois* has been noted elsewhere together with some particular echoes, but the general style of such scenes as the meeting of Charlemont and Castabella in the church (3. 1), the argument between Castabella and D'Amville (4. 3. 90 ff.), and the soliloquy of Levidulcia (4. 5. 15 ff.) are in Chapman's manner. Charlemont assures his mistress that he is alive by advising her to

> Reduce thine understanding to thine eye.

She replies

> I feel a substance warm and soft and moist
> Subject to the capacity of sense.
>   *Charlemont.* Which spirits are not: for their essence is
> Above the nature and the order of
> Those elements whereof our senses are
> Created.   (3. 1. 93 ff.)

This habit of generalisation is most incongruous in the instinctive woman, Levidulcia. There is nothing like it in *The Revenger's Tragedy*. The thinking there is either at a greater heat (as in Vindice's address to the skull) or else in tritely aphonistic couplets: these have disappeared in *The Atheist's Tragedy*.

Tourneur's construction is perhaps the most typically Elizabethan of all the tragic writers. His use of the narrative exploits all the advantages of stylisation; his adaptation of Humorous characters is more careful than Marston's. There is a constant connection between speech and action, so that the language is a living part of the story. Finally, his poetry, if not the greatest, is among the most concentrated writing of the time; in the power of a single word or a single image he is surpassed only by Shakespeare.

CHAPTER VIII

John Webster

BETWEEN Tourneur and Webster there is more of a gap than appears at first sight. Both used the Revenge convention, but in Webster's plays, as Professor Stoll has observed, it begins to crumble. He uses it intermittently, less as a vehicle than a prop.

Webster was in a sense too sophisticated; in the pejorative sense, too literary. He was concerned with perfection of detail rather than general design: this is reflected in his structure as well as the texture of his verse. For example, Webster uses the ghost for a momentary effect of terror or pathos, and does not relate it to the other supernatural suggestions of the play.

He completely dropped the traditional narrative, retaining one or two of its most effective episodes. *The White Devil* and *The Duchess of Malfi* are both based on historic facts, and this implies a different attitude to the narrative from Tourneur's. The story is not deliberately distorted; each incident in itself can be treated more naturally. The characters have the same double nature as Vindice; but instead of alternating, the two halves are blurred and run together. This also makes for naturalism. As a result, there is no pattern of characters, nor is there any structure of themes as in Tourneur's plays.

Of course there is some simplification. For example, in the two scenes where Vittoria defends her life by lying (3. 2 and 5. 6), it is so well done that the language contains no trace of dissimulation (as the duplicity of Iago can be felt behind his speeches).

> Behold, Brachiano, I that while you lived
> Did make a flaming altar of my heart

> To sacrifice unto you, now am ready
> To sacrifice heart and all.   (5. 6. 84 ff.)

The splendid bluff rings true; too true for strict dramatic effectiveness.

There is, as it were, a subordinate side of Vittoria which is innocent. Actually she is guilty, but there is a strong under-current of suggestion in the opposite direction. It never comes to the surface plainly, but it is there. Her character is a "reconciliation of opposites". The guilty side is naturally predominant; but if the various hints of the other are examined together, their cumulative weight will be found considerable. Of course this could hardly be a conscious device on Webster's part (though his evident admiration for *Sejanus* is significant).

Vittoria's part of the play is really limited to four scenes (1. 2, 3. 2, 4. 2 and 5. 6). When we first see her with Brachiano the adultery is obviously right from any but a puritanical point of view.

> Give credit, I could wish time would stand still
> And never end this interview, this hour,
> But all delight itself doth soonest devour.
> Let me into your bosom, happy lady,
> Pour out, instead of eloquence, my vows....
> > *Flaminio.* See, now they close. Most happy union.
> > > (1. 2. 192 ff.)

There is no argument against the movement and rhythm of such a passage, any more than against

> If it be love indeed, tell me how much.

Suddenly Cornelia bursts in with her jingling moralising—

> Earthquakes leave behind,
> When they have tyrannized, iron, lead or stone:
> But woe to ruin, violent lust leaves none.   (1. 2. 208–10)

Cornelia is at this point as irritating (because unconvincing) to the audience as to Flaminio. In the scene at the house of convertites Vittoria is even more sympathetically treated. Her courage in casting off Brachiano and her wounded feelings are most delicately given (4. 2. 130–98).

In the other two scenes where she appears, Vittoria lies steadily but, as has been said with no overtone of deceit, so that she hardly seems morally guilty; her "innocent-resembling boldness" as Lamb called it, is thoroughly convincing.

When she suggests a murder to Brachiano it is done by means of a dream, which, besides giving a picture of her as a victim rather than an aggressor, is vivid enough to draw off attention from its sinister purport, if the Elizabethan interest in the surface meaning of words is remembered.

It is obvious on reflection that she is an accessory if not a party to the murders; but anything obvious only on reflection was not very prominent to the Elizabethan playgoer. She does not witness the dumb shows with Brachiano, though they are in her house. Also Brachiano is made to pursue Vittoria, so that her guilt at first is little more than weakness. In a speech of Marcello's she is bracketed (by implication) with Isabella as his victim.

> O my unfortunate sister.
> I would my dagger point had cleft her heart
> When she first saw Brachiano. (3. 1. 32–4)

This at once recalls Florence's words on *his* sister:

> Thou hast a wife, our sister: would I had given
> Both her white hands to death, bound and locked fast
> In her last winding sheet when I gave thee
> But one. (2. 1. 66–9)

On the other hand Vittoria is often called a devil, even in the early part of the play—"Excellent devil" (1. 2. 246).

> Were there a second paradise to lose
> This devil would betray it. (3. 2. 72–3)

> If the devil
> Did ever take good shape, behold his picture.
>
> (3. 2. 224–5)
>
> Your beauty, oh ten thousand curses on it.
> How long have I beheld the devil in crystal. (4. 2. 88–9)

To a literal-minded Elizabethan audience the epithet would have great force. Twice it is suggested that she is possessed by devils.

> Next the devil adultery
> Enters the devil murder. (3. 2. 112–13)
>
> Thou hast a devil in thee: I will try
> If I can scare him from thee. (5. 6. 19–20)

As in the case of Gratiana in *The Revenger's Tragedy* such statements would not be sufficient to make the audience ready to take an oath, if cross-examined, that Vittoria was possessed; but then they were not accustomed to judge their impressions separately or even to analyse them out fully, and the suggestive power of these passages in a superstitious age cannot be ignored.

Finally, all Flaminio's hints about the way women forget their husbands colour the last act of the play (5. 3. 183–9, and 5. 6. 155–66). Vittoria would not, after all, sacrifice herself for Brachiano. Flaminio's comments are quite generalised, but they inevitably become attached to Vittoria.

> Had women navigable rivers in their eyes
> They would dispend them all: surely I wonder
> Why we should wish more rivers to the city
> When they sell water so good cheap. I'll tell thee
> These are but moonish shades of griefs or feares,
> There's nothing sooner dry than woman's tears.
>
> (5. 3. 184 ff.)
>
> O men,
> That lie upon your death beds and are haunted
> With howling wives, ne'er trust them, they'll remarry
> Ere the worm pierce your winding sheets, ere the spider
> Make a thin curtain for your epitaphs. (5. 6. 155 ff.)

In conclusion, Vittoria's love is dignified and heroic on all occasions, but Vittoria is also condemned outright as a monster and a devil. Perhaps some words applied to the Duchess of Malfi describe her best:

> Methinks her fault and beauty,
> Blended together, show like leprosy,
> The whiter, the fouler.

Supreme beauty and glamour are mixed with lust and selfishness. In either case Vittoria remains a splendid figure-piece rather than a natural character in spite of the realism of individual scenes. The men are more slightly drawn. To a certain extent they reduplicate each other: but they are not variations on a single theme, like Tourneur's minor figures.

Brachiano is both hero and villain. His heroic qualities are a certain magnificent swagger and his tenderness to Vittoria. In the trial scene his exit is hardly inferior to her stand; his retorts have the audacity which Webster always approved.

Cardinal. Who made you overseer?
Brachiano. Why, my charity, my charity, which should flow
From every generous and noble spirit
To orphans and to widows. (3. 2. 165 ff.)

On the other hand he bears most of the guilt. Vittoria is a beautiful but scarcely human temptress; he is the man who sins. He is given a quite mechanical brutality towards Isabella, but it is rather to heighten her pathos than to qualify his own character.

Brachiano is accompanied by a set of images turning on poison, physic and disease (which were frequently used as symbols of spiritual rottenness). He is the most frequent butt of jokes about venereal disease. He is also treacherous: the second half of Cornelia's curse, it should be noted, is addressed to him. She says to Vittoria:

If thou dishonour thus thy husband's bed,
Be thy life short as are the funeral tears
In great men's ——
  Brachiano. Fie, fie, the woman's mad. [*She turns on him.*]
  Cornelia. Be thy act Judas-like, betray in kissing. [*Turns back
   to Vittoria.*] (1. 2. 288 ff.)

The interpolation refers to the fumed picture in a prophetic
manner. Isabella was poisoned by kissing it, so that Giovanni
could not kiss her when she was dead. Finally Brachiano,
himself poisoned, says to Vittoria:

> Do not kiss me: for I shall poison thee. (5. 3. 27)

Poison was associated especially with the Machiavellian
"politician", and therefore the fact that Brachiano is often
called "poisonous" is significant. Cornelia says he blights
like a mildew (1. 2. 262) and his wife hopes to

> Charm his poison, force it to obeying
> And keep him chaste from an infected straying.
>
> (2. 1. 16–17)

It is therefore appropriate that he should die by poison since
it was "his art". He ends with:

> Mercury—
>   And copperas—
>   And quicksilver
> And other devilish 'potecary stuff
> A melting in your politic brains. (5. 3. 162 ff.)

During the last scene he is half damned. He imagines
himself in hell, and sees the devil and familiar spirits in the
form of rats. The Church ceremonial, though the priests are
conspirators disguised, would add to the visual impression,
for they condemn him, tell him he is damned and given up
to the devil. Vittoria at one point cries "O me! This place
is hell!" and her cries sound to Brachiano like those of lost
souls.

Yet even in this last scene Brachiano has been seen as
noble and heroic; he has fought in the tourney, and his

soldierly qualities, as well as his tenderness to Vittoria, have
been stressed. Florence's aside sums up the double impression:

> Noble youth,
> I pity thy sad fate. Now to the barriers.
> This shall his passage to the black lake further,
> The last good deed he did, he pardoned murther.
>
> (5. 2. 79–82)

There is a single mixed response to Brachiano and Vittoria:
Churton Collins' phrases about "blasted splendours" would
apply here. This blurring of contradictory aspects is different
from their juxtaposition, and clearly a sign of decadence.
It suggests *A King and No King* or *Love's Sacrifice*.

Flaminio is a blend too; his rôles of Malcontent and of
tool villain are not separated by a disguise, like Vindice's.
In the early part of the play he seems a complete Machiavel,
assuming an air of *bonhomie* to cajole Brachiano, Camillo or
Vittoria. He also tries (unsuccessfully) to flatter Giovanni.
The same enthusiasm is seen in his greeting to the doctor:
"Let me love thee, O thou loathsome abhominable gar-
garisme", and in his manipulation of the quarrel between
the lovers:

> Fie, fie, my lord,
> Women are caught as you take tortoises.
> She must be turned on her back—Sister, by this hand,
> I am of your side. Come, come, you have wronged her.
>
> (4. 2. 152–5)

The more serious speeches of Flaminio in the early part
describe his bitter grinding poverty: here, as in *The Revenger's
Tragedy*, gold buys the poor. He shares this attitude with
Ludovico (1. 1. 1–30; 1. 2. 301–7; 3. 1. 35–7; 3. 3. 1–9,
19–50, 81–93; 4. 1. 81–92; 5. 1. 112–40; 5. 3. 190; 5. 6. 8–16).
Flaminio's bitterness grows as his reward slips through his
fingers. He only feels safe at the marriage. Throughout the
poisoning scene he is dismayed. He has only one soliloquy;

and here his melancholy seems genuine, not like the feigned "mad humour" of Act 3:

> I have lived
> Riotously ill, like some that live in court
> And sometimes when my face was full of smiles
> Have felt the maze of conscience in my breast.
> Oft gay and honoured robes these tortures try:
> We think caged birds sing when indeed they cry.
>
> (5. 4. 112 ff.)

This mood cannot be reconciled with his earlier character. Flaminio is largely an author's mouthpiece; but he is not a formalised character like Vindice. The excuses for his moralising presuppose a naturalistic standard of characterisation; it would not have occurred to earlier writers to apologise in this manner for their characters:

> I do put on this feigned garb of mirth
> To gull suspicion....
> It may appear to some ridiculous
> Thus to talk knave and murderer: anon
> Come in with a dried sentence stuff'd with sage:
> But this allows my varying of shapes,
> Knaves do grow great by being great men's apes.
>
> (3. 1. 30–1, 4. 2. 242 ff.)

In Act 5 the varying of shapes is most pronounced. The story of the crucifix and the amour with Zanche blacken him; yet his melancholy is more genuine. His final speeches acknowledge only his disillusion.

> I am in the way to study a long silence.
> To prate were idle. I remember nothing.
> There's nothing of so infinite vexation
> As man's own thoughts. (5. 6. 204–7)

There is no consistent impression of Flaminio. The various aspects of his character are neither polarised nor reconciled.

Even Florence and Ludovico are blends. Florence is sometimes the complete Machiavel; he "winds" Brachiano,

arranges the lovers' flight and carries out a "politic" murder.
Yet in his disguise he is spoken of nobly; described as a
stoic and permitted to moralise. His love for Isabella is
insisted on. Ludovico is a serviceable villain; he reflects
Flaminio sometimes, and contrasts with him at others. He
mocks the melancholy attitude as well as using it (this
turning round on a former position is characteristic of
Webster).

The difficulty of *The White Devil* is that the feelings are
meant to be naturalistic, but the characters are not. The
impression of the parts conflicts with the impression of the
whole. The play is held together chiefly by the dominant
tone of the writing: that peculiar sardonic note that is more
matured, if not more bitter, than Tourneur's. The violence
of the action is paralleled by images of disorder. Cornelia
sees Brachiano as a calamity of nature, an "earthquake". He
retorts to her:

> Thy rash tongue
> Hath raised a fearful and prodigious storm. (1. 2. 298–9)

The Cardinal calls Ludovico a "foul black cloud" threatening
a storm. Vittoria is to Monticelso like "Shipwrecks in
calmest weather", and at her death she cries:

> My soul like to a ship in a black storm
> Is driven I know not whither. (5. 6. 248–9)

Three times she is called a "blazing star" which is to be
"prodigious" or "ominous". The use of imagery of poison
and disease in connection with Brachiano has already been
noted.

There are an extraordinary number of references to
animals in the play (I have counted more than a hundred),
and most of them belong to Flaminio. They occur in clumps
and clusters in his Malcontent speeches. The effect is of
course to reduce man to a brutish level: they are nearly

always contrasted for some repulsive quality, though sometimes (as in the images of caged birds) for their helplessness. In Act 5 alone, for example, mention is made of sparrows and pigeons; the wolf, the dog with a bottle at his tail, other dogs with fleas, Aesop's dog, hawks, hounds, geese, fowls, the screech owl, the wolf, the raven, quails, dogfish; a dogfox; rats, a dead fly-blown dog, snakes, the partridge, the peacock, the eagle and dottralls, the wolf and raven again, the screech owl again; crickets, toads, robins, field mice, moles; wolves; caged birds, the fox, braches, worms, spiders, spaniels, blackbirds, the sparrowhawk, lions caged.

This kind of imagery is much more frequent in Webster than the charnel-house kind. For disgust has been replaced by the sardonic in his writing; instead of attacking vice, he satirises it. This only illustrates at another level the particular quality of sophistication already noticed in the characterisation, vocabulary and narrative.

The Duchess of Malfi is a much more complex case of bi-focal technique. Not only the characters are invested with the curious ambivalence of *The White Devil*, but the action itself hovers in an ambiguous manner between the natural and the supernatural.

Everyone has felt a vague "suggestion" of the supernatural in the tortures of the Duchess in Act 4 and the madness of Ferdinand in Act 5. It is a shadowy feeling, but quite inescapable. For example, when the Cardinal says (5. 5. 1):

> I am puzzled in a question about hell:
> He sayes, in hell there's one material fire
> And yet it shall not burn all men alike.
> Lay him by. How tedious is a guilty conscience!
> When I look into the Fish-ponds in my Garden
> Methinks I see a thing armed with a Rake
> That seems to strike at me.

The contrast of the "material fire" and the vague reflection of a devil "armed with a Rake" is fused into a powerful suggestion of a present hell. The Elizabethan audience would be familiar with

> Why, this is hell, nor am I out of it.
> Thinkst thou that I, that saw the face of God
> And tasted the eternal joys of heaven,
> Am not tormented with ten thousand hells
> In being deprived of everlasting bliss?
>
> *(Faustus,* 1. 3. 79 ff.)

Of course there is never any categorical statement of the presence of the supernatural: there are no definite ghosts as in *The White Devil,* though, as Mr F. L. Lucas points out, the Echo scene and Antonio's vision of "a face folded in sorrow" are equivalent to an appearance of the spirit of the Duchess. The whole play is kept very delicately and firmly on the level of suggestion.

But to a suggestible and superstitious people vague implications are more horrifying than straightforward assertions. This attitude involves a very different kind of "belief" from most senses to which we are accustomed, but the Elizabethans were nearer to the Middle Ages than to us in questions of the supernatural.

The demoniacal possession of Gratiana, was, as we have seen, hinted by Tourneur: there is a picture of Brachiano already suffering the torments of the damned before his death in *The White Devil.* In *The Duchess of Malfi* there is a more lengthy application of this same technique; something of the same method was to be used in *The Changeling.*

Charles Lamb was, perhaps, nearer to approaching a direct description of the effect of the play than he realised, when he said of the tortures in Act 4:

All the several parts of the dreadful apparatus with which the Duchess' death is ushered in, are not more remote from the conceptions of ordinary vengeance, than the strange character of the sufferings which they seem to bring upon their victims, is beyond the imagination of ordinary poets. As they are not like inflictions of *this life,* so her language seems *not of this world.*

She has lived among horrors till she is become "native and endowed unto that element". She speaks the dialect of despair, her tongue has a smatch of Tartarus and the souls in bale.

There can be no doubt what the reading of Act 4 *suggested* to Lamb. Of course, as in the case of Gratiana's demoniacal possession, it is not something which can be taken as a matter of fact. It will be perhaps easier to take it as a kind of over-shadowing metaphor, but a metaphor of such force and strength that the mind is suspended between accepting it as that or between taking it as something more. The whole handling of the supernatural on the Elizabethan stage was of a delicacy and subtlety to which justice has not been done.

Mr Lucas locates Act 4, Scene 2, as "somewhere in prison", for, as he points out, there are no indications of time or space. It was the neutrality of the Elizabethan stage which made these ambivalences possible. The scene is not laid in a definite place: it is, as it were, in a different dimension; there is a curious stillness and hush about the scene, a static quality and a sense of timelessness. The Duchess herself is fixed in an attitude of grief. She says to her maid:

> Who do I look like now?
> Like to your picture in the gallery,
> A deal of life in show but none in practice....
> Very proper. (4. 2. 32 ff.)

The Duchess is not excessively self-conscious; the speech is simply meant to point out the nature of their response to the audience. Whatever it is, it is not naturalistic.

Before considering the question of the supernatural in more detail, it will be necessary to analyse at some length the character of the Duchess. For an obvious objection presents itself; the Duchess is not a criminal, and there is no reason why she should be thought of as suffering the tortures of the damned. It is true that the attitude towards her is entirely sympathetic; but it is not simple.

Painter, the immediate "source", translating Belleforest, takes an attitude which cannot be dismissed as hostile, but which is not approving. According to him, the Duchess was guilty of some indelicacy in remarrying at all; of great impropriety in marrying her servant. He appreciates both Antonio's worth, and her purity of motive, stressing her horror of fornication, but he disapproves of the marriage and not merely because of its results.

His Duchess attempted to do her duty and live a widow, but she "was moved with that desire that pricketh others that be of flesh and blood". She is bewildered by it: "I have a certain unacquainted lust and know not very well what it is that moveth me.... Pygmalion loved once a marble pillar, and I have but one desire, the colour whereof is more pale than death.... It apperteyneth me to show myself as issued from the noble house of Aragon".

Painter describes the special attractiveness of Antonio's character at more length than Webster; but he was too ready blindly to follow his "blind Fortune". In a passage that throws light on Act 4, Painter adds "as ordinarily you see that lovers conceive all things for their advantage, and fantasy dreams agreeable to their most desire, *resembling the mad and Bedlam persons* which have before their eyes the figured fancies which cause the conceit of their fury".

The Duchess and Antonio are led by their instincts, and it is perfectly possible to deprecate the attitude without condemning either the instincts or the persons. The maid blames her for lack of foresight: Painter is deploring the absence of an essential fineness which is not of the intelligence or the feelings alone, but which distinguishes the awakened self from the "natural man".

That is Painter at his highest level; at his lowest he condemns the Duchess, in the strident tones recorded by F. L. Lucas: "she made her way to pleasure, which she lusted more than marriage, the same serving her but for a mask and coverture to hide her follies and shameless lusts, for which she did the penance that her folly deserved", for she was "of those that believe they be constrained to follow the force of their mind; and may easily subdue themselves to the laws of honesty and virtue", though he always allows "they be not guided by wisdom's lore, which suffer...a young wife long to live in widow's state".

Thomas Beard, who also recorded the story, took the cruder attitude throughout. "Albeit the Cardinal's cruelty was most famous...yet God's justice bare the sway that used him as an instrument to punish those who under a veil of secret marriage thought it lawful for man to commit any villainy."

Such were the current interpretations of the Duchess' marriage. Webster had to work upon these, as Shakespeare had to work on Kyd's *Hamlet*. It is useless to pretend that he could behave as though his sources did not exist; he could modify them and he did, but that meant absorbing them into a more comprehensive whole.

There was a general theoretic objection to the remarriage of widows. Webster expresses it himself in his character of *A Virtuous Widow*: "She is like the purest gold employed for princes' medals: she never received but one man's impression.... To change her name were, she thinks, to commit a sin should make her unworthy of her husband's calling". It was a continual topic of sermons and crops up in all the manuals of conduct. So advanced a thinker as Juan Luis Vives could say:

For to condemn and reprove utterly second marriage, it were a point of heresy. How be it that better is to abstain than marry again is counselled not only by Christian pureness but by pagans.... The women of Almayne were not wont to marry but of maids, and though they were widows in their youth yet would they not marry again, and specially noble women. (*The Instructions of a Christian Woman*, Englished by R. Herde, Book 3, chap. 7.)

"Better is to marry than burn" was the best comfort a
widow could get: "none wed the second but who killed
the first" was more customary. Catholics did penance before
a second marriage.

To marry out of one's class was definitely wrong, being
contrary to the teaching of the Church, and to the whole
conception of "order" and "degree" which was still so
potent a force. To marry secretly and without the advice
of kindred was also no light offence, however it may appear
to-day: Thomas Becon, in his *Boke of Matrimony*, is particularly eloquent on this subject.

Naturally practice and theory were at variance, but that
did not discredit the theory. Satire upon the widow's wiles
is common in comedy, but it implies at least an ideal standard
to be transgressed. *The Widow's Tears*, the most mature and
complete attack, puts into the mouth of Cynthia "such
imprecations to her heart if it should ever receive a second
impression: her open and oft detestation of that incestuous
life (as she termed it) of widows' marriages...that to wed
a second was no better than to cuckold the first..." (2. 2.
25 ff.). However abstinence is bemocked, it could not have
been a target at all if it were not accepted theoretically by
the majority of people as the proper thing. Middleton's
More Dissemblers besides Women is illuminating on the subject.

The ideal was adhered to in tragedy. Shakespeare has
three widows who remarry—Tamora, Gertrude and Regan;
in his histories only the wives of Edward IV and Richard III;
in comedy only the unpleasant widow in *The Taming of the
Shrew* and Paulina in *The Winter's Tale*, who is given in
marriage by the King. Shirley makes his Duchess Rosaura a
virgin widow; and on the question of marrying one's inferior,
which is also satirised in *The Widow's Tears*, Rymer, speaking
after the Restoration for the heroic code, says: "Whether a
Lady may better marry her Brother than her Groom is a
question more easily decided in Divinity than in Poetry".

External evidence could be amassed at more length, but it has no more than an indirect relation to the play. The point is that there were three reasons against the Duchess' marriage: she was a widow; she was of royal blood and had a duty to her rank; she acted simply on her liking, without advice, without the rites of the Church and without publishing her marriage. Her brothers advance all three reasons, but the second seems by far the most potent with them (I. I. 323; 2. 5. 30–60), though it is obviously the one of which Webster takes least account: it is refuted at length by the Duchess' rhetorical remark to Bosola, "He was basely descended" (3. 2. 299), and his reply.

There is no doubt that Webster saw the action of the brothers as quite diabolical. But he utilised the conventional "case" against the Duchess as material for the tragedy.

His Duchess is warm-hearted; wilful, if charmingly so (I. I. 382–3); she relies exclusively on her likings, her immediate feelings. The directness which makes her choose Antonio:

> Let old wives report
> I winked and chose a husband—   (I. I. 389–90)

makes her favour him dangerously before the court; makes her also ready to dismiss the inevitable from her mind, and live from hand to mouth, equivocating pitifully with her brothers. Antonio feels the degradation of it:

> The Great are like the Base: nay, they are the same
> When they take shameful ways to avoid shame—
> > (2. 3. 68–9)

so does the Duchess (3. 2. 190–3). Antonio has perhaps a mingling of ambition, but his case appears desperate to Delio:

> how fearfully
> Shows his ambition now (unfortunate Fortune)!—
> They pass through whirlpooles and deep woes do shun
> Who the event weigh ere the action's done—
> > (2. 4. 105–8)

while Cariola feels that the Duchess' marriage "shows a fearful madness".

The wooing scene, which is closed with this last sinister comment, has been justly praised for its charming humanity; but the echoes of Painter are significant:

> This is flesh and blood, Sir,
> 'Tis not the figure cut in Alabaster
> Kneels at my husband's tomb.   (1. 1. 519–21)

The constant shadowing with such dark images is to be explained as the tragic consciousness of the mature mind contemplating the naïve expectation of happiness, of "living happily ever after":

> O yonge fresshe folkes, he or she,
> In which ay love upgroweth with your age...
> Thinketh all nis but a faire
> This world, that passeth sone as floures faire!

It can also be plainly felt in the wooing scene that the Duchess is not a child: she, like Chaucer's Criseyde, is blind to the outcome, but she rather ignores it than remains ignorant of it. Her widowhood, which is stressed throughout the scene (1. 1. 446–7, 464, 520–5) means that she is well awake to the direction of her feelings; she handles the situation at the same time that she is guided by it (as in Painter). The combination of experience and immaturity is a piteous thing, when the isolation of the young Duchess is added to it: again it puts her with Criseyde, as Chaucer (not as Henryson) saw her. The force of the traditional attitude in both cases required an unusually mature and full mind to absorb the cruder judgment, and present something more than a merely romantic inversion of it. The Duchess is at first frank and lovely "flesh and blood" with all the graces of that state, and without a single superadded one. Not to feel her charm is impossible; not to feel her pleased recognition or invention of an indecent joke (1. 1. 375–81, 443–5), together with

Antonio's enthusiastic tribute to her continence (1. 1. 202–9), is to miss the complexity of the situation. It is Painter's "certain unacquainted lust".

The violent abuse which Ferdinand pours upon her for two scenes, when he hears of the rumours, cannot be discounted. It has been pointed out to me that the reason was that he thought her to be unmarried; but what he thought has less effect than what he says. The audience knows that it is all false as a matter of fact, but that does not deprive it of all suggestive power. It is not necessary to invoke so mechanical a rule as Schücking's Objective Truth of Villainous Statement; the sense of moral outrage behind the lines is so strong that it carries its own force. Ferdinand sees only lechery: the Duchess defends herself on the grounds of "nature".

> Why might I not marry?
> I have not gone about in this, to create
> Any new world or custom....
> Why should I
> Of all the other princes of the world
> Be cased up, like a holy relic? I have youth
> And a little beauty.   (3. 2. 127–9, 160–3)

The mirth of the bedchamber scene is of a tone to fit this. The Duchess lives known to the common people as a strumpet; she "used religion as her riding hood" to woo Antonio, beginning her talk with laying up treasure in Heaven. Antonio is not religious (5. 2. 135–8) nor do they desire the rites of the Church for themselves (1. 1. 558) or their children (3. 3. 76): when Cariola calls the feigned pilgrimage "blasphemy" she is dismissed as a "superstitious fool" (3. 2. 367). Some of these statements are made by the Cardinal and are "unreliable"; they only confirm the general temper of the early scenes.

It is through the awakening of responsibility that the Duchess develops into a tragic figure. She faces Ferdinand's dagger, the banishment from Ancona, and the parting from Antonio. It is always she who plans: Antonio is acquiescent and at one point he ungenerously sinks to suspecting Cariola.

The pilgrims who describe their banishment from Ancona give the orthodox religious judgment:

> Who would have thought
> So great a lady would have matched herself
> Unto so mean a person? yet the Cardinal
> Bears himself much too cruel. (3. 4. 25–8)

This is an echo of the White Devil's trial:

> She hath lived ill.
> —True, but the Cardinal's too bitter.

The Duchess parts from Antonio with foreboding: "This puts me in mind of death". Antonio speaks like "a dying father" and their next meeting will be, as she hints, in "The Eternal Church". But she accepts her fate willingly:

> Yet (O Heaven) thy heavy hand is in't...
>   ...naught made me ere
> Go right but Heaven's scourge stick. (3. 5. 92–5)

This is entirely a new mood for the Duchess, and it is one which grows upon her. She never acknowledges that her brothers have the right to judge her; but she does acknowledge that she is in need of a corrected judgment. It is in this development of the Duchess that the interest of the prison scenes lie, and by this they are saved from being merely sadistic exhibitions.

Bosola, the agent of the brothers, now appears to capture her. From the first they have been described as diabolic: "the devil speaks" in the Cardinal (1. 1. 190) who corrupts Bosola with money:

> your Devils
> Which Hell calls Angels...
> And should I take these, they'll take me to Hell.
>   (1. 1. 285–8)

Bosola, however, takes them. When he appears to capture

the Duchess he is vizarded as becomes his diabolic function, and the first words he speaks are a judgment:

> You must see your husband no more. (3. 5. 115)

The Duchess denies the judge rather than the judgment:

> What *devil* art thou that counterfeitest *Heaven's thunder*?

He tells her that she is like a silly bird allured to the nets, and that his warning serves only to scare her off. The image echoes her own wistful lines on her greatness and its incompatibility with her womanliness:

> The birds that live i' the field
> On the wild benefit of nature, live
> Happier than we: for they may choose their mates
> And carol their sweet pleasures to the Spring.
>
> (3. 5. 25–8)

The Duchess now enters her purgatory. Purgatory and hell were often equated in the Elizabethan mind (the evidence of Hamlet's ghost may be recalled); so that in purgatory the souls were attended by devils, but they did not stay for ever and they willingly accepted their pain. The shift of mood to the supernatural can be felt in the tenseness of the movement and seen in the imagery.

> I have heard that Charon's boat serves to convey
> All o'er the dismal lake, but brings none back again.
>
> (3. 5. 126–7)

Superficially this is irrelevant, one of Webster's trimmings: its implications are profound.

The Duchess does not at once attain to peace. She welcomes misery, but in a bitter mood of disdain. Bosola adds that she has natural cravings; she is still both Duchess and woman:

> This restraint
> Like English mastiffs that grow fierce with tying
> Make her too passionately apprehend
> The pleasures she's kept from. (4. 1. 14–17)

This is again an echo of *The White Devil* (1. 2. 188 ff.).

The Duchess is shown sitting in darkness. Ferdinand approaches and she asks his pardon. He retorts with savage insults about her children, and she says then:

> Do you visit me for this?
> You violate a sacrament of the Church
> Shall make you howl in hell for it.　(4. 1. 45–7)

The Duchess had not sought the sacrament of marriage in the Church, or that of baptism, but she is at present experiencing the sacrament of penance.

She is tormented by the shows of her dead husband and children, which, like all the horrors of hell, are essentially unreal. At once all natural desire leaves her; to go on living is only to prolong her pain.

> There is not between heaven and earth one wish
> I stay for after this....
> That's the greatest torture souls feel in hell,
> In hell: that they must live and cannot die.
>
> 　　　　　　　　　　　(4. 1. 72–3, 82–3)

She is still imperfect of will, feeling only the pains of complete loss. She suggests various Christian ways of death in a savage jesting way; she curses the stars, the whole universe. This is near fulfilling Ferdinand's aim, to bring her "to despair" (4. 1. 140), but Bosola thinks otherwise:

> Send her a penitential garment to put on
> Next to her delicate skin, and furnish her
> With beads and prayer books.　(4. 1. 143–5)

Ferdinand is not concerned with her soul's salvation, as he says; he is feeding the bonfire of his revenge, however he persuades himself that it is "intemperate agues makes physicians cruel".

The next scene contains the famous masque of madmen. The Elizabethan theory of madness as demoniacal possession is well known; it was often used to suggest the supernatural on the stage, as in *King Lear* and *The Changeling*. Before they enter, the Duchess speaks the most Dantesque lines in Webster; they alone would be sufficient to show that her afflictions are "not of this life".

> The Heavens o'er my head seem made of molten brass,
> The Earth of flaming sulphur: yet I am not mad.
> I am acquainted with sad misery
> As the tanned galley slave is with his oar,
> Necessity makes me suffer constantly,
> And custom makes it easy.   (4. 2. 27–32)

Then the madmen come in. Their talk is of adultery and fornication: it is not worth quoting, but it is not irrelevant. The references to hell fire are frequent: "Hell is a mere glass house where the devils are constantly blowing up women's souls on hot irons and the fire never goes out".

After the dance of the madmen, Bosola enters as an old man. He has given a reason (4. 1. 161) but the larger purpose is to symbolise Time and the decay of the temporal. The procession which follows later is modelled as Mr Lucas has noted, on that of the condemned prisoners at Newgate. But first Bosola has his say. He revives the image of the caged bird, which has hitherto indicated the conflict between the Duchess' rank and her person, the "spirit of greatness" and the "spirit of woman" (1. 1. 576).

Didst thou ever behold a lark in a cage? Such is the soul in the body: this world is like her little turf of grass, and the Heaven o'er our heads like her looking glass, only gives us a miserable knowledge of the small compass of our prison.

Imprisonment is no longer the special lot of the Duchess, but that of all: "bones built in us, flesh filled, blood brimmed the curse" of Time and Place.

Then Bosola, in lines which would be unbearably cruel if the reference were conscious, recalls the jests of the bed-chamber scene about grey hairs and unquiet sleeping. But the Duchess keeps her pride of rank, though as a woman she has lost everything: "I am Duchess of Malfi still".

Bosola replies by showing that pride is a tomb, which may imprison princes even after death, and debar them from Heaven.

Princes' images on their tombs do not lie as they were wont, seeming to pray up to Heaven,...they are not carved with their eyes fixed on the stars: but as their minds were wholly bent upon the earth, the self same way they seem to turn their faces.

The three steps of Bosola's preparation may be considered irrelevant moralising, but if so, it must also be thought fortuitous that the Duchess turns from

> I am Duchess of Malfi still

to

> I have so much obedience in my blood
> I wish it in their veins to do them good. (4. 2. 167–8)

After the dirge, with its ceremonies of purification, she puts off both the woman and the Duchess. She accepts the most shameful form of death in an attitude far from the despair of the first scene:

> I perceive death, *now I am well awake*,
> Best gift is they can give or I can take...
> Pull, and pull strongly, for your able strength
> Must pull down Heaven upon me:
> Yet stay, heaven gates are not so highly arched
> As Princes' palaces—they that enter there
> Must go upon their knees. (4. 2. 230–41)

It is after this that her "innocence" is proclaimed by Ferdinand. She did no sin before the law, nor was he her judge (4. 2. 322–8). The Duchess revives for a moment, and Bosola, who feels himself damned, as Cariola had said he was, imagines the heavens open to take him up to mercy. With an exquisite natural touch the Duchess catches up the word: but it is not to Bosola that she speaks. Then she dies, and he pronounces final judgment on her and himself:

> O sacred innocence, that sweetly sleeps
> On turtles feathers: whilst a guilty conscience
> Is a black register wherein is writ
> All our good deeds and bad: a perspective
> That shows us hell.   (4. 2. 383–7)

In the last act, the Cardinal and Ferdinand are both given up to the devil: Bosola dies in a mist; the lustful Julia, who had acted as a minor foil to the Duchess, is killed by kissing a poisoned bible, on which she was swearing "most religiously" to keep the Cardinal's sin a secret.

In law, the Duchess was innocent; by social standards she was at first reckless and intemperate; by ethical and religious standards she was an instinctive creature awakened by suffering to maturity. Hers was original sin, not personal sin; like King Lear's uncontrolled greed for affection and rage of frustration. What happened to the Duchess was as little deserved as what happened to Lear: neither of them get common justice; by the end of the play neither of them desire it. For in the timeless central scenes on the heath and in the prison, both have passed outside the ordinary modes of being, and its standards no longer apply.

The guilty aspect of the Duchess is strictly subordinate. The dominant attitude is that she is innocent, but the clash of opposite views accounts for several apparent irrelevances and inconsistencies.

It is impossible to fit the content of the play into a logical narrative. The minor contradictions of fact have been recognised and accepted; for instance, the three years which elapse between Acts 2 and 3 when so much happens at Amalfi and nothing anywhere else. Webster refutes the obvious criticism by underlining the situation (3. 1. 8–11): "Methinks 'twas yesterday". It is parallel to the three years' interval in *Jude the Obscure*, when Sue's children were born, and allows a similar sense of stability in the marriage to heighten the catastrophe, besides providing a sufficiency of children for a respectable holocaust: one would have looked scanty.

Questions of fact at this level are of little importance. But there are some contradictions of a more serious kind, which involve incompatibilities in the emotional structure of the play.

At 4. 1. 66 the Duchess is shown "the artificial figures of Antonio and his children looking as if they were dead". *Children*: Antonio had only one with him, so that the plural means that the Duchess saw also the bodies of the two younger who had been captured with her. The deception is not unmasked till the very end (4. 2. 377) when Bosola tells her the truth as she is dying. The conviction that all the children are dead is behind the heavy despair of 4. 2: it justifies the complete hopelessness of that scene as compared with 4. 1, its whole fixed and rigid grief. Yet the Duchess says to Cariola:

> I prithee look thou give my little boy
> Some syrup for his cold, and let the girl
> Say her prayers ere she sleep.   (4. 2. 207–9)

Apart from the obvious and unpleasant pathos of these lines the suggestion that the Duchess knows her children to be alive removes the whole emotional prop and scaffolding of the scene. She had been in a peace "beyond hope and beyond despair": this touch of "humanity" is as out of place as it is offensive in itself. The factual contradiction is of comparatively small importance.

This is Webster's most serious fault. He was capable of extraordinary power over the single phrase, yet again and again he produces one which is irrelevant to the feeling of the scene as a whole, or to the character, or to the reader's feelings towards the characters. The felicitous phrase is there for its own sake; or, at most, the touching sentiment, the poignant feeling is there for *its* own sake, without any regard to the structure of the feelings as a whole.

The last act of *The Duchess of Malfi* is a series of wholly impressionistic scenes, for Webster had fairly exhausted himself. The torments of the mad Ferdinand, of the Cardinal who is in "despair" (5. 4. 31–2), and of Bosola have all a familiar accent; they die in "a mist" or "a storm" in which the devil "rocks his own child". The dying speech of Bosola is unnecessary after the dying speech of Flaminio.

This is the danger of the note-book method. Webster wrote slowly—"I confess I do not write with a goose quill winged with two feathers". In his best passages, though less than half the phrases may be original, they are firmly woven together, as a nest out of straw and twigs. At other times each epigrammatic phrase stands out sharply, so that sometimes Webster seems to be a collector of *mots justes* only. This lack of structure can be felt in the movement of the verse:

> Prosperity doth bewitch men, seeming clear,
> But seas do laugh, show white when rocks are near——
> We cease to grieve, cease to be fortune's slaves,
> Nay cease to die, by dying —— Art thou gone,
> And thou so near the bottom? false report
> Which says that women vie with the nine Muses
> For nine tough durable lives —— I do not look
> Who went before nor who shall follow me,
> No, at myself I will begin and end ——
> While we look up to heaven, we confound
> Knowledge with knowledge —— O, I am in a mist.

At each dash there is a break in tone and tempo. First a generalised "sentence"; then a Malcontent stoicism; then a human question tailing off into cynicism; another stoical phrase; another sententious maxim; and a poetic image in Webster's best manner. If this is compared with Vindice's address to the skull, it will be seen how much easier and more coherent is Tourneur's verse.

. This way of writing makes each speech unconnected with any other speech. It explains how, in his later work,

Webster could write passages of poetry as fine as anything he had ever done, and embed them in the middle of stuff which was of a totally different tone and temper. The dirge in *The Devil's Law Case* and one or two other speeches there are not inferior to the best parts of *The White Devil* and *The Duchess of Malfi*. This argument cannot be urged against those two plays, whose homogeneity is remarkable. But it indicates a latent danger in Webster's style, present from the beginning; a unity which is *only* a unity of tone and temper is likely to be precarious and unstable, since it is founded upon eclecticism, and dependent upon continuity of mood alone. In this respect the study of Webster should provide a corrective to those who hastily assume that poetic structure is a matter of choice of words only, and not of permanent impulses behind the choice of words—a caution which seems not unnecessary in view of the recent developments of Elizabethan dramatic criticism.

CHAPTER IX

Thomas Middleton

MIDDLETON'S tragedies are as similar in their methods of construction as they are different from the plays already considered. Rowley's name appears on the title page of *The Changeling*, but it is difficult to see the possibility of his sharing in the main plot, for its unity is of a kind which not even the most sympathetic collaboration could achieve.

The connection between the two plots of this play is, however, very carefully worked out. It is indicated even in the title, "The *Changeling*", which describes both Antonio, the innocent, and Beatrice-Joanna, the inconstant woman (a usual meaning—*vide Anything for a Quiet Life*, 2. 1. 71, and *N.E.D. sub verb.*).

The construction of the play is masked by the greater naturalism of the treatment. Compared with the characters of earlier plays, Middleton's are fuller, more natural and human. Their motives and actions may be conventionally "Italianate" (they have vestigial remains of the Revenge code in the melancholy of Tomazo the revenger and the appearance of the ghost), but their feelings and responses are normal. Beatrice-Joanna's famous outburst, when the murderer demands possession of her as a reward:

> Why 'tis impossible thou canst be so wicked
> Or shelter such a cunning cruelty
> To make his death the murderer of my honour—
>
> (3. 4. 121 ff.)

is only the most obvious illustration of Middleton's interest in the way the mind works. Deflores' brief plea to the man he has cuckolded, when he hears Beatrice-Joanna crying out in futile anger:

> Let me go to her, sir— (5. 3. 112)

is so assured of his right to calm her that the husband can
but send him in.

The construction of the play is, however, partly dependent
on themes: briefly it may be described as a study in the conflict of passion and judgment, and of the transforming power
of love. All the characters (save Alsemero) are entirely at
the mercy of their feelings, which are instinctive and un-
controllable. Judgment is blinded, so that the characters
practise all kinds of deception and self-deception to gain
their ends. Love is "a tame madness", a kind of possession
which seizes upon a man and "changes" him so that he is
no longer recognisable. In the main plot the themes are
worked out naturalistically; in the subplot the use of the
madmen, and of more literal transformations, as well as
more farcical action, makes a kind of phantasmagoria. The
key words are "change", "judgment" and "will" (in the
sense of instinctive desire, often of sensual desire, as in Shakespeare). The connection between plot and subplot is summed
up in the final scene where the structure of themes is explained.

> *Alsemero.* What an opacous body had that moon
> That last changed on us! here is beauty changed
> To ugly whoredom; here servant-obedience
> To a master-sin, imperious murder;
> I, a supposed husband, changed embraces
> With wantonness—but that was paid before—
> Your change is come too from an ignorant wrath
> To knowing friendship. Are there any more on's?
> *Antonio.* Yes sir I was changed too from a little ass as I was
> to a great fool as I am: and had like to ha' been changed to the
> gallows, but that you know my innocence always excuses me.
> *Franciscus.* I was changed from a little wit to be stark mad
> Almost for the same purpose.
> *Isabella* (*to her husband*). Your change is still behind,
> But deserve best your transformation. (5. 3. 199 ff.)

"Transformation" is a useful word to describe the character

changes in the play: people are changed in the eyes of others, and they are also changed radically in themselves by the power of love.

The play opens with Alsemero falling in love. It was "in the Temple" which he instinctively feels to be an omen (the use of omens as what would now be called promptings of the unconscious mind plays a large part in the play). In any case he is already transformed; from an ardent traveller he becomes a loiterer, from a woman hater a courtier so that his friend cries:

How now: the laws of the Medes are changed sure: salute a
woman: he kisses too: wonderful! (1. 1. 60)

This sense of shock and discovery is the same in kind (though not in intensity of course) as the "discoveries" of Beatrice-Joanna, of Isabella and of Alsemero.

The dialogue which follows states the main theme. Alsemero roundly declares his love, to which Beatrice-Joanna replies:

Be better advised, sir:
Our eyes are sentinels unto our *judgments*
And should give certain *judgment* what they see;
But they are rash sometimes and tell us wonders
Of common things, which when our *judgments* find
They can then check the eyes and call them blind.

(1. 1. 73 ff.)

Alsemero has seen her twice, however, and this he considers amply sufficient for the co-operation of eyes and judgment.

Deflores is then introduced, and Beatrice-Joanna's instinctive hatred of him. "She knows no cause for't but a peevish *will*." Beatrice-Joanna and Alsemero have a long discussion on the idiosyncratic character of the will (compare *The Merchant of Venice*, 4. 1. 44–62) and its instinctive pre-critical judgments. Beatrice-Joanna's father then appears and a conversation, in which asides and equivocations are frequent, shows to what extent Beatrice-Joanna's "will" is already transforming her. She says:

> I shall *change* my saint, I fear me: I find
> A giddy turning in me— (1. 1. 158–9)

an echo of Alsemero's "I keep the same church, same devotion" which points the contrast between them. Her father explains to Alsemero that she is betrothed to Alonzo de Piracquo: immediately his plans change, he must go away. The father will have her married at once, "I'll want my *will* else". Beatrice-Joanna adds aside, "I shall want mine if you do it". Finally Deflores, remaining to soliloquise, reveals his plight as the same one:

> I know she hates me
> Yet cannot choose but love her: no matter,
> If but to vex her, I will haunt her still:
> Though I get nothing else, I'll have my will.
>
> (1. 1. 237–40)

The second act opens with Beatrice-Joanna busily deluding her own judgment. Alsemero's friend has just arranged an assignation, and she catches at his discretion as a justification for herself.

> How wise is Alsemero in his friend,
> It is a sign he makes his choice with *judgment*:
> Then I appear in nothing more approved
> Than making choice of him.... (2. 1. 6ff.)

She loves "with intellectual eyesight" as Alsemero thought he did.

Instead of Alsemero, Deflores arrives. He describes his own infatuation coolly (he is well aware of his ugliness, so that only "intellectual eyesight" could ever endure him) yet he does not despair, and when Beatrice-Joanna turns on "this ominous ill-faced fellow" he endures her patiently. He has a certain self-knowledge which sets him above the others, if it does not give him self-mastery.

> Why am I not an ass to devise ways
> Thus to be railed at? I must see her still,
> I shall have a mad qualm within this hour again
> I know't. (2. 1. 77 ff.)

When he is gone Beatrice-Joanna enlarges on the feeling of
danger he inspires in her. The scene concludes with an interview with her unwelcome lover, Piracquo. He refuses to
recognise her very plain dislike of him, since love has over-
powered his judgment too. His brother comments on his
incredulity:

> Why, this is love's tame *madness*,

a significant link with the subplot.

All this interweaving of self-deception and self-awareness
is supported by dialogue of the greatest ease and naturalness.
There is no sustained heroic pitch as in Tourneur or Webster;
the climaxes of feeling are simply expressed, not in obviously
rich and poetic language.

> I have within my eyes all my desires.... (2. 2. 8)

>> Here was a course
> Found to bring sorrow on her way to death
> The tears would ne'er have dried till blood had
>> choked 'em. (2. 2. 37–9)

The scene in which Deflores is given the commission to kill
Piracquo is one of ironic comedy. Having seen her secret
interview with Alsemero he has hopes for himself and when
Beatrice-Joanna seems more friendly he is really deceived
into thinking her judgment is changed.

> *Beatrice-Joanna.* You've pruned yourself, methinks: you were
>> not wont
> To look so amorously.
> *Deflores.* Not I—
> 'Tis the same phisnomy to a hair and pimple
> Which she called scurvy scarce an hour ago.
> How is this?
> *Beatrice-Joanna.* Come hither; nearer, man.
> *Deflores.* I'm up to the chin in heaven! (2. 2. 74 ff.)

8

At first he coaxes her into speaking because he half
believes she is in love with him. She is trying to get her
request out naturally and he makes things easy by impor-
tuning her.

> *Beatrice-Joanna.* Oh my Deflores!
> *Deflores.* How this? she calls me hers?
> Already, my Deflores—You were about
> To sigh out somewhat, madam?...
> *Beatrice-Joanna.* Would creation—
> *Deflores. Ay well said, that's it.*
> *Beatrice-Joanna.* Had made me man.
> *Deflores.* Nay that's not it.   (2. 2. 97 ff.)

He may be ironical, but it is hardly likely. They part
mutually deceived, Beatrice-Joanna rejoicing at being rid of
him and he in having won her.

The murder is quickly done and the great discovery scene
follows. Beatrice-Joanna is congratulating herself on her
judgment

> So wisdom by degrees works out her freedom.   (3. 4. 13)

Deflores is something more than complacent as he enters
and shows her the severed finger of Piracquo. She is horrified, for she had not visualised the murder; Deflores the
hired assassin was to stand between her and the dirty business
of the stabbing. He is quite calloused physically, and cannot
understand her qualms at sight of the ring—"the first token
my father made me send him". When she tells him to keep
the jewel, however, her coarseness is exposed in turn by
his retort:

> 'Twill hardly buy a capcase for one's conscience though
> To keep it from the worm, as fine as 'tis.   (3. 4. 45–6)

His anger rises as he realises her attitude towards himself.
The barriers of her modesty, dignity and stupidity are not
easily broken; she only thinks of him as a servant and at
first actually appeals to him on those grounds.

Think but upon the distance that creation
Set 'twixt thy blood and mine and keep thee there.

(3. 4. 131–2)

Deflores' reply suggests that she has become "transformed":
she is no longer the woman she was, since her love has
altered.

'Twas chang'd from thy first love, and that's a kind
Of whoredom in the heart, and he's chang'd now
To bring thy second on, thy Alsemero. (3. 4. 144–6)

She is "the deed's creature", and one with him. It will be
seen that later both Beatrice-Joanna and Alsemero acknowledge her transformation.

Deflores' speeches have also a naturalistic interpretation.
The pain of his disillusion can be felt behind his violence;
it breaks out finally in an appeal to her pity, as direct as hers
to him:

I live in pain now: that shooting eye
Will burn my heart to cinders. (3. 4. 152–3)

When she submits he drops to a tenderness heard again in
the final scene. It is one of Middleton's most daring and
most perfectly managed modulations of feeling:

Come rise and shroud your blushes in my bosom:
Silence is one of pleasure's best receipts:
Thy peace is wrought for ever in this yielding.

(3. 4. 167–9)

The last two acts are worked out in the same manner as
the first three. Beatrice-Joanna makes the same mistake with
Diaphanta as she did with Deflores. "'Tis a nice piece gold
cannot purchase", and so she bribes her maid to take her
place on the marriage night.

Diaphanta's lust nearly wrecks the plan, as Deflores' had
done. He arrives and suggests an alarm of fire, but Beatrice-

Joanna is as slow now as heretofore to see the point of his proposals.

> *Beatrice-Joanna.* How, fire, sir? that may endanger the whole house.
> *Deflores.* You talk of danger when your fame's on fire?
> (5. 1. 33–4)

The trick of the "magic" glass of water by which Alsemero tests her virginity is not out of place, for it belongs with the "omens" and other irrational elements rather than with the naturalism of character and speech; it is also reinforced by the stronger suggestion of "magic" in the subplot.

Alsemero is the only character whose "will" does not overpower his judgment. Beatrice-Joanna fears his clear sight (4. 1. 1–17). He is contrasted with Piracquo who would not hear a word against his betrothed:

> Were she the sole glory of the earth,
> Had eyes that could shoot fire into Kings' breasts
> And touched, she sleeps not here.   (4. 2. 106–8)

The quarrel with Tomazo de Piracquo seems "ominous" to him; but his innocence relieves him. At the moment of discovery he remembers his early scruples:

> O the place itself e'er since
> Has crying been for vengeance! the Temple....
> (5. 3. 73–4)

Beatrice-Joanna now appears hideous to him, even physically hideous, and in that is akin to Deflores. Her transformation is complete, through the discovery of her deceit.

> The black mask
> That so continually was worn upon't
> Condemns the face for ugly ere't be seen.   (5. 3. 3–5)
> O thou art all deformed.   (5. 3. 78)

Beatrice-Joanna miscalculates a third time: she confesses murder but denies adultery, thinking Alsemero will pardon the greater crime, since it was done for his sake. She knows him no better than Deflores or Diaphanta; he rejects her with horror and it is left for Deflores' resolution to cut the thread, by murder and suicide. Beatrice-Joanna recognises her transformation, at first indirectly: of the word "whore" she says:

> It blasts a beauty to *deformity*
> Upon whatsoever face that breath falls
> It strikes it ugly. (5. 3. 33–5)

Finally she recognises her union with Deflores, and the significance of her first "will" to dislike him (5. 3. 157–60).

The revenge of Tomazo de Piracquo is also a matter of will. At first he likes Deflores, but later he feels an inexplicable recoil from him.

The subplot is connected with the main plot chiefly by implication. It acts as a kind of parallel or reflection in a different mode: their relationship is precisely that of masque and antimasque, say the two halves of Jonson's *Masque of Queens*. The direct links at the end have already been mentioned: there is also a scene of parallel action, first noted by Mr Empson, in which Isabella, the wife of the madhouse keeper, is detected with her lover by a servant Lollio. He proceeds to exact the same price from Isabella that Deflores did from Beatrice-Joanna:

Come, sweet rogue: kiss me, my little Lacedemonian: let me feel how thy pulses beat: thou hast a thing about thee would do a man pleasure, I'll lay my hand on it. (3. 3. 247–50)

Her reply is an inversion of Beatrice-Joanna's. She threatens in turn:

> Be silent, mute,
> Mute as a statue, or his injunctions
> For me enjoying, shall be to cut thy throat,
> I'll do't, though for no other purpose. (3. 3. 253–6)

Deflores enjoyed Beatrice-Joanna in return for cutting a throat.

Isabella has two lovers, who are disguised as a fool and a madman in order to gain access to her. Antonio, the fool, throws off his hideous disguise, which he calls a *deformity* (3. 3. 195) and appears as her lover suddenly:

> This shape of folly shrouds your dearest love,
> The truest servant to your powerful beauties,
> Whose *magic* had the force thus to *transform* me.
>
> (3. 3. 127–9)

It is parallel to Deflores' appearance as the lover of Beatrice-Joanna. The quality of the surprise is similar (not, of course, the intensity). The other lover never actually encounters her, but sends a letter in which he says:

Sweet Lady, having now cast off this counterfeit cover of a madman, I appear to your best *Judgment* a true and faithful lover of your beauty...(Love) shapes and transhapes, destroys and builds again....

In the same scene Isabella puts on the disguise of a madwoman to meet the fool; but she is only temporarily transformed. Her speeches are full of references to Dedalus and Icarus, which suggest the dangerous nature of their secret and the preciousness of the reward. But the fool does not recognise her, and so she returns to her former state, and is never actually unfaithful to her ridiculous husband.

The chorus of madmen depict the bestial element in man, rather as Caliban does, or the rout in *Comus*. At the climax of the subplot, when Isabella is hard pressed by Antonio, Lollio cries "Cuckoo! cuckoo!" and there is the direction:

> *Madmen above, some as birds, others as beasts.*

Bullen and other editors rearrange this, but it clearly means that the madmen appear on the upper stage in the masquing habits which they are to wear at their entertainment at Beatrice-Joanna's wedding. They are a symbolic presentation of evil. Isabella explains:

> They act their fantasies in any shapes [i.e. costumes]
> Suiting their present thoughts.

Already they have been heard within crying at the game of barley-break:

> Catch there: catch the last couple in hell! (3. 3. 173)

The old worn pun gains in horror when Deflores echoes it to Alsemero in the final scene:

> I coupled with your mate
> At barley-break: now we are left in hell. (5. 3. 165–6)

Vermandero adds, "It circumscribes us here", thinking of the actual chalk ring.

The supernatural element in the main plot is veiled: it depends on the omens and the "magic" effects of Alsemero's chemistry. The subplot is fantastic and pictorial. The masque of madmen, ostensibly prepared for the wedding, is actually given in rehearsal before Isabella at the end of Act 4. She is summoned to it:

> Away then, and guide them in, Lollio:
> Entreat your mistress to see this sight.

The importance of this masque can be gauged by the comparison with that in Ford's *The Lover's Melancholy* (3. 3). Here the doctor Corax has a masque of melancholy men to cure the melancholy of the Prince. The different types of the disease are taken from Burton, and each is symbolically dressed. For instance, Lycanthropia has "his face whited, with black shag hair, and long nails and with a piece of raw meat". The wanton melancholy is "a Sea-Nymph big-bellied, singing and dancing", the point of this being of course that *mermaid* was slang for prostitute.

The Prince remaining unmoved, Corax adds:

> One only kind of Melancholy
> Is left untouched: 'twas not in art
> To personate the shadow of that fancy:
> 'Tis named love-melancholy...
> Love is the tyrant of the heart: it darkens
> Reason, confounds discretion: deaf to counsel
> It runs a headlong course to desperate madness.

The Prince, like Claudius in *Hamlet*, breaks off the revels abruptly. The significance of this passage with its symbolic treatment of madmen and the connection between love and madness involved in the symbolism is perhaps all the stronger for there being no trace of any direct influence of Middleton.

Throughout the scenes of the subplot of *The Changeling*, riddling games and tableaux keep up the bizarre horror.

> Here's a fool behind a knave, that's I: and between us two fools there is a knave, that's my master: 'tis but we three, that's all.
>
> We three, we three, cousin. (I. 2. 202 ff.)

This is the husband posed between Lollio, his servant, and Antonio, his "patient", both of whom are deceiving him at the moment when they so firmly assert that he is the knave and they the fools. So Isabella is posed between her husband and her two lovers throughout the play. So Beatrice-Joanna is posed between her husband and her two lovers, Piracquo and Deflores, in the one scene where the supernatural is allowed to intrude overtly into the main plot, and the silent ghost of Alonzo appears to Deflores and Beatrice-Joanna as they plot the second murder, that of the waiting woman Diaphanta. Yet even here the tone is kept quiet: to Deflores the ghost is only a "mist of conscience", while Beatrice-Joanna does not even see it clearly enough to recognise it: it felt an "ill thing" that left a shivering sweat upon her. So firmly does each half of the play retain its own proper atmosphere, and yet so closely are they interwoven with each other.

Women, Beware Women is a slighter play than *The Changeling*. Its themes are nearer to a thesis; the moralising is sharply cut off and put into the mouth of the Cardinal in Act 5. But this play is, however, also a study in the progressive deterioration of character. The first part of the play is much more natural than the latter half; here the writing is full of little observations of daily life, not sharpened like Webster's epigrams, but entering easily and unobtrusively. The characters are humble; consequently their speech is often quite near to that of Middleton's comedies. Yet at the end the catastrophe is achieved through the old convention of murder in a masque, though this is varied by making the masquers attack each other—a method not used since *The Spanish Tragedy*.

Plot and subplot are contrasted in their action: in the main plot a love-marriage is wrecked by ambition; in the subplot a marriage of convenience cloaks an infamous love affair. They are united by the schemes of Livia who is the pander in both cases. Bianca stands between her lover, the Duke, and her husband, as Isabella does between Hippolito and the ward. Both have the innocence of ignorance at first, like Beatrice-Joanna; but the larger part played by mercenary calculations in this play (even Deflores was not mercenary) lowers the tone of it.

At the beginning Leantio introduces his new wife to his mother. His renunciation of riches (after stealing an heiress) is a little too smug; his sentiments do not sound as if they had ever been tested by experience; he is jauntily didactic.

> I find no wish in me bent sinfully
> To this man's sister or to that man's wife;
> In love's name let 'em keep their honesties
> And cleave to their own husbands: 'tis their duties.
>
> (I. I. 28 ff.)

Bianca is equally sure of herself:

> I'm as rich as virtue can be poor. (I. I. 128)

The mother's strictly practical remarks pass unheeded, yet they are shrewd enough. Leantio has wronged Bianca by bringing her to poverty, and may expect to hear of it. The scene is written in a tone of *naïveté*; all the characters have the same accent, and even the mother hardly ventures to question the enthusiastic idealism of her son.

In the next scene the contrast is evident; a marriage is being arranged. The tone is more dignified, especially in the protests of Isabella, the unfortunate subject of the bargain.

> O the heartbreakings
> Of miserable maids when love's enforced!
> Their best condition is but bad enough.
> When women have their choices, commonly,
> They do but buy their thraldoms, and bring great portions
> To men to keep them in subjection. (1. 2. 169ff.)

Even her affections are betrayed; for her uncle Hippolito, whose love she had valued, reveals that

> Blood, that should be love, is mixed with lust—
>
> (1. 2. 231)

and Isabella vows to see him no more.

The next scene shows the ingenuous lovers taking leave of each other. It is chiefly their affection which is stressed, yet the purely sensuous nature of it is significant. Leantio's debate with himself, however, is virtuous simplicity itself, though this in itself is ominous, for such an innocence is ill-armed against "policy".

The next scene opens with an equally friendly and easy discourse between Livia and her brother Hippolito; but the upshot of this affectionate exchange is that she promises to procure their niece for him. Livia's affection is sincere; but, since she is simply without moral scruples of any kind, the very kindness of it becomes horrible, and suspicion is cast over all frankness and love when it can lead to such a speech as:

> You are not the first, brother, has attempted
> Things more forbidden than this seems to be.
> I'll minister all cordials now to you
> Because I'll cheer you up, sir; (2. 1. 46ff.)

and it is underlined by the short soliloquy which follows (beginning "Beshrew you, would I loved you not so well!").

In the scene of seduction which follows Livia falsely tells
her niece that she is not bound to obey her father, and
accept the unpleasant marriage, because she is not really his
child. Not a word is said of Hippolito, but there are indirect
hints.

> What a largeness in your will and liberty
> To take or to reject or to do both!
> For fools will serve to father wise men's children.
> All that you've time to think on. (2. 1. 160 ff.)

This refers in the first place to her "father" Fabricio, but
also as a suggestion that marriage with the foolish ward may
be wisdom. Isabella is completely deceived; she receives
Hippolito willingly; and still the simple, unsophisticated
accent is preserved in her speech, even while she plots the
covering marriage, making the whole thing seem more
pitiful than criminal, and quite effectively debarring any
heroics, any idea of "magnificence in sin".

> So discretion love me,
> Desert and judgment, I've content sufficient.
> She that comes once to be a housekeeper
> Must not look every day to fare well, sir,
> Like a young waiting gentlewoman in service,
> For she feeds commonly as her lady does,
> No good bit passes her but she gets a taste on't
> But when she comes to keep house for herself
> She's glad of some choice cates then once a week
> Or twice at most, and glad if she can get 'em....
> (2. 1. 215 ff.)

This scene is immediately followed by the masterly seduction
of Bianca. Livia's methods are precisely the same as before.
Her friendly accents are those of Isabella, the old mother,
or Bianca.

> Widow, come, come, I've a great quarrel to you:
> Faith, I must chide you that you must be sent for:
> You make yourself so strange, never come at us....
> (2. 2. 142 ff.)

The courteous interchange is heightened when Bianca appears to something more polished; but when Guardiano has finally enticed away and brought her to the Duke, the tone changes abruptly. The Duke is absolutely hard; to her pleas for release, he replies:

> I think
> Thou know'st the way to please me. I affect
> A passionate pleading 'bove an easy yielding:
> But never pitied any—they deserve none—
> That will not pity me.   (2. 2. 363 ff.)

He is completely mercenary too:

> Come, play the wise wench and provide for ever.
>   (2. 2. 387)

Bianca's virtue simply collapses. It seems to be the Duke's determination at this point rather than any ambition which wins her, just as Livia, having warned Hippolito, turns round and "cheers him up".

Guardiano's comment sums up the satirical attitude of the whole scene, during which the old mother has been innocently engaged in her game of chess.

> It's a witty age;
> Never were finer snares for women's honesties
> Than are devised in these days.   (2. 2. 401 ff.)

It is an attitude wholly devoid of the "pity" and "affection" which has been shown between Bianca, Leantio and the mother, or between Livia and Hippolito or Hippolito and Isabella, but Guardiano from the first has been frankly mercenary; that was his motive here:

> Advancement,
> I venture hard to find thee.   (2. 2. 409–10)

This new, hard, mercenary, ironical tone is to become increasingly prevalent and infect all the simpler characters as ambition gains a hold on them. Their "affections" are shown to be without roots.

Bianca enters again, but she is now changed. The Duke has opened her eyes to horror. "Infections, mists and mildews hang at's eyes." In a bitter aside she upbraids Guardiano, which he counters with one of the familiar, good-tempered speeches, which from now onwards are to sound only hollow and insincere.

> Well, so the duke love me,
> I fare not much amiss then: two great feasts
> Do seldom come together in one day,
> We must not look for't. (2. 2. 449 ff.)

(Compare Isabella's words, quoted above. The "practical" tone of their worldly wisdom again takes from the horror and makes the villainy seem petty.) Livia prophesies that even this resentment will not last long: "'Tis but a qualm of honour, 'twill away".

In the third act Bianca fulfils exactly her mother-in-law's prophecies in Act 1, Scene 1. Her "affections, wills and humours" are so commonplace in their form that the scene has the same air of ironic comedy as the preceding one: it reflects back to the seriousness of Isabella's pleas for freedom in marriage.

> Wives do not give away themselves to husbands
> To the end to be quite cast away: they look
> To be the better used and tendered rather
> Highlier respected and maintained the richer:
> They're well rewarded else for the free gift
> Of their whole life to a husband. (3. 1. 47 ff.)

This is directly connected with the mother's words in Act 1, Scene 2; and Leantio's soliloquy which follows, on the delights of wedlock, in its unctuous morality and its sensuality is a malicious preparation for his cool reception, and almost justifies the demonstration of humours which Bianca gives.

> She'll be so greedy now and cling about me…
> (3. 1. 107)

is met with

> No matter for a kiss, sir: let it pass:
> 'Tis but a toy, we'll not so much as mind it.   (3. 1. 150–1)

The messenger from the Duke soon arrives and makes his danger clear to Leantio, but at first he fears only the consequence of his having stolen Bianca, and imagines that if he keeps her in hiding, all will be well; her indignant refusal to be "rude and uncivil" disillusions him. The abrupt collapse of the mother's virtue is a minor ironic underlining of the situation; a few sweetmeats are sufficient to overcome her, and Leantio is left to soliloquise again. His two soliloquies are exactly parallel. In the first:

> Honest wedlock
> Is like a banqueting house built in a garden
> On which the spring's chaste flowers take delight
> To cast their modest odours.   (3. 1. 89 ff.)

The second opens:

> O thou, the ripe time of man's misery, wedlock,
> When all his thoughts, like overladen trees
> Crack with the fruits they bear, in cares, in jealousies.
>
> (3. 1. 271 ff.)

In the following scene Leantio is bribed with an office by the Duke and forced to watch the courtship of his wife. Hippolito also is forced to display the graces of Isabella by leading a dance with her, for the benefit of the ward. The similarity of their situations is suggested in their asides.

> *Leantio.* I'm like a thing that never yet was heard of
> Half merry and half mad: much like a fellow
> That eats his meat with a good appetite
> And wears a plague sore that would fright a country.
>
> (3. 2. 52 ff.)

> *Hippolito.* Come, my life's peace—I've a strange office here...
> Like the mad misery of necessitous man,
> That parts from his good horse with many praises
> And goes on foot himself.   (3. 2. 193 ff.)

The gaiety of the scene, with its dancing, music and feasts, has the same ironic contrast with the misery of Leantio, Isabella and Hippolito, as the quietness of the chess scene with its rapid intrigue. More than a third of the scene is taken up by asides in which these characters explain their feelings, while the action all the while remains animated. Leantio's soliloquy at the departure of the Duke and Bianca is one of the finest pieces of writing in the play, expressing this time not moral indignation but the agony of outraged feelings. It is the last time that such feelings are to be heard in the play. For Livia, the bawd, has fallen in love with him and approaches him with the familiar poisonous suggestions of wealth, the attack upon such feelings.

> Young gentlemen that only love for beauty
> They love not wisely: such a marriage rather
> Proves the destruction of affection;
> It brings on want, and want's the key of whoredom.
> (3. 2. 282 ff.)

Leantio's sense of values is not immediately overthrown; he cries out:

> O my *life's wealth*, Bianca! (3. 2. 307)

For money is not yet all-prevailing with him. It is during the course of one of those soliloquies which seem to telescope a lengthy mental process that worldly values conquer, and he accepts Livia's offer.

> Do but you love enough, I'll give enough.
> Troth then, I'll love enough and take enough.

So he sinks to Bianca's level; and in the scene where they bandy insults over one another's advancement (4. 1) this equality is explicitly set forth. Her fine lodgings and his fine clothes are set against each other; and her conscience is seen to be wholly dead, while his is still in the stage of ineffective stirring as hers had been earlier (2. 3, *ad fin.*).

It is at this point, however, that a new theme is introduced, which is to swell during the last two acts: that of death and judgment. More powerfully than in *The Changeling* it is given as the "punishment" and inevitable end of sinners. Leantio threatens Bianca in a whisper:

> I speak softly now
> 'Tis manners in a noble woman's lodging
> But come I to your everlasting parting once
> Thunder shall seem soft music to that tempest.
>
> (4. 1. 86 ff.)

This, conveyed to the Duke, brings about his own death. But the note of doom is struck again in the lengthy speech of the Cardinal, when he points to the Duke's body and says:

> There's but this wall between you and destruction
> When you're at strongest, poor thin clay— (4. 1. 242–3)

and, for Bianca:

> Is she a thing
> Whom sickness dare not visit or age look on
> Or death resist? doth the worm shun her grave?
>
> (4. 1. 248–50)

It is a note which curiously enough had been sounded by Leantio (with apparent irrelevance) in the opening speech in 1. 1:

> To have the toil and grief of fourscore years
> Put up in a white sheet, tied with two knots:
> Methinks it should strike earthquakes in adulterers
> When even the very sheets they commit sin in
> May prove, for aught they know, all their last garments.
>
> (1. 1. 20 ff.)

Except as a prelude to the later passages, this appears an excrescence. It will be noted how these references make man seem something pitiable and puny, confirming the impression of the intrigue.

In the very next scene, death comes sharply. Leantio is struck almost unawares, and in dying feels his wife's curse on him, as Livia feels the punishment for her sins. Pity is dead. She reveals the incest: Guardiano will "listen to nothing but revenge and anger"; Isabella's revenge will be "acted without pity". The masque is arranged: the bawd plays the marriage goddess and the adulteress a nymph wooed by two swains.

The wedding procession of the Duke is interrupted by the Cardinal, whose speech would apply equally well to the other marriage. His attack rouses pitiless revenge in Bianca; and so the scene is set for the masque.

Here the ironic casting is supplemented by action. Isabella is killed by a shower of gold:

> Bright eyed prosperity which all couples love,
> Ay and makes love. (5. 1. 156-7)

"Prosperity", or ambition of it, has undone Bianca, Leantio, Isabella, and the rest.

The ironical series of deaths follows quickly. Guardiano is caught in his own trap; Livia and Isabella kill each other; Hippolito commits suicide; the Duke is poisoned by mistake, and Bianca commits suicide, recalling her marriage vow, as Leantio had recalled her curse (5. 1. 252-3; cf. 4. 2. 43-5).

"Measure for measure" is recognised by Hippolito and Bianca, and it is she who speaks the real epilogue:

> Pride, greatness, honour, beauty, youth, ambition,
> You must all down together, there's no help for it.
>   (5. 1. 260-1 ff.)

The huddle of murders may be improbable, but the over-hanging atmosphere of mortality in the last act makes all the method of narrative of subsidiary importance. Death in some form is felt to be inevitable. Bianca, Leantio, Hippolito, Isabella and Livia have destroyed themselves already by destroying all moral sense,[1] and physical death has been pronounced upon them by the Cardinal who speaks with the voice of Heaven (*vide infra*).

It need hardly be added that the subsidiary figures have usually something to contribute to the atmosphere of the play. The ward, like the madmen of *The Changeling*, represents the completely bestial, as Caliban does in *The Tempest*. His lustfulness is continually stressed: it is lust at its coarsest, but only there as a commentary on the lust of the Duke and Hippolito, so that although too much space may seem to be given to his obscenities they are necessary as a ground-base for the consort of themes. Guardiano's cunning and Fabricio's foolishness serve similar ends; and the Cardinal's speeches are nearly all impersonal comments on the total situation. There is not a scene in the play which is really superfluous or divorced from the pattern as a whole, which may be summed up as the conflict between love and mercenary selling of love, with self-destruction envisaged as the inevitable result of the spiritual suicide of lust and ambition.

The imagery of the two plays is not systematised to the same extent as Chapman's or Webster's, yet there are certain dominating images in the Shakespearean manner which give a distinct tone to the play. For example Deflores is constantly referred to as a "poison", implying I think the natural antipathy which the good people in the play feel for him, marking him out as opposed to the healthful and life-giving associations of food and feasts. The discussion of instinctive likes and dislikes in Act 1 centres round food: Alsemero's "poison" is "a cherry". When Beatrice-Joanna first thinks of using Deflores, she exclaims:

> Why men of art make much of poisons:
> Keep one to expel another.... (2. 2. 46–7)

[1] See Leantio's words, 1. 1. 47–8:
  "If it be known, I've lost her: do but think now
  What that loss is—life's but a trifle to it".

And when she is forced to submit to him she thinks of him as a poisonous snake who has seized her (with a hidden reflection on the legend that vipers devoured their parents, for she is the employer of Deflores):

> Was my creation in the womb so curst
> It must engender with a viper first? (3. 4. 165–6)

Alsemero knows that Beatrice-Joanna so hated Deflores that "the very sight of him is poison to her", and therefore does not credit Jasperino's suspicions. Tomazo suspects him of having poisoned his brother; he is

> so most deadly venomous
> He would go near to poison any weapon....
>   (5. 2. 17–18)

Nevertheless he challenges Deflores:

> I'd rather die like a soldier by the sword
> Than like a politician by thy poison.... (5. 2. 28–9)

And when Beatrice-Joanna finally confesses, she cries:

> I have kissed poison for it, stroked a serpent.
>   (5. 3. 67)

It is not fortuitous, I think, that Alsemero is a physician and Alibius too. There is also a significant number of images dealing with the appetite and with food and drink. Miss Spurgeon has shown how in *Troilus and Cressida* such images give a certain coarseness to the sexual feelings in that play, by equating one appetite with the other. Here the images belong chiefly to Deflores and reinforce the suggestion that his feelings for Beatrice-Joanna are essentially gross. He is even eager for the murder, as a means to an end, and says:

> I thirst for him.... (2. 2. 134)

Beatrice-Joanna comments on his eagerness:

> Belike his wants are greedy: and to such
> Gold tastes like angels' food. (2. 2. 127–8)

It is this grossness of feeling which makes him imagine
Beatrice-Joanna attracted to himself:

> Hunger and pleasure they'll commend sometime
> Slovenly dishes and feed heartily on 'em,
> Nay, which is stranger, refuse daintier for them.
> Some women are odd feeders.... (2. 2. 152 ff.)

And when he returns after the murder he cries, in anticipation:

> My thoughts are at a banquet.... (3. 4. 18)

His final triumphant assertion of his dominance over Beatrice-
Joanna is in the same form:

> it is so sweet to me
> That I have drunk up all, left none behind
> For any man to pledge me. (5. 2. 172 ff.)

Tomazo's melancholy is at once a thirst for blood (4. 20)
and an inability to "taste the benefits of life" with "relish".
The madmen in the subplot are clamorous for food (1. 2).

The images of food are much more frequent in *Women,
Beware Women*, however, as fits the coarser quality of the
feelings in that play. I have counted a total of twenty-two
passages where this imagery is used, some of which are of a
considerable length; and there are continual direct references
to feasting (especially in 2. 2, 3. 1 and 3. 2). The coarsest
characters are gluttonous; for instance, the ward wants
some of Isabella's sweetmeats and says, with a reference
which makes the symbolism apparent,

> These women when they come to sweet things once
> They forget all their friends, they grow so greedy,
> Nay, often times their husbands. (3. 2. 75 ff.)

And the mother is ready to condone adultery for the sake
of a feast.

> I'll obey the duke
> And taste of a good banquet, I'm of thy mind
> I'll step but up and fetch two handkerchiefs
> To pocket up some sweetmeats and overtake thee.
> (3. 1. 265–8)

Bianca comments on this:

> Why here's an old wench would trot into a bawd now
> For some dry sucket or a colt in marchpane.
>
> (3. 1. 269–70)

It is reminiscent of the christening scene in *A Chaste Maid in Cheapside* (3. 2).

In the first scene Bianca compares her varied fortunes to a feast where all classes of people mingle. In the next scene Livia talks of a husband's privileges—"obedience, forsooth, subjection, duty and such kickshaws"—as dishes prepared for him by his wife. She "ministers cordials" to her brother and bids him "taste of happiness", describing him in the curious lines:

> Thou art all a feast
> And she that has thee a most happy guest.   (1. 2. 152ff.)

She tells the false tale to Isabella with:

> You see your cheer, I'll make you no set feast.

Isabella compares her former cruelty to Hippolito with an *apéritif*, and goes on to describe her love in terms of feasting (*vide supra*, p. 227). In the seduction scene the pictures are "a bit to stay the appetite". Guardiano endures Bianca's anger, since two feasts do not come together, and Livia thinks she only dislikes sin because its flavour is new to her.

In the feasting scene (3. 2) the references become thicker. The ward is "coarse victuals" to Isabella while she smells "like a comfit maker's shop" to him. (In the next scene she consoles herself that he has only "a cater's place" in choosing her.)

Leantio feigns mirth like someone whose appetite hides disease (*vide supra*, p. 230). His place is "a fine bit to stay a cuckold's stomach". To the end he "eats his meat with grudging" and cannot reconcile himself to the loss of Bianca. He, like the ward, has only a cater's place; it is largely through this kind of imagery that the link between plot and subject is kept. Bianca, like Deflores, dies "tasting my last breath in a cup of love". The other chief images of the play are those drawn from plagues and diseases, from treasure and jewels, and from light and darkness. The metaphors of disease are nearly always applied to lust, reinforcing the connection between spiritual and physical death. It is like "destruction" worn in a man's bosom; a "plague" which a man brings home to his own house. Livia's love for Leantio is "a diseased part" which Hippolito must cut off. Bianca finds the Duke diseased (perhaps this is meant to be taken literally) but:

> Since my honour's leprous why should I
> Preserve that fair that caused the leprosy?
>
> (2. 2. 429–30)

And she dies recognising her foulness in words which recall those of *The Changeling*:

> My *deformity* in spirit's more foul
> A blemished face best fits a leprous soul. (5. 2. 246–7)

The metaphors of wealth need hardly be considered; their functions will be evident. Affection is the wealth of the good. Bianca, while she is chaste, is Leantio's "treasure", his "jewel", his "life's wealth". He in turn is Livia's "riches". The use of light and darkness occurs in the last two acts only: it is symbolised in the action in the scene where the Cardinal brings two candles on to the stage and shows his brother the darkness of his own life. Bianca is called "brightness" and "bright Bianca" by the Duke: Leantio's life was such that "flames were not nimbler", though to Hippolito the crown of his sin is that he is "an impudent daylight lecher". The atmosphere of darkness thickens to the close (all the revels would be by torchlight) and is mingled with imagery of blood.

It is not absolutely necessary to grasp the scheme of imagery or even the themes, in order to appreciate the plays.

They are not completely dependent upon this scheme in the way in which the plays of Tourneur are: a great deal can be got from them on the level of narrative-and-character alone. But it is difficult to grasp the connection of plots and subplots in any other way, without which Middleton must seem to combine an exceptional power of construction and a wanton disregard of its elementary principles in the most curious way. It remains true, however, that the stress which should fall upon themes and imagery is much lighter in Middleton's plays than in those of most of his contemporaries. This is not to say that Middleton's language is less poetic or less important than that of the other poets, but that he also relies upon action and characterisation in a way which no one else did (except Shakespeare). His language too gains its effects by different methods from those of the majority of the Elizabethans; he does not rely upon explicit statement or direct speech but upon implication; nor upon a gorgeous and elaborate vocabulary, but upon a pregnant simplicity which is perhaps more difficult to achieve, and is certainly found more seldom.

CHAPTER X

The Decadence

I. "BEAUMONT AND FLETCHER"

THE plays of the "Beaumont and Fletcher" group and of Massinger, for the purpose of this study, may be considered apart from questions of their authorship, for the qualities by which they may be said to be decadent are common to them all. They are positive qualities and serve to distinguish these plays from the negative decadence of attrition which is found in Ford and Shirley: there is a coarsening of the feeling (which is accompanied, inevitably, by a coarsening of the poetic fibre) together with an increased dexterity in the manipulation of the emotional effects of narrative and character.

The coarsening of the fibre may be seen in the blurring of the tragic and comic. In the earlier drama they had been juxtaposed without being confused; the strength of the writing lay in this reconciliation of opposites. In Fletcher's tragedies, there is no permanent reliance upon a scheme of values, so that the method of Tourneur and Middleton is impossible. In *Bonduca*, for example, the tragic death of the Queen so excites the admiration of the Roman Petillius that he falls in love with her memory; but this is taken as a subject for comedy, for the bluff soldier in love is always ludicrous.

> What do I ail, i' the name of Heaven? I did but see her
> And see her die: she stinks by this time strongly,
> Abominably stinks. She was a woman,
> A thing I never cared for: but to die so,
> So confidently, bravely, strongly—oh, the devil,
> I have the bots!—by Heaven, she scorned us strangely,
> All we could do, or durst do: threatened us
> With such a noble anger, and so governed
> With such a fiery spirit—the plain bots!
> A pox upon the bots, the love-bots! Hang me!

The earlier writers might have used the decay of a corpse, as tragedy, or as pure comedy, or in a sardonic spirit, but they would never have reduced tragedy to comedy in this fashion. Nor is this passage isolated. The deflection towards comedy is constant, and, which is perhaps more significant, the comedy is never critical. For criticism implies a fixed standard of judgment which these later dramatists did not possess. In the earlier scene in *Bonduca*, where the Queen's daughters are prepared to torture the Romans in revenge for their rapes, the bluff soldier Caratach joins with the enemy to turn the action to farce, and there is hardly a serious line in the whole scene.

A comparison of the senile amorousness of the old Dukes in *The Revenger's Tragedy* and *Cupid's Revenge* is illuminating. In the one case it is dismissed with curt disgust:

> O that marrowless age
> Should stuff the hollow bones with damned desires,
> And 'stead of heat, kindle infernal fires
> Within the spendthrift veins of a dry duke!
> (*The Revenger's Tragedy*, I. I. 5 ff.)

In *Cupid's Revenge*, the old Duke's courtship is extended over several scenes and is a matter for comedy; not the fierce comedy which Jonson might have made of it, or Beaumont writing alone, as he did in *The Woman Hater*, but dependent on the old Duke's pitiable appearance only. His character is quite undamaged; he is referred to as "the good old duke".

> *Duke.* Shall I fight for thee?
> This sword shall cut his throat that dares lay claim
> But to a finger of thee, but a look:
> I would see such a fellow!
> *Bacha (aside).* It would be
> But a cold sight to you! This is the father of
> St George a-footback! Can such dry mummy talk?
> *Timantus.* Before the gods, your Grace looks like Aeneas.
> *Bacha.* He looks like his old father upon his back,
> Crying to get aboard.

This attitude is no further developed than that of Shakespeare's Achilles.

> The faint defects of age
> Must be the scene of mirth: to cough and spit,
> And with a palsy fumbling on his gorget
> Shake in and out the rivet.
>
> *(Troilus and Cressida*, 1. 3. 172 ff.)

Similarly, the subject of *A King and No King* might conceivably be a subject for comedy of a savage kind, like *Volpone*. But when Arbaces asks Bessus to procure his sister for him, Bessus' assent is far more convincing than the King's indignation: Arbaces' horror is made ridiculous.

> *Arbaces.* Thou hast eyes
> Like flames of sulphur, which methinks do dart
> Infection on me: and thou hast a mouth
> Enough to take me in, where there do stand
> Four rows of iron teeth.
> *Bessus.* I feel no such thing. But 'tis no matter how I look,
> I'll do your business as well as they that look better: and when
> this is dispatched, if you have a mind to your mother, tell me,
> and you shall see I'll set it hard. (*A King and No King*, 3. 5)

The comic bawds of *Valentinian* and *Thierry and Theodoret* enjoy the same ascendancy as Bessus, while the righteous indignation of Lucina or Martell is mechanical and forced. The attitude behind these plays is not at all different from that behind *The Custom of the Country*. It is only necessary to think of *The Changeling* and *The Roaring Girl* to realise what this implied.

The coarseness of Fletcher and Massinger is offensive in a way quite impossible in the earlier period. The scene in which Bacha tempts Leucippus (*Cupid's Revenge*, 3. 1) gives only verbal counters, formal protestations to the Prince, while Bacha is drawn with a vigour and relish which would be tolerable if she were part of a system of characters (as, for instance, is Levidulcia) but which is quite intolerable in the void. It is not that a set moral condemnation is required; but Bacha might be "placed" indirectly.

Fletcher uses his coarseness with as little sense of its weight as the author of *The Birth of Merlin*, yet with as much sensuous immediacy as Tourneur. Massinger shows the same bluntness in almost every play. It is not surprising therefore to find a taste for the more extraordinary sexual themes (rapes, impotence, incest) combined with a blurring of the aesthetic difference between tragedy and comedy and the moral distinction between right and wrong. Hence Amintor is able to say, after seeing Evadne sleeping sweetly:

> I'll be guilty too,
> If these be the effects!

and Maximus, whose wife has been ravished, says of his best friend:

> Would he had ravished me! I would have paid him!

Such passages are symptomatic of the larger confusion of such plays as Middleton's *Fair Quarrel* or Ford's *Love's Sacrifice* (compare this play with Heywood's *English Traveller*), or the shift of sympathy at the end of *Valentinian* and *The Duke of Milan*. Fletcher or Massinger are never clear about their postulates; consequently, villains change into heroes or *vice versa*. The double personage of Vindice is compatible with a clear judgment upon each aspect of the character, but the double personage of Maximus or Sforza, or of Petillius in *Bonduca* is incoherent, because the two halves of the character do not stand in any relationship to each other, as the character of Bacha did not stand in any genuine relationship to the other characters in *Cupid's Revenge*. The real objection to the last act of *The Duke of Milan* is not that Sforza is here a different person from the Sforza of Act 2 who pleaded before Charles V in Massinger's most dignified heroic manner, or that a new set of facts have been introduced, but that the two halves of Sforza and the two sets of facts belong to different conventions and that their juxtaposition serves no purpose.

A fundamental indecision can be felt in most of Fletcher's plays. Otto and Leucippus are half innocent victims and half weaklings (as the bluff soldiers are half heroes and half fools). When their deaths approach, their innocence is stressed, to heighten the pathos. The very feelings of the characters themselves are made to depend upon opinion, and the judgment of others; they have no absolute standards. The ravished Lucina, the disgraced Poenius use similar accents, showing clearly the true basis of Fletcher's fundamental values of chastity and valour.

> And now I am left to scornful tales and laughters,
> To hootings at, pointings with fingers, "That's he,
> That's the brave gentleman forsook the battle,
> The most wise Poenius, the disputing coward!"
>
> *(Bonduca, 4. 3)*
>
> My family,
> Because they are honest and desire to be so,
> Must not endure me: not a neighbour know me:
> What woman now dares see me without blushes,
> And pointing as I pass "There, there behold her;
> Look on her, little children: that is she,
> That handsome lady, mark"? *(Valentinian, 3. 1)*

The difference in the depth of tragic intensity in a play where this marks the lowest depths of suffering, as compared with the dying speeches of Byron, or Cleopatra's dismissal of the Roman citizens, needs no comment. For even these characters, "blameless" as they are, are subjected to a kind of satire, which like the treatment of the Duke Leontes, reduces them to contempt while preserving a fatal good temper. Both are innocents, and the worldly wise, the bawds and Machiavels, may laugh at them. It is the difference between Shakespeare's attitude to Ajax, and his attitude to Coriolanus.

This betrays itself inevitably in the texture of the verse. Fletcher and Massinger never state anything with the detachment of perfect conviction; they argue and persuade. There is always the undissolved residuum of personal appeal; the quality of Elizabethan rhetoric had changed. The number of adjurations, addresses and tirades which occur in these plays is surprising; this form of impassioned writing replaced the soliloquy, which becomes comparatively rare. It is eloquent, full flowing, balanced and amplified, and consequently the concentration of the earlier style is lost. These are typical passages:

> Hew off my innocent hands as he commands you!
> They'll hang the faster on for death's convulsion.
> Thou seed of rocks, will nothing move thee then?
> Are all my tears lost? all my righteous prayers
> Drowned in thy drunken wrath? I stand up thus then,
> Thus boldly, bloody tyrant,
> And to thy face, in Heaven's high name, defy thee!
> And may sweet Mercy, when thy soul sighs for it,
> When under thy black mischief thy flesh trembles...etc.
>
> (*The Bloody Brother*, 3. 1)
>
> What is honour
> We all so strangely are bewitched withal?
> Can it relieve me if I want? he has;
> Can honour, 'twixt the incensed prince and envy
> Bear up the lives of worthy men? he has.
> Can honour pull the wings of fearful cowards? he has.
> And I have lived to see this, and preserved so:
> Why should this empty word incite me then
> To what is ill and cruel? let her perish....
>
> (*Valentinian*, 3. 4)

(This last, it may be remarked, is part of a debate with himself in which a husband resolves to kill his best friend, because the friend is too loyal to the King to permit the husband to revenge his wife's rape as honour dictates.)

When the emotional egg-whisk has been used in this manner, it is difficult to revert to a more controlled and

complex style. Fletcher has no choice but to pile up his
epithets and exclamation marks.

It was possible, however, by using the inarticulately heroic
bluff soldier, to make incoherence touching. Ismenus, the
rough diamond of *Cupid's Revenge*, refuses to leave the
banished Prince, and equally refuses to give reasons.

> *Leucippus.* But why wilt thou not leave me?
> *Ismenus.* Why, I will tell you, because when you are gone—
> Then—life, if I have not forgot my reason.
> Hell take me! you put me out of patience so.
> O, marry, when you are gone, then will your mother—
> A pox confound her—she ne'er comes in my head
> But she spoils my memory too. There are a hundred reasons—
> *Leucippus.* But show me one.
> *Ismenus.* Show you one (what a stir is here!)
> Why I will show you—do you think—well, well,
> I know what I know. I pray, come, come! 'Tis in vain,
> But I am sure—Devils take 'em! what do I meddle with 'em?
> You know yourself—soul, I think I am—
> Is there any man i' the world—As if you knew not this
> Already better than I! Pish, I'll give no reason.

There are a good many more lines before he bursts out:

> You know I love you but too well!

Scenes in which the bluff soldier is wheedled and coaxed
into a proper frame of mind are frequent; for "he will as
tenderly be led by the nose as asses are", and when it is all
done from pure affection, the spectacle is both touching and
amusing to the sophisticated spectator.

The bluff citizens who so often appear in interludes
(*Philaster*, Act 5; *Cupid's Revenge*, Act 4; *The Bloody Brother*,
Act 4; the soldiers of *Bonduca*) are the choric equivalent of
the bluff soldier. They too are naïve and hearty, and full
of simple affections.

The women may be divided simply into the chastely meek
and the viragoes. It is of little consequence whether the

viragoes are good or bad; their fury is of the same sort. The assertion of innocence too often involves vituperation of the guilty; the tirades of Edith or Bonduca are much more vehement than expressive of an attitude towards anything or anyone: and in the latter case they lead to the kind of coarseness which is inescapable in Fletcher.

> Show me a Roman lady
> In all your stories dare do this for her honour:
> They are cowards, eat coals like compelled cats;
> Your great saint Lucrece
> Died not for honour: Tarquin tupped her well,
> And, mad she could not hold him, bled.
>
> (*Bonduca*, 4. 4)

This scene is the equivalent of the fourth act of *The Duchess of Malfi*. There could not be a clearer case of the loss of detachment, of the substitution of assertion for statement.

The basis of these plays is an outrageous stimulation. Provided the characters are feeling intensely all the time, it does not much matter how or why. Hence the twists and reversals of the story to provide the maximum amount of sensationalism; hence also the purely passive characters whose only function is to suffer, and the grosser exhibitions of physical pain in *Valentinian*. There is often a conscious gloating over feelings, especially those which involve abasement or inflation.

> My lord,
> Give me your griefs: you are an innocent,
> A soul as white as Heaven: let not my sin
> Perish your noble youth....
> I do present myself the foulest creature,
> Most poisonous, dangerous and despised of men
> Lerna e'er bred, or Nilus! I am hell,
> Till you, my dear lord, shoot your light into me....
>
> (*The Maid's Tragedy*, 4. 1)

The final test of these plays is their language, and here they are strikingly apart from the earlier drama. There is no

verbal framework of any kind; the collapse of the poetic
is to be directly related to the collapse of the moral structure,
for they were interdependent. With the decay of the linguistic
patterns, the peculiar qualities of setting and of stock incident
decayed also. The plays of Fletcher and Massinger are set
in a kind of no man's land, whether it be France, Italy or
the Roman Empire.

The structural use of plot and subplot was likewise
abandoned. The comic citizens only provide the crudest of
comic relief, the worst case being perhaps in *The Bloody
Brother*. Structural use of tags and quotations also stopped,
though borrowing did not.

In some directions there was development. There were the
new typical characters of the bluff soldier, the forsaken maid,
the tyrant, the wicked queen, and the virago. Most of these
were originally comic types; the girl page, for instance,
being descended from the heroines of Greene and Shakespeare. The attitudes of these characters are unrealistically
intensified, but their feelings (especially when nearest to
sensations) are given with a new immediacy. Compare
Bacha's wooing of Leucippus with Eugenia's wooing of
Eleazer in *Lust's Dominion*.

The narrative is often farcical. *Cupid's Revenge*, *Thierry
and Theodoret* and *The Bloody Brother* form a group in which
the rapid intrigue is of greater interest than the sensations of
the characters, and consequently the scheming and villainous
have heavier parts than the virtuous and long-suffering. The
most effective scenes often depend on "baffling", or the
reckless deception of one character by another (*The Bloody
Brother*, 2. 3, 3. 1; *Cupid's Revenge*, 4. 1; *Thierry and Theodoret*,
3. 1). The best-known scene of this sort is in *The Maid's
Tragedy* (4. 1) where Melentius practises on Calianax by
denying aloud what he is saying aside. Such a scene owes
much, probably, to the constructive powers of Jonson (compare the end of *Volpone*).

This shows also a growing interest in the way the mind works, and, coupled with the taste for implication and suggestion in the passages dealing with the humouring of the bluff soldier (e.g. the one quoted above between Ismenus and Leucippus, and the similar ones at the end of *Bonduca* between Petillius and Junius), they may be related to the technique of Middleton.

There is a more complex manipulation of suspense than in the earlier writers. The value of keeping the audience in the dark as a method of stimulating the attention was exploited to the full. Sometimes the device is very transparently used, as in the mysterious words of Clarangé at the end of the third act of *The Lover's Progress*:

> Something I will do,
> A new born zeal and friendship prompts me to.

The second act of *Valentinian* uses suspense in a subtler way. The bustle and scurry of the servants' preparation for Lucina's arrival at court intensify the feeling that she is being trapped:

> — How now?
> — She's come.
> — Then I'll to the Emperor.
> — Do. Is the music placed well?

At the very last, Valentinian seems to repent, and tells Lucina he has only been trying her virtue, but an ambiguous aside suggests that he is only half sincere, though one repentance has been actually shown already.

> He that endeavours ill
> May well delay, but never quench his hell.

This is all extremely clever; but it is little more. It is the kind of thing which can be learnt; the reward of competence. It also implies that the action is separable from the words in which it is expressed; that is, that a split has occurred between the poetry and the drama.

It is obvious that whenever Fletcher wrote tragedy, it was against the grain. He takes every opportunity to escape a tragic treatment of the subject; the "tragedy" is often only in the catastrophe. Character and narrative are not informed and unified by a pressure of thought and feeling, and the feeling which is exuberant in his comedies becomes raucous in his tragedies. Massinger's deflection was the less violent, as his sense of the comic was more sober, but this only makes the calculated atrocities of such plays as *The Unnatural Combat* the more ineffectual.

This last play may also serve as an illustration of the decadents' inability to handle the supernatural. The appearance of the ghosts is only an episode; it is not linked to any diffused feeling of a deity shaping the ends of action; and it is purely spectacular. Fletcher's use was even less successful: his one ridiculous ghost is the ghost of the host in *The Lover's Progress*; and his introduction of Cupid as an enraged deity in *Cupid's Revenge* is reminiscent of the descent of Jupiter in *Cymbeline*.

II. JOHN FORD

Ford has received more detailed criticism than many of his predecessors. Lamb's commentary, Swinburne's fine study, and various more recent papers are sufficient evidence of his permanent importance. But the precise degree of this importance has never been quite certain, and there has been, on the whole, a tendency to examine Ford rather than to place him.

The critics are in general agreement about one quality of his writing, and that is the limited intensity of his emotional effects. Everything in Ford is focussed to a single point; his plays live at the core, but they are not wholly alive. As Swinburne says: "He wants deep water to swim well". To assume that this is a question of morals ("his power as a poet is simply a moral power") seems unwarranted; at all events, the moral power is only to be measured through the poetic and dramatic technique. It is by these means that it is possible to define the difference between Ford and Tourneur whose limited intensity does not appear as a limitation of power in the same way; and, on the other hand, the difference between Ford and Fletcher or Massinger, which makes his best work free from their defects. Ford's finest passages express what is essentially a single feeling, in an individual accent. This feeling is a personal and human love, described in simple and unimpassioned language. The contrast between the strength of the feeling and the quietness of the statement is something new in Elizabethan drama.

> In short, I know thou never wilt forget
> Whose wife thou art, nor how upon thy lips
> Thy husband at his parting stalled this kiss.
> No more. (*The Lady's Trial*, ll. 227 ff.)

> O the glory
> Of two united hearts like hers and mine....
> My world and all of happiness is here,
> And I'd not change it for Elizium.
> (*'Tis Pity She's a Whore*, ll. 2155 ff.)

> A freedom of converse, an interchange
> Of holy and chaste loves, so fixed our souls
> In a firm growth of union, that no time
> Can eat into the pledge. (*The Broken Heart*, ll. 120 ff.)

Here the tone depends upon the lack of rhetoric; the feeling has none of the passion of, say, Vittoria. The most exquisite of Ford's characters, Lady Katherine Gordon, Penthea, Susan and Winifred in *The Witch of Edmonton*, have pre-eminently this quality of devotion and reticence. Calantha's feelings are never shown at all except through their effects. The Griselda-like and quite colourless figure of the heroine in *The Queen*, and Cleophila in *The Lover's Melancholy* are first studies for the type: the final scene of *Perkin Warbeck* is probably the best piece of extended writing

in which this feeling predominates. The delicacy with which
Ford shows emotion freed from any sensuous element links
him with his old collaborator, Dekker.

It is for this reason that *'Tis Pity She's a Whore* is so successful. In his essay on Ford, Mr Eliot compared the play
with *Antony and Cleopatra*, and said, "The passion of Giovanni
and Annabella is not shown as an affinity of temperament
due to identity of blood: it hardly rises above the purely
carnal infatuation". This seems to me entirely mistaken;
there is not a passage in *'Tis Pity* where any kind of direct
presentation of "carnal infatuation" appears in the verse
itself. The lovers are supposed to be physically attracted of
course, but the feeling never informs the writing. The
wooing scene (1. 3) and the description of Annabella (2. 5)
are extraordinarily flat in their enumeration of eyes like
jewels or stars, hair like threads of gold and so on. Giovanni's
feelings are expressed in such lines as:

> O Annabella, I am quite undone!
> The love of thee, my sister, and the view
> Of thy immortal beauty have undone
> All harmony both of my rest and life.

Compare Bassanes to Penthea:

> Light of beauty,
> Deal not ungently with a desperate wound!

The appeal is enhanced by its very abstractness: it works in
terms of sentiments and not of passions, of the affections and
not of the senses. Ford uses endearments in a significant
way. Perkin calls his wife "my dearest", or "dearest" and
she calls him "my life's dearest". The power of this, like
the famous "Oh, Nan, Nan!" of *A Woman Killed with
Kindness* depends on implication, not statement, and on the
human, not the heroic, type of character. In *'Tis Pity* the
constant use of "brother" and "sister" as terms of endear-

ment is one of the ways of heightening the horror; but it works by hints, not statements.

Ford's lack of definiteness is often very striking. For example, Orgilus wishes to leave Penthea:

> To lose the memory of *something*
> Her presence makes to live in me afresh,   (ll. 172–3)

and Palador muses

> Parthenophil is lost and I would see him,
> For he is like to *something* I remember
> A great while since, a long, long time ago. (ll. 2076–8)

The deliberate reserve heightens the effect of these passages: it also makes them seem less obviously poetic and nearer to common speech, which is probably what Lamb meant when he said, "He sought for sublimity not by parcels in metaphors or visible images, but directly where she has her residence in the heart of man".

When feelings are no longer sensuously expressed, the explicitness of imagery is replaced by implication. There is an ejaculation which Ford uses three times as the climax of a scene which will illustrate the point.

> You can suspect,
> So reconciliation then is needless.
> Conclude the difference by revenge, or part
> And never more see one another: sister,
> Lend me thine arm, I have assumed a courage
> Above my force, and can hold out no longer:
> Auria, unkind, unkind! (*The Lady's Trial*, ll. 2490 ff.)
> Forgive him, Heavens, and me my sins. Farewell
> Brother unkind, unkind.—Mercy, great Heaven.
> > ('*Tis Pity She's a Whore*, ll. 2409–10)
> I am a sister, though to me this brother
> Hath been, you know, unkind, O most unkind!
> > (*The Broken Heart*, ll. 1626–7)

The penetrating quality of the word "unkind" depends upon a range of feelings to be found in Heywood, Dekker,

Shakespeare ("Commend me to my *kind* lord. O farewell!")
and Middleton, but not in the other tragic writers of the
period.

The grief which comes of wounded affection is a common
theme in Ford, but as his affections are of this softened kind,
so the grief is dignified and generalised:

> ...the sickness of a mind
> Burdened with griefs....

> On my soul
> Lies such an infinite clog of massy dulness
> As that I have not strength enough to feel it.

In *The Lover's Melancholy* it is no stronger than the charming
woes of *The Arcadia*, but in the later tragedies, circumstances
are more brutal, and unhappy love, reduced to despair, is
transmuted into a desire for death. This nostalgic death-
yearning is the second major theme of Ford's poetry: its
connections with devoted love are complex. It is expressed
in the same monosyllabic movement as the characteristic
love passages.

> When a man has been a thousand years
> Hard travelling o'er the tottering bridge of age
> He is not the thousandth part upon his way:
> All life is but a wandering to find home;
> When we're gone, we're there.
>
> > (*The Witch of Edmonton*, 5. 4)
>
> Minutes are numbered by the fall of sands,
> As by an hour glass: the span of time
> Doth waste us to our graves, and we look on it.
> An age of pleasures, ravelled out, comes home
> At last and ends in sorrow: but the life
> Weary of riot numbers every sand,
> Wailing in sighs until the last drops down,
> So to conclude calamity in rest.
>
> > (*The Lover's Melancholy*, ll. 2107ff.)
>
> Pleasures, farewell, and all you thriftless minutes
> Wherein false joys have spun a weary life!

To these my fortunes now I take my leave.
Thou precious Time, that swiftly rid'st in post
Over the world to finish up the race
Of my last fate, now stay thy restless course.
('Tis Pity She's a Whore, ll. 2054 ff.)

The Broken Heart is so full of such passages that selection is impossible. It will be noted how the metaphors in each of these three extracts emphasise the toilsomeness of life, and the recurrence of words like "weary" and "wandering". If these passages are compared with similar ones from the earlier drama (with Byron's speech on death for example) the exhausted sound of Ford's dragging lines is quite startling.

His fondness for the generalised description of feelings and his lack of sensuous immediacy have already been discussed. The finest of his songs seems in its imagery to sum up the delicate and colourless beauty of his style, and the nostalgic quality of his sentiments. It is the one sung at the death of Penthea:

> O no more, no more, too late
> Sighs are spent: the burning tapers
> Of a life as chaste as Fate,
> Pure as are unwritten papers
> Are burnt out: no heat, no light
> Now remains: 'tis ever night.

Nor have his characters an individual tone and accent which might replace poetic warmth by an interwoven pattern of speech. The dialogue is most interesting at those points where an interchange of courtesies allows Ford to use stilted language elegantly, such as the scene praised by Swinburne wherein James of Scots dismisses Perkin Warbeck. He is quite unable to manage quarrels or debates. The flyting of Soranzo and Annabella is very forced; and Ford's incapacity to depict anger is comically illustrated by his trick of making one party repeat the words of the other (e.g. *The Broken Heart*, 4. 1).

Ford's structure of narrative and characterisation differs from that of earlier writers in a way corresponding to that of his speech. In the first place, it is not assisted by any pattern in the language, such as the imagery provides in Tourneur and the themes in Middleton. The most subtle of the Elizabethan co-ordinating forces is thereby lost to Ford.

This can be seen by a comparison of *Women, Beware Women* and *'Tis Pity*. The subplot of the first play is so similar to the second play that it would seem that direct modelling on Ford's part had occurred. Annabella = Isabella; Giovanni = Hippolito; Donado = Guardiano; Hippolita = Livia; Bergetto = the ward; Poggio = Sordido. But in Ford's play there is no interconnection between the comic characters and the serious ones. Bergetto's wooing of Annabella is entirely without underlying purpose, and because the comedy is not used as comment on the tragedy, the lesser figures, such as Donado and Poggio, become mere supers. Ford, like Middleton, takes the Italianate setting, but he does not use it in the same way. Compare the masque of Hippolita with that of Livia; the first is only a makeweight, the second is linked with the rest of the play through contrasts of characters and feelings. Ford's limited intensity could not supply feeling for every part of a play; it animates single characters or single speeches. The "absence of underlying pattern or purpose" which Mr Eliot notes as a moral defect in Ford can thus be illustrated in terms of corresponding defects of technique.

An overmastering Fate is used to explain and order the narrative and character. Throughout *'Tis Pity* the lovers are thought of as doomed by some external power, but this is only sufficient to cover the action of the two main characters.

In the first scene the friar sees Giovanni's "ruin". Giovanni replies, "My fate's my god". In the next scene he accepts his "ruin", and his declaration of love begins: "O Annabella,

I am quite undone!" Annabella too cries: "I am lost".
Giovanni has already observed:

> 'Tis not, I know,
> My lust, but 'tis my fate that leads me on. (ll. 308–9)

Hence Mr Eliot's and Mrs Woolf's criticism of the characters
of Giovanni and Annabella is beside the point in so far as
it depends on inadequacy of motivation; they are doomed
in the Racinian manner, like Hermione or Phèdre. Their
love is a "possession", as Middleton had conceived it: two
lines of Giovanni have almost the ring of Deflores:

> Yet time is left you both.
>   —To embrace each other.
> Else let all time be struck quite out of number.
> She is like me and I like her resolved. (ll. 972–4)

In the last act, Giovanni, by despising ruin, surmounts it.
He says:

> I hold fate
> Clasped in my fist, (ll. 2311–12)

and

> In my fists I bear the twists of life. (l. 2509)

In *The Broken Heart* the oracle is used with similar implications, but less successfully. The seer Tecnicus is constantly
exhorting Orgilus, "Tempt not the stars", and he, when his
plots are maturing, echoes Giovanni:

> Ingenious fate has leapt into my arms. (l. 556)

Even the minor characters often make such remarks as
"Fate instructs me" by way of compliment in conversation.
The connection of the idea of an over-ruling fate with the
images of life as a journey to a fixed goal is obvious, but
the way in which the sentiment reappears at every turn of
the plays differs from the earlier sense of fate which expressed
itself in variations on the theme of "The wheel is come full
circle". In Ford, fate is arbitrary and works blindly.

In *The Broken Heart* Ford attempted also to impose a pattern of characters. The dramatis personae have "names fitted to their qualities" in the Humorous manner: Ithocles, honour of loveliness; Orgilus, angry; Bassanes, vexation; and so on. The four principals are a "Niobe group of frozen griefs", but the contrast does not work in precise and particular ways; it is not a matter of detail. The omission of comic relief, however, must be counted in Ford's favour. He tried to reduce everything in the play to different illustrations of his one type of feeling; a selfless devotion thwarted by circumstance.

In the more realistic plays, *Perkin Warbeck* and *The Witch of Edmonton*, there are no dead links or excrescences, nothing to correspond to the Philotis and Richardetto of '*Tis Pity*. All the minor characters are alive in *Perkin Warbeck*, even the servants (see especially 5. 1). In *The Witch of Edmonton* Ford had collaborators, but even in those scenes which seem entirely his, there are no false notes.

In his narrative Ford chose the oblique situation, hid his motives and worked by indirect statement. The final revelation of Calantha's character is contrary to the explicit methods of the earlier writers. In this respect I think Mr Havelock Ellis is right in calling Ford "modern". Calantha's dignity and reticence are treated in a more sophisticated way than Cordelia's (compare the latter's asides in the opening scene of *King Lear*).

Ford preferred complex motives and equivocal actions. In *The Lady's Trial* a wife is wrongly suspected, and circumstances combine against her. In *The Broken Heart* Penthea feels that, though unwillingly, she is guilty of a crime against fidelity: Orgilus, too, is "driven" to crime, and Ithocles as yet is not guilty of cruelty to Penthea. In '*Tis Pity* incest is not excused (it is no *drame à thèse*) but accepted as fit tragic material. In *Perkin Warbeck* Ford selected a most difficult situation: Perkin is an impostor, but he is a dignified one;

his self-deception is never shown as dissimulation, and it is explained in terms that almost sound like those of a psycho-analyst.

The list of "sympathetic" criminals will suffice to show how Ford enjoyed complexity of motive. They are not double characters but blended ones. At the same time one does not feel that they imply obtuseness, as in Fletcher; at the most, a desire for complexity for its own sake.

In Ford's two failures, *The Fancies Chaste and Noble* and *Love's Sacrifice*, there is an overstraining of the "difficult" situation, coupled with an attempt to deal with passions rather than affections. This Ford was simply unable to do, so that he blundered helplessly. His licentiousness has an air of frigid calculation that is worse even than the skilful lubricities of Fletcher: it is the cold-bloodedness of these plays which makes them less excusable, if less offensive, than *A King and No King* or *Cupid's Revenge*. The limitation of Ford's powers is shown as definitely in his impassioned speeches as in his attempts to be fashionably licentious. There is a kind of inflated rant, which is often quite incoherent, and which Ford almost always uses to show violent feelings.

> Thou knowest, false wanton, when my modest fame
> Stood free from stain or scandal, all the charms
> Of Hell or sorcery could not prevail
> Against the honour of my chaster bosom.
> ('*Tis Pity She's a Whore*, ll. 643 ff.)

The only meaning to be extracted from this is that before Hippolita was guilty, she was innocent. The friar's speech to Annabella (ll. 1400–30) is almost in the manner of Kyd; and Giovanni's entry with Annabella's heart upon his dagger, or the speeches with which he describes the murder try to whip up a horror in which Ford is not interested at all.

On other occasions Ford betrays his essential inattention by repetition, or, in the songs, by getting into a rhythm and rocking himself to sleep in it.

> Comforts lasting, loves increasing
> Like soft hours never ceasing:
> Plenty's pleasure, peace complying,
> Without jars or tongues envying.

Again in Orgilus' appeal to Penthea (*The Broken Heart*, ll. 903 ff.) I think Gifford's emendation unnecessary: Ford has simply used the image of incense twice over, and the only needful adjustment is the transposition of the first three words of ll. 907 and 908.

> Turn those eyes
> (The arrows of pure love) upon that fire
> Which once rose to a flame perfumed with vows
> As sweetly scented as the incense smoking
> On Vesta's altars: Virgin tears (like
> The holiest odours) sprinkled dews to feed 'em
> And to increase their fervour.

Both these vows and tears are incense to his flames (or perhaps the tears are scented oils). This kind of muddle is typical of Ford's efforts toward the explicit statement of passion. He cannot handle metaphors, as Lamb said; he cannot, that is, use the highly charged language of the earlier writers but only something which expresses simpler feelings in more tenuous language. This simplification of the language and feelings is compensated by an obliquity and complexity in motivation. In Ford there is a split between dramatic and poetic method. *Perkin Warbeck* is certainly his best play, yet it is of such subdued poetic quality that most people prefer the inequalities of his other two tragedies. There is no such division between poetry and drama in the predecessors of Ford.

His decadence may be summed up as an attrition rather than a coarsening. His faults arise from gawkiness, an attempt to deal with subjects outside his limited range. This does not prevent his producing some work which is, in a minor way, quite flawless; and his creative impulse was tragic and not comic, so that he was not tempted to the mixed effects of the tragicomedy.

Yet his relationship to the writers of the great period is that of an imitator. He took over conventions passively and therefore they were largely useless to him. Moreover, the attrition represented by *'Tis Pity She's a Whore* is serious. The Elizabethan drama had worked itself out in Ford.

III. JAMES SHIRLEY

Shirley's tragedy, like that of Fletcher and Massinger, is less important than his comedy. He has left four tragedies— *The Maid's Revenge*, *Love's Cruelty*, *The Cardinal* and *The Traitor*, and several *drames* such as *The Duke's Mistress* and *The Politician*, which are of the same stuff as the tragedies, and contain parallel themes and situations.

Shirley's interest lay in the elaborate complication of his intrigue. The central figure is often an intriguer who has several parts to play. Characters are always changing sides, doubling or twisting among different allegiances; the virtuous heroine frequently resorts to elaborate stratagems (especially Berenthia, Ardelia and Rosaura) and the spectator has no clue to their purpose.

The mystification reaches its height in *The Cardinal*. To begin with, Prologue refuses to divulge whether the play is a tragedy or a comedy, but hints that it is a comedy.

> A poet's art is to lead on your thought
> Through subtle paths and workings of a plot...
> I will say nothing positive: you may
> Think what you please: we call it but a play,
> Whether the comic muse or ladies love,
> Romance or direful tragedy it prove,
> The bill determines not: and would you be
> Persuaded, I would have't a comedy....

There are careful introductory scenes at the beginning of each act to recapitulate the course of the action, except at the beginning of Act 2, where two lords summarise it more baldly.

In the first act, the interest centres round the dissembling of the heroine, Rosaura. At first it is only plain that she is not in love with Columbo, her accepted lover: a short soliloquy provides the *volte face*.

> Forgive me, Virtue, that I have dissembled...

before she interviews her real lover Alvarez.

In Act 2 is the deceptive business of the letter with a great deal of mutual misunderstanding. In the third act, there is the horrible reversal of the murder in the masque, where the Duchess Rosaura's lover is murdered on their wedding night. The vacillations of the King between Justice and Expediency make all the rest of the scene into an elaborate game of fast-and-loose, with the Cardinal pleading ostensibly for the Duchess and actually for Columbo, the murderer.

In the fourth act, Columbo is restored to favour; the Duchess pretends to be reconciled, but in soliloquy reveals that she is not, and that she intends to act the madwoman, in the manner of the old Revenger. The Cardinal is planning to ravish the Duchess; the Duchess is plotting to murder the Cardinal; the play ends in a frenzy of plots and counter plots, of poisonings, real and pretended, of repentances true and feigned. The Cardinal, being wounded to death, says that he has offered the Duchess a poison, and repentantly produces an antidote. When both he and the Duchess have drunk the antidote, he explains that she had not been poisoned before at all: the poison itself was in the antidote, and the other a story to induce her to take it. Finally the doctor reveals that the wound was not mortal after all, and that it was only by drinking his own "antidote" that the Cardinal has killed himself.

Love's Cruelty is an earlier play, but it too depends upon peripeteia. In Act 2, Scene 3, Bellamente going, as he thinks, to release a mistress of Hippolito who is locked up in his room, finds it to be his own mistress. He has a hundred lines of grief and rage; after which the lady, Clariana, produces a sound explanation and leaves him apologising.

In Act 3, Scene 4, a servant reports the treachery of Hippolito and Clariana again: Bellamente catches them in the act, but by hiding Hippolito in a closet he makes the servant believe he was mistaken, thus preventing a scandal. He then dismisses the lovers. Throughout this scene the audience are as much in the dark as the lovers as to what Bellamente's intentions are, and his actions are at first sight inexplicable.

In Act 4, Scene 2, Hippolito is set to woo another lady, Eubella, for the Duke. Instead, she converts him to virtue, but the Duke overhears their love-making. He arrests them, threatens them with all kinds of tortures and ends:

> To-morrow, if I live, I'll see you both—
> Married.

In the last act, Bellamente surprises Hippolito and Clariana a third time. They kill themselves, and he dies suddenly and inexplicably as he is about to describe to the Duke what has happened.

The Duke's Mistress and *The Traitor* are built on a similar plan. There is an amorous Duke, a chaste lady, her outraged friends, and a cunning servant. Ardelia threatens her ravisher with a pistol (*The Duke's Mistress*, 5. 1), Amidea keeps the Duke off by threatening to kill herself (*The Traitor*, 3. 3).

Love's Cruelty is recalled in *The Duke's Mistress*, 3. 3, and *The Traitor* anticipated in 4. 1. Lorenzo of *The Traitor* is a fuller development of Leantio in *The Duke's Mistress*. The rivalry of two friends for one mistress is from *Love's Cruelty*. Petruchio is a mixture of Pallante and Valerio in *The Duke's Mistress*; Schiarra is developed from Sforza (*The Maid's Revenge*) and Sebastian (*The Duke's Mistress*). Lorenzo, the traitor, is unmasked in Act 1, but he swings himself back into the Duke's favour by an oration: the end of the scene reverses the beginning. Schiarra, by the familiar method of "trying" his sister's chastity, draws from her a set oration in its favour. The lover commands his lady to love his friend instead of himself. There is the violent peripeteia of the Duke's conversion. Lorenzo the traitor is to be unmasked by the Duke overhearing a conversation; but he suspects this, and turns the tables by denying all he had formerly said. There is a repetition of the earlier scene in which Schiarra again tempts Amidea, and finding her adamant, resolves to kill her. She, however, feigns guilt in order to make his murder of her a guiltless one.

In the final scene, her dead body is dressed up for the Duke; when he finds she is dead, he exclaims, "I prithee kill me", and Lorenzo does so, as he says, out of obedience. Schiarra is let in, but he suddenly turns on Lorenzo; they kill each other, and only a younger brother is left alive to provide the scanty remainder of the cast with explanations.

It will be seen from this rough summary how entirely the narratives of Shirley's plays depend upon a series of reversals. This is of course the method of Shirley's predecessors, of Tourneur and Middleton. Schiarra's temptation of his sister reproduces Vindice's. Bellemente and Clariana "go to it" exactly as Vittoria and Monticelso do, but Tourneur manœuvres his characters only so that he can make them say something when he has got them into position; whereas in Shirley the manœuvring itself is the only source of interest. Tourneur's means are Shirley's ends. In other words the narrative has a separate interest in Shirley. The long set speeches have an interest too, of course, but the two are not connected. Characters are wheeled into position and left to blaze away at their target, but these set speeches have no structure of their own. There is no ordering of the feelings to correspond to or justify the ordering of events.

The whole difference of the plays may be represented by the difference between the replies of Castiza and Amidea to their brothers.

> *Castiza.* False! I defy you both:
> I have endured you with an ear of fire:
> Your tongues have struck hot irons on my face.
> Mother, come from that poisonous woman there.
>
> *Gratiana.* Where?
>
> *Castiza.* Do you not see her? She's too inward then.
> Slave, perish in thy office!
>
> (*The Revenger's Tragedy*, 2.1. 257 ff.)
>
> *Amidea.* Is't not possible
> That this should be a dream? where did you drop
> Your virtue, sir? Florio, why move you not?
> Why are you slow to tell this man—for sure
> 'Tis not Schiarra—he hath talked so ill
> And so much that we may have cause to fear
> The air about's infected?...
>
> *Schiarra.* And what is your resolve?
>
> *Amidea.* To have my name
> Stand in the ivory register of virgins
> When I am dead. Before one factious thought
> Should lurk within me to betray my fame
> To such a blot, my hands shall mutiny
> And boldly with a poniard teach my heart
> To weep out my repentance. (*The Traitor*, 2. 1)

The difference in concentration of feeling between "Your tongues have struck hot irons on my face" and "The air about's infected" or "Mother, come from that poisonous woman there" and "Sure 'tis not Schiarra" represent the difference between a conviction and an opinion, between feelings "felt in the blood and felt along the heart" and their copies. Tourneur can erect an ethic upon his feelings, while Shirley's morality has no general structure, yet in all the outward matters of technique as the modern dramatist conceives it, Shirley is superior to Tourneur. His manipulation of the narrative is more ingenious, and the action is a single

one and not a series as in Tourneur. But it is significant that
Schiarra twice tempts his sister and that the effect is not one
of contrast. It is also significant that the material for tragedy
and *drame* was not different.

Compared with those of Fletcher and Massinger, Shirley's
borrowings from the older drama are direct. The adaptations
from *The Revenger's Tragedy* in *The Traitor* and from *The
Duchess of Malfi* in *The Cardinal* comprise the whole of the
Revenge convention except that living core which was its
justification, the imagery, the peculiar tone, the poetry. The
structure of incidents and characters is meaningless without
the ordering and concentration which it represented in the
earlier plays.

In *The Cardinal* the Duchess and her brothers are imitated
in Rosaura, the Cardinal and the furious Columbo. Alvarez
= Antonio. Hernando is clearly modelled on Bosola, but is
a much simpler figure. The treacherous revels are in the
Revenge tradition; there are verbal echoes:

> My heart is in a mist,　(1. 2)

and

> The mist is risen and there's none
> To steer my wandering bark,　(5. 3)

recall the same famous passage. Rosaura in one place
apostrophises her dead husband in the earlier style. It is at
the point when she assumes madness:

> Look down,
> Soul of my lord, from thine eternal shade,
> And unto all thy blest companions boast
> Thy Duchess busy to revenge thy ghost.　(4. 2)

But such detailed borrowing could be of no value to
Shirley. He did not secure concentration of interest in the
audience, because the Revenge tradition had died out, nor
for himself, for he did not utilise his borrowings to that end.

The Traitor is related in its narrative to *The Revenger's
Tragedy*. The old mood is faintly reflected:

(3. 2)

Then 'twill be just
That both their hearts weep blood to purge their lust.

> Does not
That death's head look most temptingly? the worms
Have kissed the lips off.... (3. 2)

> What winter dwells
Upon this lip! 'twas no warm kiss: I'll try
Again: the snow is not so cold: I have
Drunk ice. (5. 3)

Shirley's fondness for peripeteia, as might be expected, means that the chief relic of the older conventions of feeling is that of "the wheel is come full circle".

I have caught myself in my own engine....

I am caught with my own tools: by the same engine
I raised to the Duke's death I fall myself.

The mystery of fate! I am rewarded,
And that which was the rank part of my life,
My blood, is met withal....

Heaven is just,
Thus death pays treason and blood quencheth lust.

It will be noted how flat are the statements. The attempt at a tragic tone in the second only produces "The mystery of fate!".

In Shirley, even more than in Fletcher, Massinger or Ford, the Elizabethan tradition comes to an end. They had introduced some new forces, but Shirley's tragedies are completely derivative. The very neatness of his plotting, his most considerable virtue, suggests the orderly arrangement of specimens in a museum; and in the subtler forms of construction, such as the connection of plot and subplot, he fails completely.

To condemn Shirley would be pointless: he is an excellent writer of comedy and his tragedies are conscientious attempts to write in a manner to which he had neither personal inclination nor extra-personal encouragement.

BIBLIOGRAPHICAL NOTE

The act and scene references for the more important dramatists are to the following editions:

BEAUMONT and FLETCHER. *Dramatic Works*, ed. A. R. Waller. (Cambridge, 1906.)

CHAPMAN. *The Tragedies and Comedies*, ed. T. M. Parrott. (Routledge, 1910–14.)

FORD. *Works*, ed. S. P. Sherman and H. de Vocht. (*Materialien zur Kunde des alteren englischen Dramas*, ed. W. Bang. Louvain, 1908.)

JONSON. *Works*, ed. F. Cunningham. (1875.)

—— *Works*, ed. C. H. Herford and P. Simpson. (Oxford.)

KYD. *Works*, ed. F. S. Boas. (Oxford, 1901.)

MARLOWE. *Works*, ed. R. H. Case. (Methuen, 1931–4.)

MARSTON. *Works*, ed. A. H. Bullen. (1887.)

—— *Works*, ed. H. Harvey Wood. (Oliver and Boyd.)

MASSINGER. *Works*, ed. F. Cunningham. (Chatto and Windus, 1897.)

MIDDLETON. *Works*, ed. A. H. Bullen. (1885–6.)

SHAKESPEARE. *Works*, ed. W. J. Craig. (Oxford, 1904.)

SHIRLEY. *Works*, ed. A. Dyce. (1833.)

TOURNEUR. *Works*, ed. Allardyce Nicoll. (Fanfrolico Press, 1928.)

WEBSTER. *Works*, ed. F. L. Lucas. (Chatto and Windus, 1927.)

Spelling has been modernised in the interests of uniformity.

For modern texts of the minor dramatists, *vide* the handlists in F. E. Schelling's *Elizabethan Drama* and E. K. Chambers' *The Elizabethan Stage*.

INDEX

Plays are entered under their authors' names, or the name of the principal collaborator. Figures in heavy type indicate the most important reference.